STRATUM SERIES

French Humanism
1470–1600

STRATUM SERIES

*A series of fundamental reprints from
scholarly journals and specialised works
in European History*

GENERAL EDITOR: J. R. HALE

Forthcoming titles

POST-RENAISSANCE ITALY
Eric Cochrane

THE RECOVERY OF FRANCE: LOUIS XI TO FRANCIS I
Peter Lewis

PRE-REFORMATION GERMANY
Gerald Strauss

SPAIN IN THE FIFTEENTH CENTURY
Roger Highfield

THE REFORMATION STATE
Henry Cohn

French Humanism

1470–1600

EDITED BY

Werner L. Gundersheimer

MACMILLAN

Editorial matter and selection
© Werner L. Gundersheimer 1969

Published by
MACMILLAN AND CO LTD
Little Essex Street London W C 2
and also at Bombay Calcutta and Madras
Macmillan South Africa (Publishers) Pty Ltd Johannesburg
The Macmillan Company of Australia Pty Ltd Melbourne
Gill and Macmillan Ltd Dublin

Printed in Great Britain by
ROBERT MACLEHOSE AND CO LTD
The University Press, Glasgow

Contents

LIST OF ILLUSTRATIONS
(*between pages 208 and 209*)

PART ONE

Interpretations of
French Humanism

1 Introduction

I

"FRANCIS I was the father of good literature, of the study of the ancient languages, and of the neglected arts and sciences in France." Such, at least, was the view held by most observers of French cultural life in the sixteenth century. Jacques Amyot, the greatest of the vernacular translators from the Greek, said it in the preface to his translation of Plutarch's *Lives*, published in 1559: "the great King Francis . . . happily established and began the task in this noble realm, of bringing good letters to a new birth and flower, in which our language advances more and more every day, receiving such adornment and enrichment that neither Italian, nor Spanish, nor any other today in use in Europe, can boast of surmounting in number or in goodness our tools of wisdom, which are books . . . ."[1] Amyot's remarks are addressed to Henry II, the son and heir of Francis I. But if flattery spurred his enthusiasm, dozens of other writers echoed his judgment, and it would not be easy to find a single one in the sixteenth century who seriously questioned it. In fact, it was not until relatively recent times that scholars began to analyze the origins of the French Renaissance more closely and subtly.

There are some obvious reasons for the persistence of Amyot's point of view. The fact that it was the first general interpretation of the "renaissance des lettres," and that it enjoyed widespread acceptance during the period itself lent it strong plausibility. The prestige of its advocates was extremely great. It involved a

[1] *Les vies des hommes illustres . . . par Plutarque de Chaeronée translate de Grec en Francois* (Paris, 1559), iii–r⁰. For a survey of other contemporary views, see Wallace K. Ferguson, *The Renaissance in Historical Thought* (Boston, Mass., 1948), pp. 29–46.

relatively simple approach to historical causation, based as it was on the activity of a single "great man," and therefore had a deeply rooted popular appeal. Last, but in no way least important, the theory enjoys some factual support. Francis I was indeed the first patron of the new learning in France on a grand scale. His moving experience of Italian culture occurred early in his reign. For that, if for no other reason, it had deeper and more prolonged effects in France than the Italian journeys of his predecessors, Charles VIII and Louis XII. Then there is the visual evidence. In a literal sense we *see* the French Renaissance only in the sixteenth century, and primarily in monuments that postdate Francis I's invasion of the Italian peninsula. After studying Fontainebleau and the *châteaux* of the Loire, one is tempted to assume that the literary culture of the French Renaissance originated contemporaneously with that extraordinary efflorescence of the visual arts.

Reliance upon this kind of visual evidence can be misleading. In the present case, the student may have to resist or make allowances for its subconscious influence. For perhaps throughout all recorded history, and certainly since the invention of printing from movable type, intellectual styles and movements have tended to cross national and geographical boundaries more rapidly and easily than have artistic and architectural traditions, especially within a common linguistic region. The fact that a given cultural movement may be an easier and perhaps more inviting subject for study at its moment of highest development does not mean that it can be adequately understood before its origins have been fully explored and clarified. The kinds of patient and painstaking research required for gaining this type of understanding of a time or movement do not demand the rarest scholarly talents, but only in the last few decades have the necessary efforts begun to appear. In general, from the labors of a large and still growing number of intellectual and literary historians, textual scholars, and biographers, it has emerged that the origins of the French Renaissance are to be found in the humanistic culture of Avignon during the "Babylonian Captivity" of the fourteenth

century, and that a more or less continuous tradition of humanistic
learning and scholarship along Italian lines exists throughout
the fifteenth century in several specific French cultural *milieux*.
Indeed, as a consequence of this type of research, it has now become possible to offer a reasonably satisfactory answer to another
traditionally vexing question, namely, that concerning the
relation between the French and the Italian Renaissance.[2]

The difficulties that have arisen on this point may often be
traced to the nationalistic preferences of the scholars concerned,
though the sense in which that is true is not immediately obvious.
It should be remembered that throughout the first half of the fifteenth century the French monarch was only one of a number
of powerful overlords in the French linguistic region, and that
his energies were dissipated on the English wars and on the
consequent economic and political dislocations. Only at the very
end of the century can one even begin to talk about France as a
nation-state under a more or less unified administration, rather
than as a congeries of functionally independent and semi-
independent principalities and duchies. And even at this period,
the actual physical presence of the king and his court was often
the only guarantee of continuing loyalty to the crown in many
parts of the realm. At the same moment when the great evolu-
tionary movement toward the nation-state was taking place in
French political and institutional history, there was also a large-
scale cultural mutation. In both areas, perhaps, change was
dependent upon a new freedom from external military threats
and the emergence of a semblance of prosperity and order after
decades of economic turmoil and political confusion. Without
this new element of stability the Italian adventures of Charles VIII
and Louis XII would have been unthinkable.

If Charles VIII's invasion may be viewed as a symbol of evolving French national unification, it can also be interpreted as
evidence of Italian inability to confront the realities of the changing European structure of power. "The first-born among the

[2] For a comprehensive summary of these developments, see the article by
Henry Hornik, reprinted below, Ch. 2.

sons of modern Europe" paid with their cherished liberty for
the factionalism and jealousies that even some of their own
contemporary observers regarded as trivial.[3] Thus the symbol
of French pride and ascendancy is a token of Italian humiliation
and decline.

It is here that the nationalistic preferences, or prejudices, of
scholars have tended to prevent objective analysis of the origins
of the French Renaissance. Since the greatest achievements of
the Renaissance in France follow the Italian invasions, and since
we know that the invaders were deeply impressed by what they
found in Italy, and that they tried to bring it back with them
across the Alps, it has always been tempting to explain the
French Renaissance as an imported phenomenon. This point
of view has of course been especially appealing to Italian scholars,
who thereby salvage some national pride. On the other hand,
many French scholars have resisted this explanation of the
origins of their Renaissance and have attempted to show both
that the entire period is one of intense national fermentation,
naturally including intellectual and artistic activity, and that the
new cultural forms, far from being derivative from Italian
models, are essentially revivals of previously existing elements
in French culture that had lain dormant during the Hundred
Years' War.[4]

Yet another interpretation, generally less appealing to French
scholars, is that at the end of the fifteenth century in France a
cultural vacuum had come into existence. Owing in part to the
political catastrophes of the Hundred Years' War and in part
to their own internal dynamics, the artistic, literary, and theological forms that had achieved so formidable a vitality during
the Middle Ages now survived in various states of decay or
exhaustion. At best, it is held, the fifteenth-century productions
in these fields were competent imitations of earlier achievements;

---

[3] For this phrase and the interpretation it summarizes, see Jacob Burckhardt,
The Civilization of the Renaissance in Italy, Pt. II, Chap. 1 (Harper Torchbook
edition, Vol. 1, p. 143).

[4] Ferguson, *op. cit.* pp. 257-8.

at worst, they were ridiculous parodies of atrophied modes of expression. Vigorous and creative innovations had ceased to occur. Therefore, at precisely the time when developments in the political structure of the French nation favored new initiatives, such as the Italian expeditions, a strong urge for renewal, for new sources of inspiration and energy, came to be felt in all fields of learning and the arts. Nothing could have been more natural—so goes the theory—than to turn to Italy for inspiration and direction. In this view the French Renaissance, if not exactly an importation, is at least heavily dependent upon Italian models.

New evidence makes it possible to "save the appearances" of both these positions, as well as to abandon their crude exaggerations. Important recent work, notably that of Franco Simone, shows that the first glimmerings of the French Renaissance appeared as early as the fourteenth century, during Petrarch's stay at Avignon. Simone has proven that from this period on there never ceased to be humanistic circles of scholars, poets, and patrons who followed Italian literary, philosophical, and philological developments with the closest interest and tried to adapt them to their own needs and concerns. The French fifteenth century, then, if not a golden outpouring of new ideas and talents, was not so grimly unproductive as the old theories claimed; nor is it necessary to look back to the cathedral schools of the twelfth century to find authentic French antecedents for the humanists of the sixteenth century.[5]

Nevertheless, despite its interest and influence, the French humanism of the late fourteenth and fifteenth centuries operated within narrowly defined limits. At any given time, only a handful of individuals were involved, and they were usually clustered around the court of a single noble patron. What the movement lacked until the time of Francis I was intense, devoted, influential patronage on a large scale. Francis I was unusual in his largesse as well as in his enlightened concern. He operated on several fronts, and on each of them his patronage brought distinguished

[5] Franco Simone, *Il Rinascimento Francese* (Turin, 1961), esp. pp. 1-118.

results. French art and architecture, humanistic and linguistic culture, classical scholarship, legal studies, belles-lettres—all underwent fundamental changes during his reign. Not basically authoritarian in matters of culture, he tolerated considerable diversity, even to the point (in religious thought) where its expression tended to threaten public discipline. From the beginning of his long reign through to the 1570's, one can follow the effects of his interests and his patronage.

II

The purpose of this book is to make available to the general public interesting and important brief works of scholarship on the French Renaissance. A great part of the most useful research done in this field in recent years has been in the form of articles, most of which are to be found only in journals and books not readily available to students. Much of this literature is in French and other foreign languages. Six of the twelve articles included here have been translated from the French. Of course, hundreds of articles relevant to the study of fifteenth- and sixteenth-century French cultural history appear every year. Though each article reprinted here has a useful contribution to make, the editor has had to be selective, often painfully so.

Therefore, although this book is comprised primarily of specialized articles originally intended for professional scholars, it is meant to serve only as an introduction to some of the themes and problems that currently occupy specialists in the field. In order to provide some broad unifying themes, the book is divided into five parts, each focused on a different aspect of French Renaissance culture. Henry Hornik's useful study, "Three Interpretations of the French Renaissance," which concludes this introductory part, presents a more critical and comprehensive discussion of the main existing interpretations than is possible here.

Part II, "French Humanism and Its Urban Setting," attempts to provide the reader with some sense of the physical and social setting of the French Renaissance. N. M. Sutherland's brief but evocative characterization of "Parisian Life in the Sixteenth Century" gives needed background. "Paris from 1494 to 1517," by Augustin Renaudet, one of the greatest scholars of the French Renaissance, provides a broad and illuminating summary of Parisian intellectual and religious life in the early sixteenth century. This article may serve as a useful introduction to Renaudet's classic *Préréforme et humanisme à Paris pendant les premieres guerres de l'Italie (1494–1517)*, where the problem of Italo-French cultural contacts during this period is explored in considerable detail. To complement these discussions of Paris, Lucien Romier's "Lyons and Cosmopolitanism at the Beginning of the French Renaissance" provides a lucid introduction to the second city of French humanism in its formative period—in fact the close reader of Romier's brilliant article may decide that it is Paris that should be called the "second city." This author makes particularly suggestive connections between the topographical and economic life of the city and the stimulating cultural environment that was its most impressive characteristic. He also notices German contributions to the development of the French Renaissance, which are often obscured by the search for borrowings from Italy. It should be pointed out that a full treatment of the urban setting of French humanism would have to take numerous provincial centers into account. Bourges, Orleans, Toulouse, Rouen, Strasbourg, and many other cities were of great importance.

Part III, "French Humanism and the Printed Book," is devoted to presenting several views of the problem of the relationship between literary culture and books, the raw materials which make it public. Rudolf Hirsch, in "Printing in France and Humanism, 1470–1480," surveys the overall production of books by early French printers in an effort to determine the importance of humanistic writings in comparison with other kinds of publications. This work provides insight into the influence and importance of the humanists as consumers in the French book market. H.-J. Martin approaches the problem of book production and its relationship to contemporary culture from a different point of view. In "What Parisians Read in the Sixteenth Century", he presents the results of research on inventories of private libraries. Such inventories were usually drawn up by notaries to provide an accurate record of a man's estate for the purpose of executing his will. Actually, Martin's article is a review and analysis of the detailed studies of three other scholars, R. Doucet, A. H. Schutz, and F. Lehoux, in which the author goes on to point out certain limitations governing the use of such inventories as sources. "Lyons and Geneva in the Sixteenth Century: The Fairs and Printing," by Paul F. Geisendorf, returns us to the general theme of Romier's article, though in a later period and with somewhat more specialized concern. Geisendorf has studied the economic and political developments in Lyons and Geneva over a long period, and attempts to trace their effects on the movements of individual printers. This kind of research, of which much has been done in recent years, has striking implications for cultural history, many of which remain to be fully explored.

Part IV presents three approaches to the intellectual content of French humanism in the sixteenth century. The articles included bear to some extent upon a common problem uppermost in the minds of northern Renaissance humanists: What is the proper relationship between Christianity on the one hand, and classical or secular studies on the other? But in presenting materials that illuminate this problematical area, these articles deal with a great number of humanists and their works. The study by Eugene F. Rice, Jr. treats an essential aspect of the thought of Lefèvre d'Étaples and of the disciples of this most influential humanist of the early sixteenth century. Classical scholar, theologian, and philosopher, Lefèvre attempted to synthesize his various interests into a coherent pattern of intellectual activity centering upon the writings of the church Fathers. His vast learning and personal attractiveness made him the center of an important group that shared his interests. "A Re-evaluation of Hellenism in the French Renaissance," by Linton C. Stevens, is a brief survey of the major trends during the Greek phase of the classical revival in France. The author considers and classifies the main areas of achievement and activity of humanists and literary writers and indicates many of the important works of scholarship concerning these aspects of the period. Raymond Lebègue's "Christian Interpretations of Pagan Authors" presents an interesting corrective argument against the common assertion of the secularism of Renaissance culture. Lebègue selects particular pagan authors and shows how their works were Christianized by their French interpreters during the Renaissance. This illuminating example of a "medieval" practice carried on into the sixteenth century serves as a useful reminder of the basically arbitrary character of most periodic concepts in intellectual history.

The last two selections deal in very different ways with the artistic and literary culture of France in the sixteenth century. The first, a chapter entitled "The Ancient and the Gothic Revival in French Art and Literature," from Otto Benesch's invaluable book, *The Art of the Renaissance in Northern Europe*, should serve as an introduction not only to the visual arts of the French Renaissance, but to the problem of their relationship to other forms of cultural expression. Lucien Febvre's fascinating study of Amiens concludes the volume. Using local archives in a particularly imaginative and resourceful way, Febvre was able to reveal changes in ideology and literary and artistic taste by scrutinizing such documents as estate inventories and baptismal records. A somewhat eccentric style of writing is more than compensated for by the highly suggestive character of his methods and findings.

III

Because of the need for selectivity, and the editor's decision to construct this anthology around a few central themes and topics, a number of important aspects of French Renaissance civilization are slighted or completely passed over. The reader would do well to remember that the following receive little or no attention in these pages:

- architectural style
- artistic and architectural theory
- economic or political thought
- humanist studies of medicine
- humanist studies of music
- ideas of history
- legal studies and jurisprudence
- literary theory
- popular religion

However, a selective bibliography will make it possible for the interested reader to achieve a rapid and reliable introduction to all of these subjects.

The French Renaissance is a richly complicated and gloriously productive epoch in European cultural history. Remarkable personages appear in virtually every field of human endeavor. Political writers from Commynes to Bodin, poets from Charles d'Orleans to Ronsard and the *Pléiade*, rulers from Louis XI to Henry IV, humanists and classicists from Gaguin and Fichet to Amyot and Le Roy, philosophers from Lefèvre to Ramus—this period, beginning about 1470 and ending in 1600, is bounded by such formidable talents and peopled with many others. Rabelais, Montaigne, Budé, Calvin, Hôpital, Marguerite of Navarre— these are just a few of the men and women of sixteenth-century France whose lives and works provide endless sources of pleasure, challenge, and discovery. If this volume succeeds in introducing this period and some of its important scholarly authorities and problems to a wide audience of new and enthusiastic students and general readers, it will have amply served its purpose.

2 Three Interpretations of the French Renaissance [1]

HENRY HORNIK

WHATEVER chronological limits be determined for the French Renaissance, its history, scholarship, and literature are at least characterized by a clearly discernible attitude which distinguishes them from the work of preceding centuries. This atmosphere is perhaps best expressed by Rabelais in the letter from Gargantua to Pantagruel. Gargantua writes: "Maintenant toutes disciplines sont restituées, les langues instaurées ...."[2] He claims with enthusiasm that "Tout le monde est plein de gens savants, de precepteurs très doctes ... Je voy les brigans, les boureaulx, les avanturiers, les palefreniers de maintenant plus doctes que les docteurs et prescheurs de mon temps",[3] and concludes: "Somme que je voy un abysme de science."[4]

This attitude contrasts vividly with Gargantua's opening reference to his own youth when "Le temps estoit encores tenebreux et sentant l'infelicité et la calamité des Gothz, qui avoient

---

[1] This paper was read, in a modified version, to the Columbia University Seminar on the Renaissance. Its particular orientation is the result of a reconsideration of French Renaissance theory from the perspective of a previous article ("On Change in Literature," *Journal of Aesthetics and Art Criticism*, XVIII, 1959, 330–42) in which I seek to determine the limits within which objective characterization of a "period" in literature may be possible. It is not my intention to attempt the absurd, to rival the already great number of Renaissance bibliographies (in *Bibliothèque d'Humanisme et Renaissance, PMLA, Studi Francesi, Studies in Philology*, etc.). I must mention, however, one of the most complete studies of the Renaissance problem, Wallace K. Ferguson's *The Renaissance in Historical Thought* (Boston, Mass. 1948). Its exact historical study and selective but thorough bibliography provide a valuable guide for all future Renaissance studies.

[2] *Œuvres*, III, ed. Abel Lefranc (Paris, 1922), 103.

[3] *Ibid.*, pp. 103–4.

[4] *Ibid.*, p. 108.

mis à destruction toute bonne literature",[5] and has been considered a criterion for the recognition of this period, whether we uphold the primacy of the concepts Renaissance, humanism, or Reformation, or whether we dispute the significance of Italy's contribution.[6] Since, however, the contemporaries for obvious reasons are often thought to lack the detachment necessary to view their period objectively, subsequent observation and scholarship have resulted in three essentially different perspectives.

The first perspective originated during the Renaissance itself. It emphasizes the assumed contrast between the Middle Ages and the Renaissance, between the "Dark Ages" and the "enlightened" modern era. The concept, stressing the element of rupture with the past, has become the *traditional* interpretation. Jules Michelet, France's most famous defender of this position, synthesizes its *leitmotif* in the contention that "La révolution du xvie siècle, arrivée plus de cent ans après le décès de la philosophie d'alors, rencontra une mort incroyable, un néant, et partit de rien."[7] Generally ignoring the significant contributions of medieval man to the Renaissance and emphasizing the cultural differences between France and Italy, Michelet concludes: "Il ne fallait pas moins que cette absurdité [of the sudden encounter of two different civilizations], ce violent miracle contre la nature et la vraisemblance pour enlever l'esprit humain hors du vieux sillon scolastique, hors des voies raisonneuses, stériles et plates, et le

---

[5] *Ibid.*, p. 102. Cf. Eugenio Garin, *L'educazione in Europa (1400–1600)* (Bari, 1957), especially pp. 71–85.

[6] Recent support of this position may be found in Herbert Weisinger's articles, e.g., "The Self-awareness of the Renaissance as a Criterion of the Renaissance," *Papers of the Michigan Academy of Science, Arts, and Letters*, xxix (1943), 561–7, and Verdun L. Saulnier's preface to the French translation of W. K. Ferguson's book (note 1) published in Paris, 1950. Prof. Saulnier, for example, writes (p. xi): "La nouveauté est dans l'accent."

[7] *La Renaissance*, Vol. ix of his *Histoire de France* (new rev. and augmented ed., Paris, 1879), p. 15. For more recent evaluations of the Italian Renaissance see, among others, the "debate" by H. Baron, E. Cassirer, D. Durand, F. R. Johnson, P. O. Kristeller, D. P. Lockwood, and L. Thorndike in the *Journal of the History of Ideas*, iv (1943), 1–74; also E. Panofsky, "Renaissance and Renascences," *Kenyon Review*, vi (1944), 201–36.

lancer sur des ailes nouvelles dans la haute sphère de la raison."[8]

Wallace K. Ferguson, upon evaluation of pertinent material, concludes that the men of the Renaissance themselves were responsible for viewing their time as a "period of rebirth after centuries of medieval darkness".[9] Attributing their attitudes to the contemporaries' natural lack of historical perspective when attempting an evaluation of their own period, Professor Ferguson shows them responsible for the perpetuation of this "fallacy" through to the nineteenth century.

Scholarship, spearheaded by the work of Charles H. Haskins, Johan Huizinga, and others[10], has brought about a reconsideration, a revision of the contributions of the Middle Ages and culminated in the emphasis on *continuity*, with the Italian Renaissance emerging as an important but secondary contributing factor to the French Renaissance. An extreme view of this school of thought is Jacques Boulenger's, who insists: "La *renaissance* ne commence nullement au xve siècle et son aspect proprement italien n'est que l'un de ses aspects tardifs: elle débute au xiie siècle à peu près. Bref, il n'y a pas de moyen âge des lettres et des arts: il n'y a eu qu'une renaissance; diversement jalonnée, elle commence en l'an 1100 ou environ."[11]

The third perspective generally grants the significance of the

---

[8] P. 175.

[9] *Op. cit.*, p. 1. Cf. Franco Simone, *La coscienza della Rinascita negli umanisti rancesi* (Rome, 1949), Ch. ii, and "Per una nuova valutazione del quattrocento francese," *Studi Francesi*, i (1957), 5–25, for an analysis of this and other perspectives of Renaissance historicism. Prof. Simone concludes on the need for reconciliation of the "Italian" and the "continuity" orientations.

[10] See, among others, Charles H. Haskins, *The Renaissance of the Twelfth Century* (Cambridge, Mass., 1927), Johan Huizinga, *The Waning of the Middle Ages: a Study of the Forms of Life, Thought and Art in France and the Netherlands in the XIVth and XVth Centuries*, tr. F. Hopman (London, 1924), D. Murăraşu, *La Poésie néo-latine et la renaissance des lettres antiques en France (1500–1549)* (2nd ed., Paris, 1928), Johan Nordstroem, *Moyen âge et Renaissance*, tr. Fr. Hammar (Paris, 1933).

[11] "Le vrai siècle de la Renaissance," *Humanisme et Renaissance*, i (1934), p. 9. Cf. Panofsky, *op. cit.*, M. Françon, *Leçons et notes* (Paris, 1957), pp. 112 f., and W. L. Wiley, "The French Renaissance Gallicized: an Emphasis on National Tradition," *Studies in Philology*, xxxiv (1937), 248–58.

fundamental arguments of the traditionalists as well as those of the upholders of continuity. It inclines, however, to avoid the extreme of either position; for example, Franco Simone stresses the change of "les tendances spirituelles".[12] It might be called the school of *conciliation*.

The relative validity of these three theories must be considered if we are to understand the intellectual and social *milieu* of the literature of the period.

A. THE TRADITIONALISTS

I. The word "Renaissance"

In support of the traditionalists appears to be the very origin of the word "Renaissance" [13] Franco Simone's studies of French humanism reveal that "Furono gli umanisti, infatti, che adattarono per primi ad un significato letterario una immagine che fino alloro era stata usata per esprimere idée religiose e furono ancora essi che la trasmisero, talvolta persino traducendola in volgare, agli scrittori della Rinascenza."[14] Petrarch subsequently became the focal point of terrestrial admiration and was credited by most humanists with initiating the revival of letters and learning.

---

[12] "Le Moyen-âge, la Renaissance et la critique moderne," *Revue de Littérature Comparée*, XVIII (1938), 427, and *La coscienza* (cited in note 9), Ch. IV.

[13] Konrad Burdach, a revisionist, thought to trace the concept back to the Middle Ages and the idea of rebirth in God in *Reformation, Renaissance, Humanismus* (2nd rev. ed., Berlin-Leipzig, 1926). Prof. Kristeller, however, in *Studies in Renaissance Thought and Letters* (Rome, 1956), p. 554, cites a secular example of 1330 and challenges Burdach's attempt to derive the general Renaissance concept from specific religious sources via Cola di Rienzo. Among other scholars concerned with tracing the origin and meaning of the word were J. Huizinga, "Le Problème de la Renaissance," *Revue des Cours et Conférences* Dec. 30, 1939; E. Langevin, "Sur le mot *Renaissance*," in R. Morçay, *La Renaissance*, I (Paris, 1933, *Histoire de la littérature française*, ed. J. Calvet, II-III), 497 f.; A. Lefranc, "Diverses définitions de la Renaissance," *Revue des Cours et Conférences*, XVIII (1910), 490 f.; J. Plattard, "Restitution des bonnes lettres et Renaissance," *Mélanges Lanson* (Paris, 1922); L. Thorndike, "Renaissance or Prenaissance?", *Journal of the History of Ideas*, IV (1943), 65–74.

[14] "La coscienza della Rinascita negli umanisti," *Rinascita*, II (1939), p. 839; cf. also his "La coscienza storico del Rinascimento francese e il suo significato culturale," *Convivium* (1954), pp. 156–70, and note 9 above.

Professor Simone's examples from the work of Italian and French humanists are convincing by their number and the directness of expressed indebtedness. He cites Boccaccio, Nicolas de Clémenges, Lorenzo Valla, Guillaume Tardif, Erasmus, Rabelais, among others, crediting Valla particularly with directing effective propaganda to the second generation of French humanists, to Guillaume Fichet, Robert Gaguin, and their disciples. Valla's advocacy of "il concetto del ritorno della supremazia della lingua latina [a primary concern of the first generation of French humanists], era non solo di facile divulgazione, ma di perfetto gradimento come quello che sintetizzava in quei teologi più raffinati dei loro colleghi, i nuovi gusti estetici e le rinate tendenze letterarie." He thereby avoided the purely Italian theme of the "ritorno della spiritualità romana,"[15] which would certainly have displeased the increasingly nationalistic French, who later were to credit persons other than Petrarch, usually the king or the Maecenas, with the restoration of letters.[16]

It appears, therefore, that a new Italian *concept*, perhaps originally employed with a universal religious meaning, crossed the frontier during the fifteenth century through the aid of the more cosmopolitan humanists, who used it to express an idea in France similar to its *new* use in Italy. The transmission of this word might indeed have involved more than the idea of revival of learning, for, in the opinion of Johan Nordstroem, it "sanctionne l'idée que les Italiens de cette époque eux-mêmes se faisaient de la valeur et de la portée de leur civilisation; cette conception portait l'empreinte de l'attitude traditionellement supérieure—et souvent dédaigneuse—qu'affectaient les Italiens à l'égard des 'barbares' vivant au-delà des Alpes."[17] However, mere superiority of a culture or its propaganda alone may not be enough to persuade a country of the value of another's culture and to effect imitation. The will or the need to imitate must exist. And the men of the Italian Renaissance disposed of no twentieth-century propaganda

---

[15] *Ibid.*, p. 852. Cf. also G. Toffanin, *Storia dell'umanesimo* (Naples, 1933), pp. 306–7.

[16] E.g., Plattard, *op. cit.*, pp. 128–31.   [17] *Op. cit.*, p. 15.

devices. Their initial persuasive efforts influenced only the relatively small circle of French humanists, not the more powerful Sorbonne or the country at large.

II. The traditional interpretation

The traditional interpretation features three basic ideas succinctly summarized by Wallace K. Ferguson as follows: "That the Renaissance began in Italy and later spread across the Alps, altering its character somewhat in each country it entered; that the revival of antiquity was everywhere a dominant factor; and, finally, that it marked the end of medieval civilization and the dawn of the modern age."[18] This interpretation, whose history is fully developed in Professor Ferguson's book, has many renowned adherents, among them Jules Michelet, Pierre Imbart de La Tour, Gustave Lanson, Émile Faguet, Ferdinand Brunetière, Joel Spingarn, Arthur Tilley, Henri Chamard, and, more recently, Raoul Morçay.[19]

The central work of this school remains Jacob Burckhardt's *magnum opus*, which credits Italy with lifting the medieval veil that obscured man's vision of himself and the world. "In Italien zuerst," he wrote, "verweht dieser Schleier in die Lüfte; es erwacht eine objektive Betrachtung und Behandlung des Staates und der sämmtlichen Dinge dieser Welt überhaupt; daneben aber erhebt sich mit voller Macht das Subjektive, der Mensch wird geistiges Individuum und erkennt sich als solches."[20] He explains this metamorphosis as the result mainly of certain political and social circumstances: the disintegration of political unity, the rise of the tyrant with the resulting political indifference

---

[18] *Op. cit.*, p. 253; cf. also pp. 258–62.

[19] See Ferguson, pp. 259–61 for bibliography and discussion.

[20] *Die Cultur der Renaissance in Italien* (Basel, 1860), p. 131. Among the many scholars who share Burckhardt's view are Henri Hauser, *Les Débuts de l'âge moderne* (Paris, 1929), and Philippe Monnier, *Le Quattrocento, étude sur le XVᵉ siècle littéraire italien* (Paris, 1901). Cf. also Hans Baron, "Renaissance in Italien. Literaturbericht," *Archiv für Kulturgeschichte*, XVII (1927), 226–56, XXI (1931), 95–128, 215–39, 340–56; Delio Cantimori, "Sulla storia del concetto di Rinascimento," *Annali della R. Scuola Normale Superiore di Pisa*, Serie II, I (1932), 229–68; P. O. Kristeller, *op. cit.*; W. K. Ferguson, *op. cit.*

of the citizenry, the concurrent growth of individuality as a means of self-preservation, as well as the favorable geographic and economic conditions.

In view of the relative mediocrity of fifteenth-century French literature, the obvious superiority of Italian culture, and the Italian wars (which greatly increased facilities for cultural exchange), these traditionalist critics, then, agree upon the Italian conquest of the French spirit and the resulting emergence of a new attitude toward life, nature, and man.

If they are in general accord about the historical facts and circumstances, the problem is the time and degree of "conquest" and the reasons for French "submission." Thus Jules Michelet emphasizes the importance of contact with "la France entière, une petite France complète, de toute province et de toute classe".[21] Arthur Tilley seconds the view that the revival of Greek learning was the true starting point of the Renaissance, since it alone introduced the textually correct knowledge of ancient philosophy, architecture, literature, and even the Bible.[22] Pierre Villey emphasizes the popularization of antiquity when he writes: "A vrai dire, pour s'exprimer avec propriété, il ne faudrait pas parler de renaissance, mais de vulgarisation. . . . C'était moins le lettre qu'il fallait ressusciter que l'esprit, et voilà ce que l'Italie à fait excellemment pour nous."[23] And Raoul Morçay stresses the greater and logically more immediate social effect of the contact with Italy.[24]

Edouard Bourciez, rivaling Professor Morçay's eclecticism— a justified attitude, in view of the multiple possibilities of influence—credits France's contact with classical antiquity and the new understanding directly derived from Italy with a major effect on the Renaissance of French literature. The sentiment of beauty, of truth, the true knowledge of the works derived from critical study of the texts —"Tout ce qui avait manqué au moyen

[21] Op. cit. (note 7 above), pp. 174–5.
[22] The Literature of the French Renaissance (Cambridge, 1885), p. 14.
[23] Les Sources d'idées au XVI² siècle (Paris, 1912), p. 3.
[24] Op. cit. (note 13 above), I, 30.

âge, à notre langue pour exprimer les idées générales, comme au latin barbare et baroque de l'École, on le trouvait dans la langue grecque; une douceur harmonieuse, une simplicité grave, une clarté également répandue, et que n'offusque aucun ombre."[25] The rediscovered ancients offered a multitude of ethical, moral, and secular considerations free from the medieval love of moralization which had accommodated them to a different *Weltanschauung*.[26]

This introduction, through Italy, of Greek and Latin texts resulted in the recognized loss of much originality during the initial stages of contact as well as in the emergence of a return to nature, of a cult of paganism. "C'est plus qu'une altération savante des formes du christianisme," writes Bourciez, "c'est un culte nouveau qui réapparaît, ce sont des symboles rajeunis qui tentent de reconquérir le monde."[27] Greek poetry, he continues, was pagan, devoted to the divinization of nature. "La renaissance antique ne pouvait être complète au xviiᵉ siècle chez nous, sans qu'on vit aussi se reproduire dans les esprits un idéal analogue de la beauté, et sans qu'on essayât de le traduire aux yeux."[28] As modern Italian counterparts of Greek nature worship he cites the Roman Academy of Pomponius Laetus, the annual Romulus festivals, the predominance of Greek deities in the Medici collections, the example of Pope Leo X and his Ciceronian secretaries Sadoleto and Bembo, as well as the mixture of paganism with Christianity in the poetry of Sannazaro and his contemporaries.[29]

Henri Chamard, an equally ardent defender of Italy's leadership in the Renaissance, adds to these possible influences the further element of "la politesse telle qu'on l'observe dans les cours",[30] though he recalls that the *esprit courtois* had its origin in the south of France many centuries before its re-emergence in Italy.

[25] *Les Mœurs polies et la littérature de cour sous Henri II* (Paris, 1886), p. 139.

[26] The role of humanism in its relevance to this discussion is treated further on. See note 80 for the bibliography.

[27] *Op. cit.*, p. 160.   [28] P. 156.   [29] Pp. 156–76.

[30] *Les Origines de la poésie française de la Renaissance* (Paris, 1920), p. 65. This is the position he maintains in the study of the predecessors of the Pléiade in Vol. 1 of his *Histoire de la Pléiade* (Paris, 1939).

In conclusion to the tradionalist interpretation we might say, therefore, that the French writers of the sixteenth century repeated the Italo-French humanist dictum of contrast between Middle Ages and Renaissance, of restoration of letters after many centuries of neglect. It was also noted—by Professor Ferguson, among others—that "Most of the French writers generously acknowledged the priority of the Italians as the original agents of the literary revival."[31] We have also seen that Renaissance scholars have continued to echo this originally Italian interpretation of the Renaissance. Italy is credited principally with revelation of a different, comparatively more pleasing mode of life, with rediscovery, popularization, and contextually sound appreciation of Greco-Roman antiquity, with secularization of letters, and with effecting this revelation upon a representative and impressively large number of Frenchmen, thereby making change an inevitable consequence.

B. THE ARGUMENT FOR CONTINUITY

The supporters of continuity base their argument on two allied facts: the high level of achievement of the French twelfth-century Renaissance as revealed, for example, through the recognized authority of Charles H. Haskins; and the examination of the persistence of its influence on French and Italian culture as demonstrated in the work of Paul Spaak, Jacques Boulenger, Marcel Françon, and others.[32] Their conclusions are based on newly discovered evidence and more thorough examination and reconsideration of literary, social, economic, and political factors.

Thus Johan Nordstroem holds that "La Renaissance italienne n'est pas une victoire remportée sur le 'moyen âge,' elle ne constitue pas une rénovation de la vie civilisée et de l'humanité grâce à une résurrection de la culture antique. Elle est elle-même une branche fleurie sur l'arbre puissant de la culture médiévale."[33]

[31] *Op. cit.*, p. 31.
[32] See notes 10 and 11 above. Spaak's position is stated in the introduction to his *Jean Lemaire de Belges: sa vie, son œuvre et ses meilleures pages* (Paris, 1926).
[33] *Op. cit.* (note 10 above), p. 8.

He insists the essentials had already been discovered and developed, as indicated in Étienne Gilson's, Georg Voigt's, and John E. Sandys's respective studies of medieval, Renaissance, and classical scholarship and philosophy,[34] and maintains that France herself was the prime mover of the northern revival of learning which precipitated the Italian Renaissance.[35] This reasoning finds impassioned support by Paul Spaak, who maintains that Greek scholarship, the Italian wars, the invention of movable type merely *conditioned* the French Renaissance and that "ce qu'elle [France] devait à des influences étrangères apparaissait, enfin, plutôt superficiel."[36] It is also defended by Jacques Boulenger, who holds: "Et si la France, qui fut le principal lieu de la première renaissance, a cédé plus tard à l'Italie sa place à la tête de la civilisation européenne, c'est la guerre de Cent Ans qui en est la cause, la plus sinistre calamité, de beaucoup, que notre pays ait jamais connue."[37] He concludes with reference to the undeniably significant impact of French Provençal literature on Italian poetry, particularly Dante and his contemporaries. And Istvàn Frank insists: "Ce fut précisément au contact de la poésie provençale, et à son imitation, que prirent naissance les premiers essais d'une poésie artistique et aristocratique en langue italienne."[38] Dante's predilection for troubadour poetry (he not only imitated but also praised it in the *Divine Comedy* and in his other work[39])

[34] Étienne Gilson, *La Philosophie au moyen âge, des origines à la fin du XIVe siècle* (2nd rev. and augmented ed., Paris, 1944); Georg Voigt, *Die Wiederbelebung des classischen Alterthums oder das erste Jahrhundert des Humanismus* (3rd rev. ed., Berlin, 1893); John E. Sandys, *A History of Classical Scholarship* (Cambridge, 1900–18), especially the second volume.

[35] A position not necessarily in keeping with evidence presented by scholars like Augustin Renaudet in *Préreforme et humanisme à Paris* (2nd rev. and augmented ed., Paris, 1953), especially pp. 80 f., 114 f., 130 f., 472 f., 500 f. See also Bollea, "Reflets d'humanisme italien," *Études Italiennes*, IX (1926), 217–18, and Eugène Picot, "Pour et contre l'influence italienne," *Études Italiennes*, II (1920), 17–25.

[36] *Op. cit.* (note 32 above), p. 2.   [37] *Op. cit.* (note 11 above), p. 9.

[38] "Du rôle des troubadours dans la formation de la poésie lyrique moderne," *Mélanges Mario Roques*, I (Paris, 1950), 74.

[39] *Ibid.*, p. 77. See also H. Hoepffner, "Dante et les troubadours (à propos de quelques publications récentes)," *Études Italiennes*, IV (1922), 193–210; H. Hauvette, "La France et la Provence dans l'œuvre de Dante: Dante et la poésie

was the key to its success in Italy. His successors, among them Petrarch, Cariteo, Bembo, imitated the troubadours freely, were even ardent collectors of their manuscripts.[40] The contribution of the Provençal poets, Frank maintains, and herein is sustained by Alfred Jeanroy and C. S. Lewis,[41] was the creation of the man of letters, the affirmation of individuality, the recurrent use of a recognizable favorite theme or *leitmotif*, titled poems, the stress upon technique, universality, and cosmopolitanism.[42] For the first time since classical antiquity the world witnessed the unique combination of personal or lyric poetry written in popular language by known authors.

And Henri Chamard further demonstrates the persistence late into the French Renaissance of the medieval *esprit gaulois*, satire of the church, woman, marriage, and love in the work of Clément Marot, Rabelais, Pierre de Ronsard, Jacques Pelletier du Mans, and Joachim du Bellay.[43] And though, as we have seen, he upholds the significance of Italy's influence, he restricts it to one primarily of example, of atmosphere.

Jean Seznec similarly demonstrates that the gods of antiquity had never completely disappeared from French literature; they were merely rediscovered at the beginning of the Renaissance, albeit through the influence of Italian humanists, whose compilations were valuable source books for French scholars and poets alike.[44] The significance of this iconographic revival was

---

provençale," *Revue des cours et conférences* (1929), pp. 37–52, 239–56, 299–320. Hoepffner insists (p. 199) "c'est avec soin qu'il a dû étudier cet art dont il s'est lui-même si fortement imprégné," but that his imitation was far from slavish.

[40] Frank, pp. 78 ff.

[41] See the introduction and pp. 315–27 of the second volume, as well as the bibliography of Jeanroy's *La Poésie lyrique des troubadours* (Paris-Toulouse, 1935) and the introductory discussion and conclusion of Lewis's *Allegory of Love* (Oxford, 1936).

[42] *Op. cit.*, pp. 67–71.

[43] *Les Origines*, pp. 44–54, and Vol. I, Ch. I of the *Histoire de la Pléiade*. Obviously these themes have little direct relevance to this study as they represent neither the predominant nor the new themes, nor their causes.

[44] *La Survivance des dieux antiques* (London, 1940), especially pp. 181–8, 278–9, 287–8.

"la réintégration d'un sujet antique dans une forme antique."[45]

Georges Doutrepont seems to state the focal argument for continuity. It is the insistence on better comprehension and greater utilization of Greco-Roman sources. "S'il existe," he writes, "une différence au point de vue de l'utilisation de l'Antiquité sous la forme de l'allusion et de la citation, entre les Christine de Pisan, les Alain Chartier, les Martin Le Franc, les Georges Chastellain, d'une part, et les Ronsard, les Joachim du Bellay, de l'autre c'est que d'un siècle au suivant, un *renforcement* c'est produit."[46]

However, even this—the perspective of continuity or at least of reaction against granting Italy the leading role in stimulating the French revival of letters—had parallels, strangely similar to the modern point of view, in the sixteenth century itself when, according to Franco Simone, "une nette réaction contre la reconnaissance d'une primauté de la culture humaniste italienne"[47] developed as a direct result of the king's struggle with the popes, the rise of nationalism, and occasionally because of the poets' submission to the political position of the Maecenas. After all, the continued popularity of the *Roman de la Rose*, the prose epics, and so on, attests to the fact that all medieval literature was not rejected. The writers of the French Renaissance seemed to scorn "surtout, et résolument, la dernière heure du moyen âge, celle des scléroses et des formes figées."[48]

The supporters of continuity therefore maintain the doctrine of relatively unbroken influence of the twelfth-century French Renaissance which, though perhaps temporarily diminished in

[45] *Ibid.*, p. 181.

[46] *Jean Lemaire de Belges et la Renaissance* (Brussels, 1934, Académie Belgique, XXXII), p. 317. Cf. *Le Temple d'honneur et de vertus*, ed. H. Hornik (Geneva-Paris, 1957), introduction, and my review of M. Bambeck's article, "Aus alter Form zum neuen Leben," *Zeitschrift für französische Sprache und Literatur*, LXVIII (1958), 1–42, in *Bibliothèque d'Humanisme et Renaissance*, XX (1958), 586–7.

[47] "Sur quelques rapports entre l'humanisme italien et l'humanisme français," *Pensée humaniste et tradition chrétienne aux XVe et XVIe siècles* (Paris, 1950), pp. 242–3.

[48] Saulnier, *op. cit.* (note 6 above), p. iii.

France, had a major effect on the Italian Renaissance and thereby returned to France in the sixteenth century. They also insist that much medieval influence persists throughout the Renaissance, that much of the supposed new in thought and in literature was known or anticipated during the Middle Ages, that the sixteenth-century French Renaissance was at best a new vision of the old.

C. THE PERSPECTIVE OF CONCILIATION

The third perspective we believe and hope to demonstrate upholds some of the most basic views of both "traditionalists" and "revisionists" and offers an approach which might eliminate unnecessary emphasis upon particularist conclusions. This perspective results from the necessary reconsideration of certain historical, social, cultural, and literary phenomena with a view to utilizing, possibly reconciling where they diverge, their respective contributions to our knowledge about the French Renaissance.

I. Historical considerations [49]

Established are the relative superiority of Italian over French culture of the fourteenth and fifteenth centuries, the evident effect of the wars with Italy, the influence of the Italian humanists in persuading French scholars—the first to be affected by the new current—of the rupture with the past and return to antiquity, and in inspiring them with the example of a greater individualism. But what are the specific causes of imitation? How did the wars with Italy or the example of Italy cause the change from the work of a Guillaume Crétin to that of a Clément Marot? Granted the natural attraction of the new and different, how were these

[49] The following works form the basis for this section: Henri Hauser and Augustin Renaudet, Les Débuts de l'âge moderne (Paris, 1929); Pierre Imbart de La Tour, Vol. III of G. Hanotaux's Histoire de la nation française: histoire politique (Paris, [1920]); Ernest Lavisse, Histoire de France illustrée: depuis les origines jusqu'à la Révolution, v (Paris, 1926); Louis Batiffol, Le Siècle de la Renaissance (Paris, [1947]), as well as the other works cited in the text and the notes.

revealed to France, why and to what degree should the French poets have sought to modify their cultural heritage?

II. Political and social changes

The circumstances which form the prelude to the sixteenth-century French Renaissance are familiar to all students of modern European history. From the twelfth- and thirteenth-century climax of superlative accomplishment in literature, politics, and philosophy emerges a gradual modification brought about by many factors, chief among them social changes marked by the rapid rise of the middle class, political changes distinguished by the Hundred Years' War, and philosophic and religious changes noteworthy through the contributions of Thomas Aquinas, scholasticism, and the religio-political dissensions culminating in the papal schism and ultimately the Reformation.

The hereditary monarchies, taking advantage of the landed aristocracy's constant struggles, gradually seized more power and evolved toward political absolutism. In this they were aided by the middle class which, in need of peace and order to pursue profitable commerce, strove to impose its own relatively unsophisticated political, social, and cultural standards. This was especially true of France toward the end of the Middle Ages.

By the end of the fifteenth century the king of France had become more than a monarch in name only, however small his territory because of the power of Burgundy, Aquitania, and other provinces. Unlike most European rulers, he had become powerful owing to legal reforms initiated by Louis XI, the Gallican tradition which, in conjunction with the expulsion of the English invader, had strengthened nationalism, the weakening of the nobility as result of their ceaseless struggles for power, the administrative work of Charles VII and Louis XI, and the growing wealth of France resulting from greater exploitation of her resources and increases in foreign commerce.[50]

In the opinion of Jules Michelet, this centralization which

[50] See Henri Sée, *Histoire économique de la France* (Paris, 1939), especially the first volume.

centuries later proved to be the source of France's strength was
at first no more than the substitution of one tyrant for another.
"A l'oppression locale d'un seigneur du voisinage, on croirait
pouvoir résister. Le seigneur universel, lointain, mystérieux, le
roi, qui paraît au XIIIe siècle, armé de la double puissance de
l'État et de l'Église, est-il quelqu'un d'assez fou pour vouloir
lutter contre lui?"[51] Yet Michelet exaggerates when he suggests
that by the beginning of the sixteenth century "Le mystère de la
digestion trône au sommet de la politique."[52] It is a fact, however,
that much of the king's power and wealth was derived from the
support be it of French or Italian merchants and bankers or the
"merchant nobility," many of whom had but recently been
rewarded with their title for extending the monarch financial
support in return for these and other privileges.[53] Michelet
cites *Pathelin* as a classic example of the resulting social, cultural,
and moral climate. It is, in his opinion, the "Noble enseignement
mutuel de la bourgeoisie au peuple."[54] And he claims that "De
même qu'en philosophie la victoire du bon sens sur la scholastique
n'a rien produit qu'un grand vide; ainsi, dans l'ordre politique,
l'avènement de la justice, l'ascension des classes inférieures, ne
crée rien de vraiment vital, rien qu'une classe amphibie, bâtarde,
servilement imitatrice, qui ne veut que faire fortune et devenir
une noblesse."[55]

The role of scholasticism and the rise of the *bourgeoisie* is not to
be disputed. It is, however, doubtful whether these factors alone
contributed to the equally undisputable decline in the excellence
of artistic creation since its twelfth- and thirteenth-century peak
and whether the growth of middle-class influence was really as
nefarious, especially to literature, as Michelet would have us
believe. The chaos of the Hundred Years' War, the secularization
of the church as well as the constant waves of epidemics also
contributed to the general cultural upheaval. Hence Gaston

---

[51] *Op. cit.* (note 7 above), p. 30.   [52] P. 94.
[53] See Marc Bloch, *L'Ennoblissement en France sous François Ier* (Paris, n.d.), for
a detailed discussion. Cf. H. Sée, *op. cit.*
[54] *Op. cit.*, p. 94.   [55] P. 95.

B   F.H.

Paris concludes that by the fifteenth century "il reste peu de place pour l'activité littéraire. Celle-ci ne persiste que dans certaines provinces plus épargnées, dans quelques villes protégées par leurs murailles, à la cour de quelques princes qui trouvent moyen, dans la détresse générale, de déployer une magnificence supérieure à tout ce qu'avaient connu les âges précédents."[56] Thus the fifteenth century would appear to prepare the modern era through the disintegration of the Middle Ages.[57]

A microcosmic illustration of the appearance and effect of these various factors is the history of the city of Lyon, situated at the crossroads of Europe.[58] It was essentially a merchant city, governed by a merchant aristocracy in name and influence. As a result of its nearness to Italy and the major trade routes of the period it became an international center of commerce and culture, especially favored by the king as a source of revenue and base of operations for the conquest of Italy. Yet it was relatively free of political, religious, and social restrictions, primarily because of the cosmopolitan atmosphere resulting from a large foreign colony and continued international contacts, as well as the absence of strict control by the religious authorities of Paris, especially the Sorbonne. So favored was Lyon's position that "pendant une décade ou deux, [the city] devait concurrencer Paris et lui disputer le titre de capitale du royaume."[59] For some fifteen years its citizens witnessed the triumphant entries—a curious mixture of medieval and modern pomp—of the various royal dignitaries as well as the arrival of Europe's greatest scholars, who were drawn there by the relative freedom of the city, its international atmosphere, and the promise of employment due

[56] *Esquisse historique de la littérature française au moyen âge* (4th rev. ed., Paris, 1926), p. 208.

[57] *Ibid.*, p. 242.

[58] See Vol. I, *Des Origines à 1595* (Lyon, 1939), of the *Histoire de Lyon* (now in process of publication under the editorship of A. Kleinclausz) especially pp. 357–70, 381–8, 486–534. Also important are Henry Guy's *École des rhétoriqueurs* (Paris, 1910), particularly the first chapter, and V. L. Saulnier's *Maurice Scève* (Paris, 1948), especially the introduction and the first two chapters. [See articles v and viii, below. Ed.]

[59] Kleinclausz, p. 358.

to the presence of printing establishments, which had almost doubled in number during the first fifteen years of the sixteenth century.[60]

The city was not spared the changes and disturbances which might result from such radically rapid social changes; thus there was the *Grande Rebeyne* of 1529 and the gradual disappearance of the old hereditary aristocracy, with its replacement by the upper middle class. The new governing class demanded *culture* more in keeping with its practical interests. The larger number of books produced at first consisted mainly, therefore, of prose romances or ostentatiously decorated missals. However, free of tradition as well as eager to rival the nobles whose heritage they had not yet replaced, they also cultivated the classics, founded a college, had literary circles, and built villas, some of which rivaled those of Florence in beauty and magnificence.

III. Internal, "atmospheric" changes

In order to better understand the effect on literature of the transformations just discussed, it is important to understand the attitudes of the people for whom the poets wrote. Thus it is well to remember that medieval man lived in a relatively un-changing world in which God and the devil, birth and death, rank and fortune, time and infinity occupied a relatively fixed place in society.[61]

Johan Huizinga has recreated the general tenor of life in France at the end of the Middle Ages. "Is it surprising," he asks, "that the people could see their fate and that of the world only as an endless succession of evils? . . . The feeling of general insecurity which was caused by the chronic form wars were apt to take, by the constant menace of the dangerous classes, by the mistrust of justice, was further aggravated by the obsession of the coming end of the world, and by the fear of hell, of sorcerers and of

[60] *Ibid.*, pp. 496, 534.
[61] The fallacy of applying this generalization to *all* aspects of medieval life is obvious. The statement is true, however, if we grant the change in attitude, if we admit that there is a difference between medieval and modern man.

devils. The background of all life in the world seems black."[62]

The hour, the day, the year, life itself was "encompassed and measured by the rich efflorescence of the liturgy."[63] Art, as demonstrated in all the world's museums, played a major functional role in this perpetual ceremony. But all emotions required rigidly enforced conventionality of form because "The passionate and violent soul of the age, always vacillating between tearful piety and frigid cruelty, between respect and insolence, between despondency and wantonness, could not dispense with the severest rules and strictest formalism."[64] Thus sublimation was the *leitmotif.* Formalism was its mate, formalism as the sign of the restraint of passion and the futile attempt to revitalize a moribund era.

The declining Middle Ages is further marked by "an incredible superficiality and feebleness. The complexity of things is ignored by it in a truly astounding manner. It proceeds to generalizations unhesitatingly on the strength of a single instance. Its liability to wrong judgment is extreme. Inexactitude, credulity, levity, inconsistency, are common features of medieval reasoning. All these defects are rooted in its fundamental formalism."[65] And despite the political and social changes so significant for the future, feudal and hierarchal pride continue. They are even abetted by cupidity because of the increased circulation of wealth.

But the formalism extended even to love and its expression in literature. "In the Middle Ages the choice lay, in principle, only between God and the world, between contempt or eager acceptance, at the peril of one's soul, of all that makes up the beauty and charm of earthly life. All terrestrial beauty bore the stain of sin .... To be admitted as elements of higher culture all these things had to be ennobled and raised to the rank of virtue."[66] Clearly, the *rhétoriqueurs' songe* or the scholastic's tortuous speculations were not the answer, as they created little new except form and merely perpetuated the old answers.

Of course, aesthetic emotion was not dead. Even modern man,

[62] *Op. cit.*, p. 21.   [63] *Ibid.*, p. 223.   [64] *Ibid.*, p. 40.
[65] *Ibid.*, p. 214.   [66] *Ibid.*, p. 30.

just like his medieval brother, derives aesthetic pleasure from the formal pomp of marching soldiers or from the ceremony of a monarch's assumption of power. At the close of the Middle Ages "Art had not yet fled to transcendental heights; it formed an integral part of social life."[67] Therefore almost all aspects of life were the expression of this craving, even the costume, extravagant though it was by modern standards.

And with decline, the simple enjoyment of beauty for its own sake became "on the one hand, an appreciation which is rather religious than artistic; on the other hand, a naïve wonder hardly entitled to rank as artistic emotion."[68]

Also typical of the waning Middle Ages is the renaissance of chivalry.[69] Chivalry and the correlative quest of honor, related as they are to hero-worship, also anticipate, in the opinion of Huizinga, the Renaissance.

Thus the art and the life of the late Middle Ages are an expression of an unquenched thirst for a beauty whose nature was as yet unknown. And since the means prevail over the possibility of attaining a goal, "Burgundo-French culture of the expiring Middle Ages," concludes Professor Huizinga, "tends to oust beauty by magnificence. The art of this period exactly reflects this spirit. . . . The flamboyant style of architecture is like the postlude of an organist who cannot conclude. It decomposes all the formal elements endlessly; it interlaces all the details; there is not a line which has not its counter-line. . . . A *horror vacui* reigns, always a symptom of artistic decline. All this means that the border-line between pomp and beauty is being obliterated."[70] Is there any need to recall the literary parallel of *rhétoriqueur* poetry?

[67] *Ibid.*, p. 44.
[68] *Ibid.*, p. 243. Prof. Huizinga cites several examples of fifteenth- and sixteenth-century "art appreciation" by members of the educated classes. I grant that aesthetic response may not be much more refined today.
[69] *Ibid.*, pp. 59, 67. See also the discussion in Georges Doutrepont, *La Littérature française à la cour des ducs de Bourgogne* (Paris, 1909), and Henri Weber, *La Création poétique au XVIe siècle en France de Maurice Scève à Agrippa d'Aubigné* (Paris, 1956).
[70] *Op. cit.*, pp. 226–8.

IV. The poet

These changes were not without effect on the poet. In the midst of all this misery "on ne voit plus les ménéstrels rassembler la foule sur les places publiques pour lui raconter les exploits de Roland ou les ruses divertissantes de maître Renart. Aux vifs et mordants couplets du sirvente, aux récits naïfs et malins du fabliau, succèdent l'interminable roman en prose, chef-d'œuvre de stérilité et d'ennui; le pamphlet violent, haineux; le mystère et la farce assaisonnés de platitudes et de grossièretés. La vieille gaieté française a disparu un moment, étouffée par l'excès des maux publics."[71] This depressing state of literary affairs has been fully described in the studies of Henry Guy, Georges Doutrepont, and others concerned with French literature of the fifteenth century.[72]

The poet's material circumstances have also changed. The popular poetry, except for thematic variations of contemporaneity, perpetuates or distorts the traditional forms.[73] With the increasing importance of urban life and the disappearance of the smaller courts the poet must seek the support of the king and the princes.[74] More poets now sign their work. Men of letters appear. And the courts welcome the poets since through their work "a splendid court could, better than anything else, convince rivals of the high rank the dukes claimed to occupy among the princes of Europe."[75] The motive—Huizinga's comment was made about Burgundy—applies to most of the courts of the period.

More than ever, it is art created at the command of the Maecenas. And in keeping with the prevailing taste, the poets moralize ad nauseam or eulogize the keeper of the purse. "D'après les ordres qui lui sont transmis ou les profits qu'on lui fait entrevoir, . . . [the poet] compose un épithalame ou un éloge funèbre, joue

[71] Charles Lenient, La Satire en France au moyen âge (Paris, 1893), p. 261.
[72] See notes 58, 69 above.
[73] Lenient, op. cit., p. 261; G. Paris, op. cit. (note 56 above), pp. 209 f.
[74] G. Paris, p. 211; Huizinga, p. 31; Doutrepont, op. cit. (note 69 above), p. 367; Guy, op. cit. (note 58 above), pp. 61 f.
[75] Huizinga, p. 31.

un air de triomphe ou décoche un couplet de combat."[76] Politics in the narrow sense of gaining the Maecenas' favor and in the broad sense of attacking his foe permeates the literature of the time. However, even Henry Guy, who has not showered the *rhétoriqueurs* with praise, recognizes the force of these circumstances. "Comment," he asks, "nourris par les rois, les poètes ne les auraient-ils pas célébrés?"[77]

The praise the *rhétoriqueurs* as well as their successors, the contemporaries of Clément Marot, heaped upon their sponsors was apparently not of much avail. The poets' material condition remained bad. The Saint-Gelays, Alamannis, or Aléandres who managed to amass fortunes were the exception. "Neuf fois sur dix," reports Guy, "ces aubaines passaient loin de lui, et on le récompensait en lui donnant un emploi. Ainsi la destinée commune des peintres, des musiciens, des orateurs, des poètes, c'était de figurer sur 'l'état' des domestiques en qualité soit de secrétaires, soit de héraut d'armes, soit de valets de chambre, etc., et de toucher non des honoraires pour les ouvrages qu'ils produisaient, mais les émoluments annuels de leur charge officielle."[78] They could, however, often depend on a new wardrobe each season, medical care when ill, food from the lord's table, and extra compensation for a particularly pleasing poem.

Insecurity haunted them constantly. And the quest for security often caused the poet to change masters; and with the masters, his political views.[79] Even the great Ronsard happily sang the praises of a series of kings. The case of Jean Lemaire de Belges is more classic and more unsavory, since his allegiance complied with the vicissitudes of his master's whims. And he had so many masters.

V. Humanism and Neo-Latin poetry

If the quality of French letters seemed almost to rival the discouraging material condition of the poets, the former at least

[76] Doutrepont, p. 367.
[77] *Op. cit.* (note 58 above), p. 61. Cf. also Murărașu, *op. cit.* (note 10 above), pp. 99–104.
[78] *Ibid.*, p. 46.   [79] *Ibid.*, p. 47.

was scheduled for a revival in which the efforts of the humanists and the Neo-Latin poets played a major role.

Most scholars today would agree on the importance of the humanists in any analysis of the Renaissance, French or Italian.[80] Certainly it is no longer possible to speak of a complete void in the world of letters in the light of the significant contributions of humanism. A more appropriate characterization might be "a change of orientation."

If, for many reasons, much of French humanism derived its ideational inspiration from the north (the mystic, reform, and generally new exegetic orientation),[81] the "new" Occeamist nominalism, which more distinctly than before seemed to distinguish between faith and reason, did not satisfy the new generation of humanists, who objected to what they considered inauthentic sources and interpretations.

The very first group of humanists, the associates of Gontier and Pierre Col, as well as Jean Gerson, Nicolas de Clémenges, and later still Guillaume Fichet, Robert Gaguin, Guillaume Tardif, Jacques Lefèvre d'Étaples, Guillaume Budé and Étienne Dolet, all were impressed and strongly influenced by the work and thought of their Italian predecessors and contemporaries.[82] Their correspondence, their studies, and their visits to Italy itself had convinced them of the need to reform both the language and the subject matter, that is, to emulate the methods and style of the

[80] Cf. especially Burckhardt, op. cit.; A. Coville, Gontier et Pierre Col et l'humanisme en France au temps de Charles VI (Paris, 1934); L. Delaruelle, Études sur l'humanisme français: Guillaume Budé (Paris, 1907); W. K. Ferguson, op. cit.; E. Garin, op. cit. (note 5 above); É. Gilson, op. cit. (note 34 above); M. P. Gilmore, The World of Humanism, 1453–1517 (New York, [1952]); P. O. Kristeller, "The Place of Classical Humanism in Renaissance Thought," Studies in Renaissance Thought and Letters (Rome, 1956), pp. 11–15; P. de Nolhac, Ronsard et l'humanisme (Paris, 1921); A. Renaudet, Préreforme et humanisme (note 35 above); F. Simone, La coscienza (note 9 above); G. Toffanin, op. cit. (note 15 above); G. Voigt, op. cit. (note 34 above). These form the basis of the following discussion.

[81] See, e.g., A. Renaudet, Préreforme et humanisme, pp. 64 ff.; F. Simone, La coscienza, Ch. III.

[82] Cf. A. Coville, op. cit.; A. Renaudet, Préreforme et humanisme, especially pp. 53–290, 500–84; F. Simone, La coscienza, Ch. III.

ancients (especially Cicero) as well as their thought. Since, however, they were aware of their own progress in this direction they
applied the term "barbarian" (often used by the Italian humanists
in reference to northern scholarship) to their contemporaries, to
those who opposed them or failed to see the need for a revival.[83]
And since the French humanists were, in addition, profoundly
concerned with theological reform, unlike the Italians, who considered Boethius the last classical author, they attacked their more
immediate predecessors while recognizing the contributions of
the twelfth-century Renaissance.[84] Hence it was only in the third
decade of the sixteenth century, after the effects of the increasing
cultural exchange due to the Italian wars and visits of teachers and
students, that humanists like Budé (in the preface to *De philologia*
or *De studio litterarum*) and Dolet became "purist" and began to
affirm the autonomy of literary studies.[85]

The same intellectual *milieu* which gave rise to the new
humanism nurtured a movement of poetry which sought to soar
on sparrows' wings.[86] At first and casual glance the Neo-Latin
writers might appear as the Latin counterpart of the *rhétoriqueurs*
and, much like them, as successors to the declining medieval
traditions. However, inspired like their fellow humanists by the
recently revived interest in classical antiquity and all it implied,
their work was "modern" in that it was created by artists of
distinct and individual personality who, imitating classical
models or their Italian emulators, sought to create works
of art.[87] Scornful, like the humanists who also wrote Latin
verse, of their medieval predecessors, they also found
in Italy and through their teachers (F. Andrelini, G. Balbi,

---

[83] F. Simone, *La coscienza*, pp. 46 f.   [84] *Ibid.*, especially pp. 50–7.

[85] L. Delaruelle, *op. cit.*, pp. 3–26; A. Renaudet, *Préreforme et humanisme*, p. 690
and elsewhere; F. Simone, *La coscienza*, pp. 118–57. For an analysis of French
and Italian travel and study during the Renaissance cf. Émile Picot, *Français
italianisants au XVIᵉ siècle* (Paris, 1906), and the articles on "Les Italiens en France
au XVIᵉ siècle" in *Bulletin Italien*, I–IV, XVII–XVIII (1901–4, 1917–18).

[86] See especially Murăraşu, *op. cit.* (note 10 above), and Paul Van Tieghem,
La Littérature latine de la Renaissance (Paris, 1944).

[87] Murăraşu, especially pp. 1–26, 138; Van Tieghem, especially pp. 14–17.

J. Aléandre, and others) the inspiration for their creations.

Doubtless they were part of an intellectual élite, part of a world apart, but for that very reason they could avoid the dangers of excessive traditionalism and were, in fact, an integral part of the general Renaissance current and in close contact with writers (the *Marotiques* and *l'école lyonnaise*) who were later to create newly inspired French literature.[88] Their influence on their contemporaries was hardly minor if, as Paul Van Tieghem points out, we realize that, even ignoring editions of the classics or of medieval works, "les libraires devraient offrir à leurs clients, comme nouveautés, au moins autant, et peut-être un plus grand nombre, de volumes latins que de volumes en langue du pays."[89] Latin was, after all, the language of cultural expression during the Renaissance. And if the Dolets or Macrins were unique and Latin was to yield to the vernacular, these writers were no less a part of their time and a significant link with the *Pléiade* and all it represents.

VI. Italy

France had never broken contact with Italy. Word of Dante, Petrarch, and Boccaccio had reached the French humanists before the wars opened wide the avenues to a broader exchange of ideas. But for a long time France had been far too occupied with her own problems to be concerned with activities across the border. Here and there Italy had emerged in French poetry. However, the influence, if symptomatic, was insignificant. Christine de Pisan, of Italian birth, had imitated Dante. The first generation of French humanists[90] traveled widely, carried on extensive correspondence with Italians, and had more direct contact with Italian culture at the court of Avignon. But these were the exception; they either had no influence or were concerned exclusively with Latin style and language.

By the end of the fifteenth century France was strong and

[88] Cf. Delaruelle, *op. cit.*, pp. 20–6; Murăraşu, pp. 11 ff., 23 f., 39, 128, 138; Renaudet, *Préreforme et humanisme*, pp. 80 ff., 130 ff.; Van Tieghem, p. 36.
[89] P. 32.　　　　　[90] See, e.g., Coville, *op. cit.*, and É. Picot, *op. cit.*

united, whereas Italy was a political vacuum eagerly viewed by her neighbor with covetous eyes. The kings of France were interested in seizing the thrones of Naples and Milan.

The "northern barbarians" were not ignorant of what lay beyond the mountains. Italy was then, as it has been throughout all these centuries, the lost paradise. "La vieille tradition de la romanité, les sentiments qui entraînent les pèlerins sur les routes au bout desquelles ils contempleront les *mirabilia urbis Romae*, le prestige du siège de Pierre, et aussi le désir plus profane—le *dahin* goethéen—d'aller voir le pays béni où la vie semble douce, facile, joyeuse et brillante, il y a de tout cela dans l'espèce de nostalgie de l'Italie que l'on rencontre chez tous les 'barbares' d'outremont."[91]

Yet Italy lacked the one assurance of survival: political unity. Her forces had been exhausted by the violence of her internal struggles.[92] By the end of the fifteenth century the country was a patchwork of sovereign courts, each jealous of the other, each desirous of surpassing the other in brilliance. "L'excès de la décentralisation correspondait à un excès d'émulation."[93]

A political vacuum existed. It was only natural that France attempted to fill it. It is noteworthy that "le goût du luxe, la bonne humeur ou l'esprit,"[94] of which France had an abundance, had not been enough to raise the level of her artistic production.[95] Direct contact seemed needed, contact on a large scale. That contact was provided through the wars with Italy.

The Frenchmen of the fifteenth century who had in the past traveled very little—only the citizens of the Midi, the clergy, many of whom were humanists or diplomats, had regular contact with Italy—suddenly saw *das Land wo die Zitronen blüh'n*.

Jules Michelet very brilliantly evokes what may well have been the image of this collision of cultures. The conquerors, he writes,

---

[91] Hauser-Renaudet, *op. cit.* (note 49 above), pp. 35–8.
[92] See Eugene Müntz, *La Renaissance en Italie et en France à l'époque de Charles VIII* (Paris, 1885), introduction and pp. 31 f.
[93] *Ibid.*, p. 44.   [94] *Ibid.*, p. 437.
[95] *Ibid.* Müntz's study has interesting comparative statistics to prove his point.

"étaient éblouis, intimidés, de la nouveauté des objets. Devant ces tableaux, ces églises de marbre, ces vignes délicieuses peuplées de statues, devant ces vivantes statues, ces belles filles couronnées de fleurs qui venaient, les palmes en main, leur apporter les clefs des villes, ils restaient muets de stupeur. Puis leur joie éclatait dans une vivacité bruyante."[96]

This time it was the entire country that saw Italy. And if we may doubt these soldiers spent much time among the ruins of Italy, no one will question the soldiers' interest in the more social aspects of Italian life. The French could not fail to be impressed by the brilliant life, the costumes, gardens, palaces, by all that was and still is Italy; by much that was then lacking in France. And if we remember that the wars lasted some twenty years, "on peut dire que la civilisation italienne exerça constamment sa séduction sur les seigneurs français et sur nos rois, mais qu'ils fixèrent surtout leur attention sur ce qui se voit, ce qui paraît, ce qui brille, ce qui donne de l'éclat à la vie des hautes classes."[97]

The material importation of Italian culture has been reported in varying detail by all Renaissance scholars; brought back to France were poets and painters, architects and scholars, household servants and dancing masters, paintings and books, manners, and even the vocabulary. The intellectual influence, these same scholars emphasize,[98] was gradual, the immediate general effect was social, and the first cultural impact affected the humanists.

D. CONCLUSION

Following are the conclusions which seem objectively valid for the determination of the causes of literary change during the French Renaissance.

Johan Huizinga, fully aware of the significance of both the traditionalist and the continuity arguments, maintains there is "a

[96] *Op. cit.* (note 7 above), p. 147; Müntz, pp. 502 f.; notes 20, 22, 23, 30 above.

[97] Morçay, *op. cit.* (note 13 above), 1, 75. See also Villey, *op. cit.* (note 23 above), p. 2.

[98] See, e.g., Morçay, 1, 79; Müntz, pp. 503, 518; Murǎrașu, pp. 24, 138; Villey, p. 2.

difference which we feel to be essential, though hard to define, just as it is impossible to express the difference of taste between a strawberry and an apple."[99] As the difference exists, the critic must assume the responsibility of attempting to identify it.

Rather than agree completely with Franco Simone's position that the contemporaries erred in the exaggerated impressions of a break with the past—"toutes ces craintes et . . . toutes ces sombres descriptions de l'époque"[100] are to him evidence of the historical fallacy—we might approve his conciliatory contention about change of the "tendances spirituelles."[101] For though French humanism, for example, existed prior to the "discovery" of Italy, the ancients, or the Italian humanists, a significant change at least of perspective, of attitude had occurred. The classics, formerly adapted to a particular religious attitude, gradually became relatively independent of ideational modification. There is much difference between *Ovide moralisé* and the Renaissance editions or translations of Ovid.

There is, then, one fact on which all may agree; it is the change of perspective. And this change is expressed by the Renaissance "fallacy" of the break with the immediate past. We might even be so daring as to ask whether this "opinion" was not really fact? For it was fact, as we have seen, to the people who believed it.[102] But if it was fact can we conclude that the Renaissance was its own cause? Or can we maintain with any degree of objectivity that the Renaissance of the twelfth century really had any meaning to the writers, to the people of the late fifteenth and early sixteenth century, absorbed as they were by the "grandeur" of their own period. "Au vrai," comments Professor Saulnier, "chaque

99 *Op. cit.* (note 10 above), p. 252. Cf. P. O. Kristeller, *op. cit.* (note 80 above), p. 11, who writes that "there seems to be no doubt about the distinctive physiognomy of the Renaissance" and that the Renaissance problem "is largely a pseudo-problem."

100 "Le Moyen-âge, la Renaissance et la critique moderne," *Revue de Littérature Comparée*, XVIII (1938), 421.

101 *Ibid.*, p. 427.

102 V. L. Saulnier, *Préface* (note 6 above), p. xi, writes: "Ce qu'une époque a pensé d'elle-même peut-être illusion, mais cette illusion est déjà un fait historique." See also Weisinger, *op. cit.* (note 6 above), p. 567.

moment existe, et produit pour lui-même."[103] The historical perspective remains, in the long run, the historian's domain.

There are, however, definite undisputed facts and causes relevant to this analysis on which we may conclude positively in view of our preceding discussion.

French literature of the fifteenth century was in a state of relative decline owing to certain social, cultural, and political changes which affected the poets as well as their readers. The political changes had strengthened the country through national unity, yet weakened it because of the war with England. The social changes had created a new society, consequently a new public as well as new artists. The over-all picture of France during the fifteenth century is one of growing political strength but *generally* declining culture.

There was need, therefore, of a renascence, of a change as expressed in the life and work of the period. France could, indeed, have found expression and fulfillment of her need gradually, though perhaps still through the guidance of Italy.[104] For the country was a neighbor and set a far superior example. As it happened, a political vacuum existed. France invaded Italy. The possibilities and reasons for cultural contact multiplied.

It appears, then, that the sequence of motivations for literary transformation in France was political, social, and, finally, artistic. Political circumstances were largely responsible both for the immediate decline as well as the more rapid revitalization of French life and letters. The need for new modes of expression emerged as the result of the new public which, in turn, developed in consequence to these political and social changes. These very changes, affecting the quantity and relative excellence of literature, in turn were responsible for its renascence. And this renascence, no matter what its prior expression, received its major impulse from the humanist propaganda, the new demands of the Maecenas, who had discovered a lost paradise, and the

[103] Saulnier, p. xiv.
[104] Saulnier (p. xi) stresses that, however important the Italian influence, it "fut loin de tout submerger."

direct experience of the poet himself, who must have looked with favor upon a civilization where the poet was a statesman, not a member of the household.

As the future seemed then to hold little promise in France, pessimism—witness the morbid preoccupation with death—prevailed. Italy both before and after the wars offered the two-fold solution of a glorious past, antiquity, as well as the immediate realization of a better present and future. A. Dupront emphasizes the paradox of the French Renaissance, of the "temps à rebours," of the dreams of man "qui marche lourdement à reculons dans la nostalgie du paradis perdu. . . . Il fallait pour la libération et pour qu'elle ne soit pas anarchie, un ordre de révérence."[105] The worship of antiquity from Jean Lemaire through to Racine became the *leitmotif* of this new order of reverence.

[105] "Espace et humanisme," *Bibliothèque d'Humanisme et Renaissance*, VIII (1946), 10.

PART TWO

French Humanism and Its Urban Setting

3 Parisian Life in the Sixteenth Century

N. M. SUTHERLAND

"PARIS is the chief town and capital of the most fertile kingdom of France," wrote Braun and Hagenberg in the description of Paris for their great pictorial atlas of the sixteenth century, *Civitates Orbis Terrarum.* "Owing to its incredible size," they went on, "the multitude of nobles, merchants, citizens, the great number of its students and the magnificence of its buildings, it is superior not merely to all the cities of France and Italy but also to those of the rest of Europe." Other observers were equally flattering. In 1599 the traveller Thomas Platter remarked that Paris could justifiably be called a little world apart, or "Paris sans pair." It would be difficult, he said, in all Christendom to find so agreeable a town, where the air was mild and the climate regular, according to the season of the year. The surrounding countryside he described as among the most fertile in France; the Ile-de-France was charming and especially rich in fruit. In it were many *châteaux* and pleasure houses, set amid gardens with orchards and ponds.

At the end of the century the circumference of Paris was estimated at about seven miles. Because the city was surrounded by walls—those of Charles V (1364–80) on the right bank and those of Philippe Auguste (1180–1223) on the left—all the actual expansion took place in the *faubourgs* outside. The secretary to the Venetian ambassador reported in 1577 that there were continually more than a million people in the city, adding that the floating population, the general coming and going, and the people's habit of moving house every three months, made it impossible to give an accurate figure. This estimate is almost certainly greatly exaggerated, but it establishes the point that Paris was extremely crowded.

In 1549 a census revealed that there were ten thousand houses in Paris, mostly built of wood and cement, not counting those on the bridges, the colleges, religious foundations, or the houses of other communities. Although there were many hotels and inns, they were continually full and, then as now, lodgings were hard to find and rents tended to be high. Anyone who required only simple accommodation was apt to be treated casually and in an offhand manner. But for a client who wanted luxury, and who was willing to pay for it, there was nothing, however exotic, that the landlord was unwilling to do. Most of the foreigners and students lodged with private people, paying by the month, and sometimes combining with each other to share a maid who would buy and prepare their meals. In the region of the Palace, which, of course, was central, rents were particularly high at six, seven, and even eight or more crowns a month. The poorest little room—*chambrette*—could cost two or three *écus*. Unfurnished houses were cheaper, but then, when it came to selling furniture second-hand, it fetched only one-third of its value. Nobles often let their houses fully furnished on very short leases, for they were never certain when they might be summoned to court or when the court might visit Paris. Even so, they frequently had to beg hospitality of each other. Often the concierge let out a number of the rooms, which might have to be hurriedly vacated. Thus it happened that Salviati, a Papal Nuncio, was once obliged to move his lodgings three times in two months.

The court, when it traveled, resembled a whole city on the move; but its departure made no difference to the appearance of Paris, where the streets were always crowded, active, and noisy. Being unpaved, they were also extremely dirty, often ankle-deep in mud and other filth, and the smell was liable to make country dwellers ill. But, although dirty, the streets were undeniably picturesque, sometimes darkened or almost enclosed by the overhang of the houses, which were out of alignment, and the multiplicity of signs, both large and small, that were affixed to them. The use of signs in Paris dated from the thirteenth century; they became general in the fourteenth and lasted until the eighteenth century, when the houses were numbered. Until then it was necessary, when looking for someone, to know the name of the street, the sign of the house, and the floor on which he lived. The signs were made of metal, wood, or stone, attached by rings to metal arms that creaked and clanked eerily in the wind. Jostling with each other for the most advantageous position, they often stuck several feet out into the middle of the street and, as some of them were immensely heavy, they were a source of continual danger to those who passed underneath them. Many of the signs were naïve pictures painted on wood. Others had considerable artistic merit. Some were of wrought iron, some sculpted and some carved. Others in plaster, terra cotta, enamel, or faience were placed, like plaques, flat on the wall. They might represent anything from a saint to a saucepan. Many of the names of streets were taken from the principal signs to be found in them, as for instance in the case of the rue de la Harpe, and this custom is almost certainly the explanation of so bizarre a street name as the rue du Chat qui Pêche. In the same way, the signs sometimes became attached to the name of the owner of the house, as in the case of the celebrated sixteenth-century architect, Jacques Androuet, known to posterity as Androuet du Cerceau, from the circle that served as the sign of his house.[1]

The noise and activity in the streets is said to have continued even after nightfall, when their perils and hazards were greatly increased, although as early as 1525, Parisians were required to place a burning lantern before their doors at night. Later, the inhabitants of each street had to supply or pay for candles to be placed in their windows at night, but these burnt out by about two o'clock. The lights were designed to help the watch, known as the *guet*, in its dangerous and almost hopeless task. For Paris was constantly a prey to sedition, violence, brigandage, and intolerable abuses. Assassinations were commonplace, and no one went to the assistance of the victim of an assault. Early in the century, there was a band of masked thieves, known as *mauvais garçons*, who pillaged the city, stole boats on the river, and beat

[1] A few of these signs may now be seen in the Musée Carnavalet.

up the watch, even in broad daylight, and at night moved out with their loot. Pages, lackeys, valets, clerks, and students, as well as numbers of vagabonds and disbanded troops, also disturbed the peace, brawling with sticks, swords, pistols, daggers, and poignards, and this in spite of the *Parlement*'s most ferocious edicts against the carrying of arms. Peace and good order could not be enforced because too many different bodies and individuals were responsible for it. Their powers and duties were never properly defined, and instead of co-operating, they disputed each other's jurisdictions. Consequently, it was said to be far less dangerous to venture into a virgin forest at night than into the streets of Paris after the candles had guttered out.

By day, most of the bustle in the narrow, cluttered streets was caused by horsemen, pedestrians and the street vendors' barrows. Begging monks and pilgrims jostled with the itinerant salesmen of both sexes, peddlers of everything under the sun, from songs and pamphlets to dead bodies—all of them lustily crying their wares, while above the confused shouting could be heard the constant clanging of the bells of many churches, colleges, and other institutions. Five thousand porters added to this noisy throng. They could be found in every street, and for a few pence would carry wood, leather, and other goods to any destination. The porters were an organized body. They often became rich and able to settle considerable sums on their daughters in marriage. Not least of their daily tasks was that of carrying water, which they had to draw and have ready for delivery to their clients at certain appointed hours. A few favored houses could boast of brackish wells, but in general Paris was supplied with water from sixteen public fountains, to which it was distributed in lead pipes from a number of springs and from the Seine. The water supply was carefully controlled and the keys of the fountains—there were over sixty of them—were entrusted to a plumber.

Besides supplying Paris with much of its water, the Seine was also the city's commercial lifeline, and when control of the rivers fell into enemy hands, Paris could be effectively blockaded.

Merchants flocked there from all over the known world, and normally such vast quantities of goods were brought to Paris that what could not be found there, it was said, could not be found anywhere. The Germans in particular marveled at this great abundance of all kinds of commodities. Sometimes the whole surface of the river seemed to be covered with boats. In summer food was brought in by water from Normandy, Auvergne, Burgundy, Champagne, and Picardy. In winter it often came in carts or on horses. Certain heavy goods, like leather, coal, wood, and fodder, which always arrived by water, were sold on the embankments direct from the boats. In winter, when the river froze or flooded, there might be a serious shortage of fuel and fodder, for the immediate neighborhood could not produce nearly enough for the capital's needs—there were said to be about a hundred thousand horses in Paris alone.

A poultry market was held twice a week, on Wednesdays and Saturdays, when two thousand horses entered Paris loaded with enormous quantities of poultry, game, rabbits, hares, and young wild boar, which was nevertheless all sold, at so much a piece, within two hours. Nothing brought in for one market was ever sold off at the next. Pork was eaten by the very poor; mutton, beef, veal, kid, and venison were preferred, as well as geese, chicken, pheasant, partridge, wood pigeon, and woodcock, not to mention a host of more exotic game, such as heron, spoonbill, bittern, lark, plover, wild duck, teal, and rock dove. Turkeys were introduced about the middle of the century; fish was not greatly esteemed, no doubt because it was associated with fast days. Sea fish were preferred to fresh-water fish. Salmon and pike as well as cod and turbot were eaten, and oysters were available in Paris almost all the year round. Pâtés were made from carp, and salt herrings were imported from the Netherlands. Thomas Platter estimated in 1599 that Paris consumed 200 bulls, 2,000 sheep, and 70,000 chickens and pigeons a day. It will therefore come as no surprise that it was customary to serve as many as two, three, and even four dozen different meat dishes at one meal, which Jean Bodin described as "une infinté de viandes sophistiquées pour aiguiser l'appétit et irriter la nature," for they were heavily spiced and flavored. Rice and lentils were consumed, and fresh butter and milk. Yet in spite of the vast quantities of milk available, in the sixteenth century the French had not yet learned the art of making good cheese. If any good cheeses were to be found, they were invariably made by an Italian, and the best of them came from Milan. (This, however, was the opinion of an Italian.) Pastry was consumed in large quantities, but this generally meant meats baked in pastry rather than sweets, cakes, and jams. These were highly prized, but sugar was still an exotic and costly luxury. Rather few vegetables were eaten, but there were supplies of artichokes, asparagus, cabbage, peas and beans, lettuce, and cucumber. Even in the winter vegetables could be bought, and the salad habit was apparently well established. Fruits, in their season, were very popular, especially apples, pears, apricots, cherries, greengages, and strawberries, and the little, wild *fraises des bois* were already considered a delicacy.

With all this food, cider, beer, and wine were drunk, but hardly any water. Wine was sent from Orleans, Burgundy, and elsewhere. It was already being made in most of the wine districts now known to us, but also in other places such as Brittany and, in the region of Paris, at Argenton, Sèvres, Issy, Auteuil, Saint-Cloud, Montmartre, Vannes, and Meudon. These wines of the north were not among the best, but for Parisians, at least, they must have been the cheapest.

Food was important; indeed, it was said that the French would spend money on food more readily than on anything else. Thus it is not surprising to find that there was a great confusion and multiplicity of butchers, master roasters, *pâtissiers*, retailers, and caterers. Food could be bought anywhere—all over Paris, at any hour—just as it came from the market, ready prepared for the oven, or ready to serve on the table from shops called *cuisines*, similar no doubt to the delicatessen shops known in Paris today as *les Italiens*, where large selections of cooked foods can always be obtained. At short notice one could order either the simplest meal or the most elaborate banquet. Except on

Sundays and holidays, banquets could be prepared and served in private houses. One could also hire a dining room or a banqueting hall where everything was supplied, including tapestries, music, and sometimes even a comedy. The roasters purveyed the meats, the *pâtissiers*, tarts, entrées, and desserts, and the *cuisines* contributed jellies, sauces, and stews. One had only to name one's price per head, one or two *testons* or a number of *écus*. But for twenty *écus*, one could have "manna soup" and "roasted phoenix"—or, at any rate, the rarest things in the world. For the ordinary person, who ate well enough without aspiring to roasted phoenix, there were numbers of restaurants where cards and dice were played, where fighting might take place, and from which loose women were not excluded, as well as the taverns and cabarets, which were wine shops where bread and fish might also be obtained. These, which were doubtless cheap, were much frequented by students. One could also eat and drink in the *pâtisseries* as well as in the hotels.

Besides the Wednesday and Saturday poultry market, there were many other markets, some permanent and some with their special days. A wine market was held on Wednesdays in the Place de Grève, and the horse market took place on Saturdays to the north of the Bastille, on the former site of the Tournelles, where several thousand horses looked for all the world like a military parade—or so one observer thought. In 1546 there were at least four bread markets in Paris, and in 1566 seventeen shops of the *marché neuf* were completed somewhere near the Pont Saint-Michel: in this market fish was available.

Of all strange places, the great hall of the Palace also formed a kind of covered market. It was a popular rendezvous where a great crowd of ladies and gentlemen constantly gathered, sometimes for diversion and sometimes on business. Silk, velvet and jewels, hats, pictures, and books were sold there, and it was said to be very difficult to walk through without buying anything because of the skill, importunity, and persuasiveness of the stall-holders. These astute salesmen quickly noted who had money and who had none, and were by no means too discreet to comment upon what one lacked, or what one was wearing that might be worn out or behind the fashion. Gentlemen must often have repented taking a lady there.

The most densely populated quarter of Paris was the commercial one around the Halles. There were to be found the *fripiers* or *fripons* in the rue la Fripperie, who made a terrible din selling new and old clothes. They also acted as receivers of stolen goods and as pawnbrokers, hiring out to others the clothes they held in pawn. Next to them were the cloth merchants, and in the rue de la Lingerie, which still bears that name, were the sellers of the fine and beautiful materials so highly prized by the nobles and the rich *bourgeoisie*.

The social classes in Paris fell into much the same pattern as those in any other urban community, and they were remarkably fluid. In 1552 the *avocat général* of the *Parlement* informed the king that there were eight to nine thousand poor in Paris without any means of support. Apart from these unfortunates, the vast majority of the people of Paris were engaged in the work of the shops and markets or in industry. Paris was a center for some of the luxury trades: among other skilled artisans there were fullers, weavers of linen, and makers of gloves, scabbards, and playing cards. These, if hand-painted, could command enormous prices.

Some of the richer merchants and tradesmen were socially much on a level with the middle classes, who, as at all times, consisted of professional men and intellectuals, bankers, clerks, secretaries, administrators, lawyers—who were very numerous indeed—and doctors, who were rather few. In 1550 there were said to be about seventy doctors in Paris. They generally wore black, with yellow gloves, and visited the sick for many hours a day on horseback, muleback, or on foot. They were heavily overworked, for almost every year there were outbreaks of plague or other epidemic sickness, which was said to be worse in the region of the cemeteries because of the inadequate burial of corpses.

The more prosperous members of the middle classes were often barely distinguishable from the lesser nobility, into whose ranks they frequently penetrated. The nobility, however, was not Parisian in the same way as the middle classes and the people. They stayed in the city from time to time, and increasingly as the century advanced. For although their homes and their real strength were still centered in their rural *châteaux*, the higher nobility had begun to build those magnificent Renaissance town houses so much admired by foreign visitors. During this century there was an amazing increase in domestic comfort, luxury, and ostentation, not only in personal attire—in the splendor of which the wealthy *bourgeoisie*, who were often the richer, dared to rival the nobility—but also in furniture, pictures, tapestries, sculpture, and the pleasures of the table.

The rules of good breeding in polite society date from this period, and the manners to be observed at table were carefully defined. Before a meal, hands were washed in the presence of the whole company in bowls of scented water, and many bowls of this period have survived. Knives were used for cutting meat, but until the end of the century one ate with one's fingers, with a napkin placed on the shoulder or over the left arm. These were sometimes warmed in cold weather, and in the best company might be changed with every course. In Europe forks were first introduced in Venice, where Henry III used one on his return from Poland. When there was only one communal glass, diners were expected to wipe their mouths before drinking from it. In France men wore hats at table, and it was considered polite to chew with one's mouth open. Some of the Italians thought little of the eating habits of the French, claiming that they ate far too much and too many times a day. This, no doubt, depended upon the household. At the end of the meal, hands were washed again and dried on a clean napkin.

When they were in Paris with the court, the nobles would often amuse themselves in martial exercises, jousts, and tournaments, and tennis, or the *jeu de paume*, was a favorite pastime. The name derived from the original manner of hitting the ball with the palm of the hand. Later a glove was used, and finally a pear-shaped racquet. About 1578 there were said to be as many as eighteen hundred tennis courts in Paris, and as much as a thousand *écus* was spent on the game every day. No doubt both these figures are considerably exaggerated, but frequently, when a house was demolished, it proved more profitable to build a tennis court on the site than to rebuild the house. Already under Francis I, tennis was the fashion at court and the story is told—whether true or false—of how the king once played with a monk who, by his prowess, won the game, at which the king declared: "Voilà bien un coup de moine." "Sire," replied the quick-witted monk, "quand il plaira à Votre Majesté, ce sera un coup d'Abbé." The king was amused, and at the first opportunity, the monk was gratified. Henry II excelled at this game, and Charles IX was said to have been playing it when he received the news of the assault upon Admiral Coligny.

In the evenings at court there was often music and dancing, or masques and comedies. Although the theater was not considered respectable, plays enjoyed a growing popularity. At the Hôtel de Bourgogne, which stood by the river on the east side of the Louvre, an actor was engaged by Henry III to put on farces and comedies every day. These were topical skits and satires that were no doubt audacious and highly entertaining. Occasionally, visiting players came from England or Italy, but they met with the hostility of the *Confrérie de la Passion*, a troup of players that already existed under Francis I. The players were generally supported by the king and the court but persecuted by the *Parlement*, although they frequently produced mysteries and moralities, as well as bawdy and licentious pieces. For those who could not afford a few *sous* to see the players, there were comedians who moved from street to street, collecting an audience where they could, and there were also those perennial monsters of humanity, trading upon hideous deformities, who performed circus antics and strong-man acts.

When the court was in Paris, it sometimes joined in the diversions of the common people. Thus it might turn out in strength to witness the burning of a heretic or the hanging of a prisoner in one of the public pillories and the stringing up of his

ADDENDUM

Acknowledgments

H. HORNIK, "Three Interpretations of the French Renaissance," from *Studies in the Renaissance*, VII (1960), 43–66. Reprinted by permission of the Renaissance Society of America, Inc., New York.

N. M. SUTHERLAND, "Parisian Life in the Sixteenth Century," from *History Today*, IX (1959), 541–50. Reprinted by permission of the editors of *History Today* and of the author.

A. RENAUDET, "Paris de 1494 à 1517: Église et Université: Réformes religieuses: Culture et critique humaniste," from A. Renaudet *et al.*, *Courants religieux et humanisme à la fin du XVe siècle*: Colloque de Strasbourg, 9–11 mai 1957 (Paris: Presses Universitaires de France, 1959). Reprinted by permission of the publisher.

L. ROMIER, "Lyon et le Cosmopolitanisme au début de la Renaissance Française," *Bibliothèque d'Humanisme et Renaissance*, XI:1 (1949). Reprinted by permission of Librairie Droz S.A., Geneva.

R. HIRSCH, "Printing in France and Humanism, 1470–1480," from *Library Quarterly*, XXX (1960), 111–23. Reprinted by permission of the University of Chicago Press.

H. J. MARTIN, "Ce qu'on lisait à Paris au XVIe siècle," from *Bibliothèque d'Humanisme et Renaissance*, XXI:1 (1959), 222–30. Reprinted by permission of Librairie Droz S.A., Geneva.

P. F. GEISENDORF, "Lyon et Genève du XVIe au XVIIIe siècle: les foires et l'imprimerie," from *Cahiers d'Histoire*, V (1960), 65–76. Reprinted by permission of Imprimerie Allier, Grenoble.

E. F. RICE, JR., "The Humanist Idea of Christian Antiquity: Lefèvre d'Étaples and his Circle," from *Studies in the Renaissance*, IX (1962), 126–141. Reprinted by permission of the Renaissance Society of America, Inc., New York.

L. C. STEVENS, "A Re-evaluation of Hellenism in the French Renaissance," from *Studies in Philosophy*, LVIII (1961), 115–29. Reprinted by permission of the University of North Carolina Press.

R. LEBÈGUE, "Interpretations chrétiennes d'auteurs paiens," from A: Renaudet *et al.*, *Courants religieux et humanisme à la fin du XVe et au début du XVIe siècle*: Colloque de Strasbourg, 9–11 mai 1957 (Paris: Presses Universitaires de France, 1959). Reprinted by permission of the publisher.

O. BENESCH, "The Ancient and the Gothic Revival in French Art and Literature," from Otto Benesch, *The Art of the Renaissance in Northern Europe*, chap. VII (London: Phaidon Press Ltd., 1965). Reprinted by permission of the publishers.

L. FEBVRE, "Changement de climat; A Amiens: de la Renaissance à la Contre-Reforme," from L. Febvre, *Au cœur religieux du XVIe siècle* (Paris. S.E.V.P.E.N., 1957), 274–90. Reprinted by permission of L'École des Hautes Études.

lifeless body to rot. It might equally join them in some of the many religious processions, a usual way of expressing joy, thanksgiving, fear, or repentance, which were a frequent sight in the streets of Paris. On occasions of public rejoicing, such as the birth of a prince, the people of Paris would demonstrate their loyalty by lighting bonfires in the streets in each part of the town. Thus when Charles (later Charles IX) was born on February 3, 1549, the municipality had an enormous bonfire of wood and straw prepared in the Place de Grève. It was built in the form of a round tower, and at the moment it was lighted, the master of the artillery fired a salute of fifty guns. Some of the guns were actually placed on the Hôtel de Ville itself and others round about it, and the noise was so great that many windows were shattered. The king's artillery, near the Arsenal, replied so lustily that it, in turn, shattered the windows of the nearby Célestins. Undismayed, the town council let off fireworks while the huge bonfire blazed, and similar celebrations took place in each of the sixteen *quartiers* of Paris. On such occasions it was customary for the town council to provide a certain measure of wine and six dozen loaves of bread, which were freely distributed to anyone who came to the door of the Hôtel de Ville crying, "Vive le Roy."

It was also customary for the town council to prepare a great bonfire in the Place de Grève on December 26, the eve of the Feast of Saint John. They placed a tree as much as sixty feet high in the center of the square, banked up on all sides—dangerously, one must suppose—with wood and straw, on which a barrel, a wheel, and flowers and garlands were placed. Attached to the tree was a basket containing two dozen cats and a fox to be burned alive "for the king's pleasure." The city magistrates, the *prévôt des marchands*, and the *echevins* approached the bonfire carrying burning torches of yellow wax. If the king were in Paris at the time, the court attended the ceremony, and the king was presented with a torch of white wax, wrapped in red velvet, with which, to the accompaniment of a fanfare of trumpets, he solemnly lighted the bonfire. There followed fireworks and salvoes of guns. After the fire had died down a little, the king was entertained

in the Hôtel de Ville to a selection of strange and costly refresh-
ments such as pickles, dried fruits, scented sweets, tarts, creams,
and elaborate confections in sugar, after which there was
dancing. This curious celebration was an ancient custom, relating
to the pagan feast of the winter solstice.

One of the most universally popular forms of diversion at this
period, enjoyed by the court and the citizens of Paris alike, was
the organization of expensive mock battles, which sometimes
became dangerously realistic. Thus, on the evening of July 2, 1549,
the king and queen boarded a boat on the Seine, prepared for
them by the town council, from which they watched no less
than thirty-three galleys float down the river. These were painted
in different colors and manned by soldiers. In single file they passed
in the front of a fort that had been specially constructed on the
end of the Ile Louviers, saluting it with a prolonged firing of
guns. Then, attacked by seven galleys issuing from the little
harbor next to the fort, they pretended to retreat, only to return
and violently assail the fort itself. The defendants, considering
their position untenable, set fire to one of the towers of the fort.
This, together with the guns, caused such dense clouds of smoke
as to spoil the entertainment for the large crowds of spectators
massed on all sides. Many of the soldiers from the galleys landed
and invested the fort, which was bravely defended by the Duke
of Aumâle—better known as the Duke of Guise—until nightfall
at ten o'clock.

No account of Paris from the thirteenth century onward
could fail to mention the university, which formed so prominent
a feature of the capital, or the lawless students who contributed
so much to its disorders. About the middle of the century, there
were said to have been between 30,000 and 50,000 students,
though this figure is probably exaggerated. They were divided
into four groups—French, Picards, Normans, and Germans—
and included students from England, Scotland, Italy, Spain,
Portugal, and Scandinavia. They were obliged to live in the
university quarter, although some of them were boarded out in
lodgings or with families. Their lives were hard and strenuous

and their food barely adequate. Many of them performed menial tasks to obtain enough money to pay for their studies. Courses began at five o'clock in the summer and six o'clock in the winter. The bell of the parish church was tolled as a rising bell. The students got up and dressed, and washed their hands and faces in the courtyard. There was no breakfast. Paris was principally a center for theology, philosophy, and dialectic. Every week there was a formal debate, or "dispute," as it was called, among the students of each faculty.

But if some of them disputed in Latin, others disputed in the streets and taverns—for which they could be fined—the market places and the bawdy houses, dashing about the town brandishing swords, creating an uproar and a dangerous disturbance. Each year they were in the habit of electing a "king"—always a model of dissipation—whom they paraded about the streets in arms. The university authorities tried to put a stop to this, and so the students contemptuously elected an "abbot" instead, and continued to behave in the same way.

From time immemorial the students had regarded the Pré-aux-Clercs as their sports ground. This was a large field, extending from the south side of Saint-Germain-des-Prés down to the river. During the 1550's, when the *faubourg* was expanding, houses were built in the rue de Seine along the eastern edge of the field, which resulted in a constant feud between the students and the encroachers. There were many riotous incidents, the students being fearless and holding no one in respect. In May, 1557, they actually set fire to three of these houses. The rector of the university was many times sent for by the *Parlement*, and he replied to his questioners with a long dissertation in Latin. He said on one occasion that he was not only disobeyed; he was actually menaced with violence by his students. It was difficult to keep them from hurling stones, tiles, and other projectiles out of the windows. Certainly they gave their teachers and those responsible for their moral welfare a most fatiguing time. They were evidently more than usually out of control upon the occasion of the burning of the houses, for two weeks later the king wrote from Villers

Cotterêts to say that he was sending ten companies of foot and two hundred men at arms to deal with the students and to protect the Pré-aux-Clercs. The students then turned their unwelcome attentions to ravaging the vineyards in the neighboring villages, and later in the same year, they attacked an assembly of protestants that had gathered in the disputed field, yelling after them "Aux voleurs, aux brigands." Whether they ever learned anything is a matter for conjecture. No doubt some colleges and some faculties were worse than others.

Fortunately, the reputation of a university is based more on the quality of its staff than on the conduct of its students, and Paris in the sixteenth century was already cosmopolitan and the intellectual capital of Europe. It was also a great legal center, and the jurisdiction of the *Parlement* of Paris stretched over a vast area. The outstanding quality that Paris did not yet possess was political importance, for at this time the government followed the king. What distinguished Paris above all other cities—apart from its antiquity—was its wealth and commercial development. The city's fundamental importance to the crown lay in the fabulous sums of money that it surrendered, more or less willingly, to its acknowledged sovereign and protector. But once the loyalty and devotion of the proud, turbulent, and fiercely Catholic citizens —led by their freely elected officers and town council—was lost to the king, as happened during the civil wars, then the city of Paris became a powerful and ruthless enemy, and without her submission there could be no lasting peace in France.

4 Paris from 1494 to 1517—Church and University; Religious Reforms; Culture and the Humanists' Critiques

AUGUSTIN RENAUDET

IT might have seemed that the intention behind the writing of *Préréforme et humanisme* was to make a contribution to the history of the origins of the Reformation in France.[1] The word "Pre-Reformation," in fact, did not imply any intention to search through the twenty-three years which elapsed between Charles VIII's descent upon Rome and the appearance of Luther in order to discover men who ought to be considered as "precursors of the Reformation." The real question was of much wider historical significance. During that period a vast attempt was being made to effect a restoration of Christianity. The leading minds behind this attempt were quite varied; and while it is important to be clear about the differences of opinion among them, it must also be remembered that they all shared a desire to avoid disrupting the unity of the Church. Their real aim was to rejuvenate its teachings and activities. It became immediately evident that this attempt took place within the framework of that vast design for human renovation which inspired the work of the Renaissance. Religious and intellectual history are closely bound up together, and for this reason it was necessary to trace the evolution of general ideas and doctrines by referring to the efforts being made to express and assert specifically Christian ways of thought, which were then in the process of evolving. Since the humanist school between 1494 and 1517 entered unhesitatingly into questions of cognition, ethics, and faith,

---

[1] The author refers here to his magisterial study, *Préréforme et humanisme à Paris pendant les premières guerres d'Italie*, 2nd ed. (Paris, 1953). The present article summarizes aspects of the late Prof. Renaudet's pioneering studies in this area.

C   F.H.

produced some of the most highly significant works, and trained some of the most vigorous intellects of the age, it was necessary to follow its development with special attention, without neglecting the schools which either resisted its influence or reluctantly gave way to it. Political events, both at home and abroad—such as the Italian wars, the relations of the French Church with the State and the Holy See, and the Gallican disputes—all combined to provide a setting for this study.

I

It is known that the French Church did not in reality have any firm legal footing, since the Pragmatic Sanction signed by Charles VII at Bourges in 1438 was not put into effect, and since moves to replace it by a Concordat came to nothing. The Pragmatic Sanction had asserted the superiority of a council over the Pope, the rights of the national Church, and freedom in the matter of elections and the bestowal of benefices. These doctrines were jealously upheld by the Gallicans in the chapter of Notre-Dame, at the university and in the *Parlement*, and they continued to be taught in the faculty of law. But the government and the Holy See ignored them altogether. Nominations of prelates and appointments of canons and urban curates were from Rome, or by royal or seigneurial favor. Most of the high ecclesiastical positions gave rise to endless lawsuits before the *Parlement*, and religious life threatened to disintegrate completely. The monasteries of the great religious orders saw their numbers dwindle and their rules and studies fall increasingly by the wayside.

There is no need to go into detail about the disorder which reigned among the Dominicans of the rue Saint-Jacques, or among the Cordeliers in their great Parisian convent, or among the Benedictines of Saint-Martin-des-Champs, the Cluniac college, or Saint-Germain-des-Prés, or among the canons regular of Saint-Victor. Nor is there any need to go into the negligent management of the secular colleges or even the great theological institutes of the Sorbonne and the Collège de Navarre.

On May 15, 1492, the faculty of theology officially acknowledged that the studies were in a state of chaos.

Something, however, should be said about the work of
reform which had been growing for several decades in a number
of important monastic communities. In 1458 Cluny had rediscovered its rule, thanks to the abbot, Jean de Bourbon. In 1477
the Benedictine monastery at Chezal-Benoist, near Bourges, had
been reformed by a number of Cluniac missionaries; in 1491
Abbot Pierre Dumas founded a congregation there, from which
Saint-Maur was to emerge in the seventeenth century. A similar
labor was being carried out among the Cistercians; on February
15, 1494, Abbot Jean de Cirey published statutes of reform which
were soon imposed on all the monasteries of the order. But this
attempt at monastic reform made very little headway in Paris;
it was only with much difficulty that the Cistercians of the
Collège Saint-Bernard were brought back to their rule in 1493.
The Cluniac reform had not yet affected the capital, and the
Benedictines of Chezal-Benoist were able to find only a few
isolated supporters. Among the Franciscans the quarrel between
Observantines and Conventuals served only to perpetuate the
disorder. While St. Francis of Paola, who had been sent for by
Louis XI, had been able to found two monasteries in Touraine,
it was only toward the end of 1494 that the monastery of Nigeon
was opened on the hill of Passy. But consideration had been
given in Paris to one urgent problem at least: that of restoring
discipline among the secular clergy, who had remained primitive
and uneducated. John Standonck of Brabant, the director of the
Collège de Montaigu, who had been a pupil of the Brethren of
the Common Life and had inherited their tradition, seems to have
been the first to think of seminaries; in 1491 he had begun to
set up in his college a community of poor clerics who, under an
extremely rigorous rule, were preparing to become priests and
reformed monks.

The dislocation of studies had been brought about very largely
by intellectual causes. Ever since the middle of the fifteenth
century the triumph of Occamist criticism in the faculty of arts

had been leading to its inevitable consequences. For several decades it had seemed to provide the basis for a positive science of physics, and in Paris a brilliant but short-lived school had come into being. The new nominalism narrowed itself into the study of formal logic. The philosophical work of the moderns, or "terminists," was taken by the Renaissance humanists as the very symbol of barbarism and confusion. At the same time, in Paris, Heidelberg, Freiburg, and Basel alike, a conflict had arisen between the ancients and the moderns, between masters who had gone back to the Thomist tradition and those who continued the teachings of Occam. From 1472 to 1482 Occamism had been proscribed by the royal government, but it soon regained its authority and once more dominated the teaching of philosophy.

Theological studies were hardly promoted by Occamism, which was the reason why they became so feeble in the last years of the fifteenth century. Absorbed as the Parisian masters were in turning out endless commentaries on Peter Lombard, they no longer sought to draw any genuinely vital religious ideas from the Bible or the writings of the Fathers. In producing editions of sacred or patristic texts, or even of the most important schoolmen, Paris lagged behind Cologne, Basel, Venice, and Rome. On the other hand, since the need for religious consolation remained as strong as ever among all classes of society, a line of mystical thought was being kept up around the edges of a theology which seemed to have exhausted itself. French, Dutch, and German spiritual writings were very energetically published in Paris, though not in such numbers as in Strasbourg or Cologne. This preservation of lofty spiritual traditions in the face of the official schools was doubtless the mark of a conviction, as yet incoherently expressed, that the things of the spirit were being neglected.

There was an equally serious, though more boldly expressed, conviction that the things of the intellect were being neglected also, as is shown by the progress of humanism. Petrarch had been known in Paris since the end of the fourteenth century; a number of men like Jean de Montreuil and Gontier Col had caught the Italian enthusiasm for ancient literature. But the attitude of the university remained hostile for a long time. The man who really introduced Italian humanism to Paris was Guillaume Fichet [1433–80]. A native of Savoy, and educated at a college in Avignon and at the Sorbonne, he was familiar with the work of Petrarch and the humanists. Involved in diplomatic life and engaged at the same time both as a professor of philosophy and, more willingly, of literature, he had introduced printing at the Sorbonne and had published works of the Latin historians and philosophers as well as Lorenzo Valla's *De elegantiis linguae latinae*. Taking Plato's side, he had followed the dispute waged in the Italian schools between Platonists and Aristotelians. In 1472 he settled in Rome, to which he had been called by Sixtus IV, and he appears not to have returned to France. Robert Gaguin, a Flemish Trinitarian [a religious order founded in the twelfth century], carried on Fichet's work. He was general of his order as well as a diplomat, and he knew Italy. Dean of the faculty of law, a writer of Latin and French verse, and an opponent of nominalism, he gathered round him lovers of the ancient world, among whom were Parisian masters and prelates, officers of the crown, and members of the *Parlement*. This first school was essentially Petrarchan. Filippo Beroaldo, Girolamo Balbi, and Fausto Andrelini, who had come to France from Italy, helped the French discover classical Latin usage, though without always satisfying their profound curiosity, because they would have liked also to follow the philosophical work of the Italian schools; they also wanted to move on from the program of Ciceronian revival and get to know more about Florentine Neoplatonism. They had had an opportunity of meeting Pico della Mirandola, and Robert Gaguin corresponded with Marsilio Ficino. It was at this time that Lefèvre d'Étaples took up his philosophical and religious career.

Lefèvre was born in about 1450 at Étaples on the coast of Picardy. He never became a doctor of theology, and he did not publish his first book until he was in his forties. He was not greatly devoted to elegant Latin, but he did at least take Greek lessons fairly early on from a refugee from Sparta called George Hermonymos. What interested him most in the work being carried out by Italian humanism was the restoration of Greek philosophy. In 1490 he had started preparing a clear, methodical, and simple introduction to Aristotle's *Metaphysics*, but he did not publish it until 1494. In 1491, however, he read the *Contemplations* of Raymond Lull and remained for a long time under the influence of this genius who was at once a reasoner and a mystic. His intellectual tendencies were already clearly taking shape. He had not wanted to break with the nominalist school, but the only things he now retained from it were certain critical and dialectical habits of mind. Lull helped him to go beyond Occamism. Like Gerson before him, he felt ready to bring nominalist empiricism to fulfillment through a doctrine of divine love. This he sought from Pico della Mirandola, and it was for this reason that he went to Italy in the winter of 1491–2; in Florence he saw Pico and Ficino, and in Rome, Ermolao Barbaro; and he became acquainted with the latter's meticulous yet always Christian Aristotelianism. On his return he used Ermolao's method in his *Périphrases* on Aristotle's *Physics* and, in 1494, in his summary of the *Magna Moralia*. By now he had learned how Aristotelianism could be joined, in the spirit of Pico and Ficino, to a Neoplatonic mysticism.

II

It must be clearly stated that from 1494 to 1516 no serious attempt was made to remedy the disorder in the Gallican Church. But it cannot be said that the royal government had totally neglected the problem; it had, indeed, even gone so far as to look beyond the national horizon and, in conformity with an already ancient tradition, to consider the possibility of reforming the Church both in head and members. When Charles VIII entered Rome, various cardinals urged him to depose Alexander VI and call a council, but he did not dare to undertake an enterprise

which was too much for his resources. As Commynes concluded:
"It is not for me to say whether the king did right or wrong. In
my own opinion, however, he did the best thing possible in
delaying; for he was young and did not have sufficient backing . . .
but had he been in a position to carry it through, I believe that all
people of understanding and right reason would have held it to
be a good and great and most holy action." Four years later, on
January 11, 1498, while preparing a second expedition for the
conquest of Naples, he asked for and obtained official recognition
from the University of Paris of the right by which, in the eyes of
the universal Church, the king of France was authorized to call
an ecumenical council in defiance of the pope and even to hold
it without the presence of other national churches.

At the very beginning of his reign Louis XII had chosen as his
principal adviser Georges d'Amboise, Archbishop of Rouen and
later cardinal. Alexander VI was not long in appointing him as
legate to the kingdom. As a result of the powers entrusted to
d'Amboise the Church of France was made subject to his authority
in matters of supervision and reform, and thus, despite certain
immunities which had never been abolished, was brought very
closely under the control of the royal government. The cardinal,
however, was quite unable to push through to their logical conclusion the events then drawing the Church from the dead letter
of the Pragmatic Sanction and leading it nearer to the Concordat,
the terms of which still remained to be settled. At the end of
1501 the chapter of Notre-Dame, the university, and the Paris
Parlement began to protest against these excessive powers and
appealed to the rights of the Gallican Church. One of Julius II's
first concerns was to renew all the cardinal's powers by means of a
bull, which the chapter and university deemed illegal, and which
the *Parlement*, appealing to long-established custom in the realm,
only registered with very clearly stated reservations, after long
debates, and in defiance of royal summonses. These reservations
had little effect. There was no talk of providing a new constitution
for the Church; the government was too pre-occupied with
politics and war.

Georges d'Amboise died on May 25, 1510. Affairs in Italy provoked a violent quarrel between Louis XII and Julius II; in
France the barely dormant Gallican passions, which were by that
time being stirred up to fever pitch by the government, inspired
performances in public places of farces mocking the pope, as well
as doctrinal treatises at the theological faculty in defense of Gallican immunities. The theological consultation of 1498 was remembered, and the king, with Maximilian's approval, decided
to summon a universal council in Pisa to force Julius II to reform
the Church, or to depose him if he refused. But Rome once again
carried the day. The assembly broke up without having settled
on a program of reform; its ineffectiveness had deeply disturbed
the religious life of the French capital. Its leading lights were not
long in submitting, and Louis XII disowned it on October 26,
1512. Before the opening of the council in the Lateran Palace on
May 3, 1512, Julius II had announced his intention to proceed at
last with the long-awaited reform of the universal Church. Leo X,
who succeeded him on March 13, 1513, carefully preserved the
same attitude.

The new pope, allied as he was with Spain and the Swiss cantons, was among those defeated at Marignano. But in September,
1515, there was no Savonarola to urge Francis I to take the
reform of the Church in hand, and the French government had
no plans to put forward. The young king's advisers were states-
men who took the realist view and considered it more expedient
to negotiate. Therefore, at the Bologna conferences, held from
December 11 to December 15, it was decided to annul the Pragmatic Sanction and draw up a Concordat "which would be
similar." On August 18, 1516, after fairly long negotiations, Leo
X signed the text which remained the statute of the Gallican
Church up to the time of the French Revolution. Canons and
religious of both sexes were deprived of their long-cherished
but precarious right to elect their own superiors. The king was
to appoint the heads of the secular and religious hierarchy, and
the pope would grant bulls of investiture. Fairly strict conditions
of age and experience were henceforward to be observed.

Available benefices were to be placed at the disposal of the grantors, who, according to the regulations laid down by the Pragmatic Sanction, were to bestow a third of them on university graduates. The Concordat, furthermore, upheld the legal regulations by which all lawsuits, except for a few special cases provided for in canon law, were to be decided within the realm. Thus began a new chapter in the history of the French Church. The disorders it continued to endure, the appointments all too often made of favorites of one power group or another, the pluralism of high offices, and the rapid multiplication of abbeys *in commendam* right up to the end of the *Ancien Régime* are all too well known for there to be any idea that the Church had at last found the status it had been seeking ever since the ineffective law of Charles VII.

III

It must at least be acknowledged that the disciplinary reform put through between 1494 and 1517 among the regular and secular clergy was not in vain; among the clergy of the capital it left behind some elements of renovation which became active during the Reformation, and were even more so during the Counter-Reformation.

Despite the intense vitality of the national churches, the Roman Church preserved a universal character which revealed itself both in the religious activity of the monastic congregations and in the intellectual life of the universities. For this reason national history alone is insufficient to account either for the monastic and clerical reforms or for the attempts to bring about new developments in philosophical and theological thought, and in scholastic and humanist culture. All these labors of mind and conscience were influenced as much by foreign currents as they were by traditional French ones. This is evident in religious history; it will soon appear that it is no less evident in intellectual history.

The least vigorous influences came from Italy; of all the rigorists whose activities the Church in Paris was to undergo, the Minims [a mendicant religious order founded in the fifteenth century] were the most humble in spirit. Their founder had not permitted them to lay any claim to intellectual dominion; the recluses of Nigeon, who were scarcely qualified to write or teach and were not even very skillful at popular preaching, were able to give some counsels of spiritual perfection to John Standonck and to Jean Quentin, the penitentiary of Notre-Dame. St. Francis of Paola died at Plessis-lès-Tours on April 2, 1507, and the new general, François Binet, was a Frenchman. The "bonshommes de Passy" were to lose their transalpine character fairly quickly; for a time they were occupied completely with the canonization process of their founder.

The Carmelites of the Place Maubert could also look to Italy for an example of regular observance. Battista Spagnuoli [sometimes called Mantuanus], admired throughout Europe as a Christian Vergil, had founded the most vigorous of the observant congregations; after his election as general he continued to rule the order until 1516. A new congregation was founded at Albi, and on June 18, 1502, it received from Georges d'Amboise a set of statutes inspired by those of the Mantuan; in July, 1507—not without difficulties, and thanks to the support of the *Parlement* and Georges d'Amboise—it succeeded in incorporating the Parisian monastery.

Much more important was the success obtained in Paris and throughout France by the canons regular of Windesheim. Their congregation was at this time a powerful force in Western Europe. All its schools and communities were governed by the same ascetic and mystical ideas; these were expressed in a whole spiritual literature, at once active and contemplative, in which the virtues of the founders and great masters were brought to life again, while more modest disciples endeavored to practise the imitation of Christ. In the middle of the fifteenth century Nicholas of Cusa had counted on Windesheim to carry out the reform of the German dioceses. By 1479 its constitutions had spread throughout sixteen dioceses in Germany and the Low Countries.

By 1496 Windesheim administered about one hundred abbeys. The conversion of a commendatory abbot, Jean d'Aubusson, who in that same year decided to reform his priory at Château-Landon in the diocese of Sens, was to determine the involvement of the canons of Windesheim.

It was Standonck who journeyed to the Low Countries and asked them to come to France. They hesitated at first, since they had never set foot in the realm and did not know the language; but by the beginning of autumn they were in Paris and had installed themselves at Château-Landon. Their leader, John Mauburnus, had made himself known through a considerable number of devotional treatises, written in the style of the Brethren of the Common Life, and especially through his *Rosetum Exercitiorum Spritualium*, a detailed and often artificial manual of Christian meditation, reprinted several times since 1491, the technique of which may be seen in some respects in the *Spiritual Exercises* of Ignatius Loyola. Mauburnus was made abbot of Château-Landon by regular election toward the middle of 1497; and preparations were already afoot to establish the Windesheim canons in Paris in the ancient abbey of Saint-Victor, which had been rendered illustrious by Hugh and Richard. A further mission arrived in Paris on March 10, 1497. Only Cornelius Geerd, a mystic and humanist, is known to us, through his correspondence with a young Dutch monk of the monastery of Steyn, Erasmus of Rotterdam. But the Victorines refused to countenance any risk of their house passing into the hands of another congregation, and despite efforts made by Standonck, several members of the chapter, and a number of parliamentary counselors, who only succeeded in obtaining a semblance of reform, the Dutchmen had to withdraw on August 16, 1498. The abbey of Livry was reformed, though not without some difficulty, by Mauburnus, who received the title of abbot there in December, 1499; it was here that he died toward the end of December, 1501. Two other monasteries, Saint-Sauveur of Melun and Cysoing in the diocese of Tournai, joined themselves in spirit at this time to Livry and Château-Landon. With the authorization of Georges d'Amboise, the delegates of the four reformed houses, led by Martin Deschamps, abbot of Livry since the spring of 1504, drew up in January, 1506, the statutes of a new community of observant canons which had become increasingly independent of the Low Countries and now wished to develop exclusively within the Gallican Church.

It now became possible to try once more to reform Saint-Victor, with greater chances of success. The monastery seemed materially prosperous; the abbot, Nicaise de l'Orme, a great builder, had had the library reconstructed. But the lack of discipline was still serious, and a group of the monks, led by Marc de Grandval, appeared in the summer of 1513 demanding a reform, and later a union with Livry. Nicaise de l'Orme, then old and in bad health, stepped down in the autumn of 1514. After some fairly sharp quarrels, his successor, Jean Bordier, was compelled by the bishop of Paris, Étienne Poncher, to accept the incorporation of Saint-Victor and its dependent priories into the union, which continued under the direction of Martin Deschamps. On May 6, 1515, agreement was reached; the reformed congregation would henceforward bear the name of Saint-Victor. The final details were settled on December 22, 1516. The abbey kept its students and masters; its theological schools, thanks to the lectures of Marc de Grandval, had recently regained a little of their former prestige.

From Holland too came the Dominicans, who had been called on by Jean Clérée, a friend of Standonck, to reform the great monastery in the rue Saint-Jacques. In 1464 John of Uijtenhoven had set up a congregation which, after establishing itself first in Holland and Overijssel, had spread its influence throughout Germany and even reached the French-speaking countries, where the spirit of the Dominicans made common cause with that of Windesheim. A first mission was introduced in 1501 and appeared to score some success, though this did not last very long since the young students of Saint-Jacques asserted that "austerity of life and continual work are two opposite and incompatible things."

Georges d'Amboise had to intervene with his authority as legate, and the *Parlement*, in the second half of 1502, took measures to support those who had reformed. It must be acknowledged that at least the level of studies was raised, and Thomism once again found some interpreters at Saint-Jacques. Pierre Crockart of Brussels, who died in 1514, left behind some writings and also a tradition; it was in his school that Francisco de Vitoria [Spanish Dominican theologian, 1480–1546] was trained.

It had not been possible to reform the Cordeliers. In 1502 the French provincial, Olivier Maillard, together with the Paris *Parlement* and a number of prelates, attempted several times to impose a disciplinary reform on the great monastery in Paris. The Cordeliers were able to appeal to their rights and customs and refused to allow the Observants to intervene. The quarrel which divided the Franciscan world remained incurable, and Scotist studies did not recover from their decline.

A reform which was French in both spirit and origin had had its center in Cluny since the middle of the fifteenth century. Its tireless promoter was the theologian Jean Raulin. This forceful preacher from Navarre, stern, austere and impassioned, had resigned his chair and left the nominalist school, which looked on him as a master, in order to seek the peace of the interior life at Cluny. From the beginning of 1501 he undertook the reform of the great Parisian priory of Saint-Martin-des-Champs. He sent to Cluny for Philippe Bourgoing and thirteen other monks and established them in the priory. An action was brought against him before the *Parlement* by Jean d'Espinay, who, in addition to the bishoprics of Valence and Die, had been accumulating a number of abbeys and was laying a claim also to Saint-Martin. In the following year it was necessary for Georges d'Amboise to step in and secure his withdrawal, and Philippe Bourgoing remained prior. Several months previously Raulin and Bourgoing had restored discipline in the Collège de Cluny. The Cluniacs in Paris, whose numbers had grown, practised in their theology a very liberal eclecticism which embraced the ancient world, the recent schools of humanism, Marsilio Ficino, and even Savonarola. At about the same time Raulin attempted to introduce the Cluniac reform to Saint-Germain-des-Prés. The commendatory abbot, Geoffrey Floreau, bishop of Châlons, called him there together with Bourgoing and thirteen monks of Saint-Martin-des-Champs. Here they established themselves, though not without a measure of force, and despite a lawsuit, they did not leave until the death of Floreau and the installation of a new commendatory abbot, Guillaume Briçonnet, archbishop of Rheims, on January 2, 1504. On October 1, 1507, Briçonnet obtained from Julius II a bull permitting him to pass on the abbey to his son Guillaume, bishop of Lodève, who was a friend of the humanists and supporter of a reform which wanted the removal of Raulin and Bourgoing. In spite of quite a spirited resistance on the part of the monks and the election, on June 8, 1508, of one among their number, whom the *Parlement* compelled to step down, the young bishop was able to promulgate several reformatory statutes. In the same year, Lefèvre d'Étaples, who was to become his spiritual adviser, took up lodgings at Saint-Germain. When Guillaume Briçonnet returned from the Council of Pisa at the end of 1513, Lefèvre may quite possibly have drawn his attention to the need to carry through the reform of Saint-Germain-des-Prés. There was no longer any question of Cluny; the idea was to turn to Chezal-Benoist, which from very early on had kept up friendly relations with the Parisian humanists, and no doubt with Lefèvre. The negotiations went off quickly and smoothly. An extraordinary chapter was held at Saint-Sulpice in Bourges, which delegated two abbots to go to Paris and come to an agreement with Briçonnet. Louis XII, Anne of Brittany, and Louise of Savoy were interested in the undertaking. Thirty Benedictines of Saint-Sulpice entered Saint-Germain on January 23, 1514; some of the old monks took to flight and were not greatly missed. At last, on May 8, 1515, came the signing of the Concordat uniting the ancient Merovingian abbey to Chezal-Benoist. Lefèvre d'Étaples, who probably supported the missionaries from Berry with his advice, would hardly have been without some influence on the restored studies of the monks.

Very little had been done to reform the secular clergy. The Parisian preachers such as Olivier Maillard, Jean Raulin, Jean Clérée, and John Standonck had, in all probability, not failed to point the finger of scorn and censure; but the real problem was the founding of seminaries, and only Standonck had made some provision for this.

The community of Poor Clerics at Montaigu had been growing up on the fringes of the college, under a discipline similar to that of a prison. The rector [Standonck], schooled by long hardship, was a terrible, pitiless man to whom all elegant cultivation of the mind was utterly foreign. It was he who had introduced the canons of Windesheim to Paris, and traces of his activity are to be found in all the monastic reforms in the capital. But he knew that if order and discipline were to be imposed a start had to be made among those from whom the prelates of the future would be drawn. In 1497 he attempted something which turned all eyes. On June 24 the archbishop of Rheims, Robert Briçonnet, had died, and his brother Guillaume was canvassing for the succession. "Never," said an advocate before the Paris *Parlement*, "was greater pressure put upon the electors." Despite the protests of chapter and people alike, one canon voted for Standonck. The rigorist party, whose leader was the rector of Montaigu himself, advised him to go to law, and Raulin gave him energetic support. The appeal, fought out before the Paris *Parlement*, could only be terminated by the victory of Briçonnet, and Standonck stood down on February 26, 1498. His attitude in the matter of the royal divorce, which he disapproved of and which one of the masters at Montaigu, Thomas Warnet, denounced from the pulpit, drew down the anger of Louis XII. Following a series of university disturbances provoked by a pontifical tithe, Standonck and Warnet were sent into exile and withdrew to the Low Countries.

It was then that Standonck conceived the project of setting up a congregation of indigent clerics destined to work for the reform of the Church "through a better practice of poverty." Four new houses were opened in Cambrai, Valenciennes, Malines, and Louvain.

Letters of pardon signed by the king on April 17, 1500, enabled Standonck to return to his college, his pupils and his friends. Supported by a party which looked on him as an apostle, he now prepared definitive statutes for Montaigu and its daughter-houses. These were approved by the chapter of Notre-Dame on January 30, 1503, and constitute one of the outstanding monuments of Catholic reform at the beginning of the sixteenth century. Standonck's seminarists were crushed beneath an oppressive discipline of passive obedience and humility. The rector died at Montaigu on February 5, 1504, and his work was not destined to live on. Under the rule of Noel Beda, and thanks to professors like John Major and Antonio Coronel, the college was able to become one of the most active centers of nominalism in Paris. But in 1509 the daughter-houses in the Low Countries started to gain their liberty. The college which Standonck had wished to see poor became rich; and the community of indigents, much diminished in numbers, continued to lead an obscure and sterile existence, under the brutal direction of masters devoid of scholarship and talent, right up to the time of the [Catholic] League. Erasmus and Rabelais had long condemned Standonck and the ignorance and humiliation on which his teaching methods were based.

IV

The evolution of humanism in Paris between 1494 and 1516 can only be understood in the light of that domination which Italy had exercised for half a century over all modern thinking in the Western world. The work of Lefèvre d'Étaples, and his love and understanding—not only of the ancient philosophies, but also, to a large extent, of Christian thought—are to be accounted for by the lessons he had learned from Italy. In the work of Erasmus, the criticism of society and human institutions may be accounted for principally by the example of the ancient moralists and the impressions formed by a traveler familiar with several of the great countries of Europe; but his religious criticism, and the method he applied to the study of the texts upon which Christian traditions and the Church itself were based, were the outcome of a liberality of mind which was essentially Italian. The other French humanists, whether followers of Lefèvre or Erasmus, were all, with the possible exception of Charles de Bovelles, disciples of Italy.

After his return from Rome Lefèvre had undertaken the task of making Aristotle's scientific and philosophical works available to the Parisians through the translations and commentaries of the Italian masters; in this way he carried on the work of Ermolao in France. The *Physics* appeared in 1494, the *Nicomachaean Ethic* in 1497, the *Organon* in 1503, the *Politics* in 1506, and the *Metaphysics* in 1515.

There can be no question here of entering into an examination of Lefèvre's Italian Aristotle in all its editions and commentaries. In his introduction to the *Physics* he detected in the philosopher's descriptions a sense of divine harmony and a clear perception of metaphysical reality. But the edition of the *Ethics* certainly deserves attention. It may well be that all he was seeking to extract from Aristotle was a compendium of lively and active humanism; but his reflections in this case appear singularly rich, and are filled with references to the historians, rhetoricians, and poets. No one before him in France had shown such a familiarity with the ancient world, and a number of passages seem to anticipate the *Adages* of Erasmus and the *Essays* of Montaigne. The conclusions he reached were those of a Christian thinker who was following Pico della Mirandola in the quest for a mystical fulfillment to all human endeavor. The edition of the *Organon* is preceded by an eloquent preface which expresses the holy anger both of a defender of truth toward the Goths and of a restorer of genuine logic toward the intellectual games of modern logicians. In truth, Aristotle's logic did not offer a method of investigation or a means of exploring the world of reality; it simply taught the art of deduction and induction, and Lefèvre realized that Aristotle alone was not enough. The edition of the *Politics* afforded him an opportunity to reread the *Republic* and the *Laws* of Plato.

He had long thought that the Neoplatonists would help him find a way of progressing beyond Aristotle, and for this reason he had published Ficino's version of the *Hermetic Books* in 1494. But in 1499, after editing Ambrogio Traversari's version of Pseudo-Dionysius, he became convinced that the Alexandrian school had done nothing other than plagiarize St. Paul and his disciple, and from that time onward he would have nothing more to do with it. He remained an enthusiastic admirer of Lull with his inspired dialectic and his mystical theology, and in 1505 he published the *Contemplations*. Yet, after 1501, it was Nicholas of Cusa who came to have an ever-increasing hold on his mind. He would appear to have collaborated with Charles de Bovelles, his most powerfully talented pupil, when he began his study of the many and complex writings of the Cardinal of Brixen. Lefèvre was familiar with mathematics, and Bovelles was a mathematician, physicist, and logician. Like his master, Bovelles was also drawn by the mysticism of the Christian spiritual writers to progress beyond Aristotle and even become reconciled with Plato. In the spirit of Nicholas of Cusa, he now sought to make a synthesis of rational philosophy, boxed up as it was in the study of the laws of conjecture, with intellectual philosophy, the aim of which was to strive after knowledge of that infinite unity in which all contradictions are ultimately resolved. The two volumes printed in Strasbourg in 1489 and 1490 were far from representing the sum total of work whose value was well understood by Lefèvre and Bovelles. The master had probably thought very early on in terms of a more complete collection. The edition he offered in 1510 of Richard of Saint-Victor's *De Trinitate* belongs to the same cycle of ideas. During a journey through the Rhineland in that year (he had already been back to Italy twice, in 1500 and 1507), he discovered several new treatises unknown to the Strasbourg publishers; and during this time Bovelles, who had been going through monasteries and libraries in Switzerland, wrote off short commentaries on the fundamental propositions of Nicholas of Cusa. The edition, which had been collaborated on by several German friends of Lefèvre, appeared in three volumes during the summer of 1514. With this fine achievement the philosophical work of Lefèvre d'Étaples may be considered at an end. After this, the *Metaphysics* of Aristotle, printed in the following year, could hardly be anything more than a handy compendium.

On February 6, 1499, when Lefèvre published the works attributed to Dionysius the Areopagite, he wrote the words *Theologia vivificans* as an epigraph to the two new volumes. He was not a doctor of theology, nor had he ever wished to become one; he felt completely out of sympathy with the professors of the modern schools who proudly served up courses of instruction based on Peter Lombard. The meaning of the divine words revealed itself only to souls who had prepared themselves by mystical meditation. Through his reading of the Areopagite, Lefèvre was drawn to the texts of the first Patristic Age, which for him were living witnesses from generations still close in time to Christ. In addition to Pseudo-Dionysius he published the *Epistles* of St. Ignatius and St. Polycarp, and on July 15, 1504, those of Clement of Rome and Anacletus; among these texts, however, were some which were being printed for the first time and were neither authentic nor of any great value. But Lefèvre sincerely believed he would be doing something useful if he exhorted modern Christians to give a hearing to words which had for so long remained forgotten. The first edition of the *Theology* of John of Damascus, an almost completely unknown monk of the eighth century, does perhaps represent an effort to provide the men of the West with a dogmatic summary somewhat nearer in time to the origins of Christianity than the four books of the Lombard. In this way Lefèvre found himself gradually being led toward a study of the Bible. Was he, perhaps, taking the advice which Erasmus had recently given to theology students? In 1509, anticipating the biblical works of Erasmus, he completed the printing of his *Quincuplex Psalmorum*, in which he gave the four Latin versions read by the moderns, as well as a fifth, in a rather timid attempt to reconcile the other four with one another with the aid of a slender knowledge of Hebrew; he also wrote a commentary in which he deliberately set aside all theological considerations and spoke only in terms of the interior life. Three years later, during the Christmas of 1512, he published the *Epistles* of St. Paul. People have claimed to see this as the first Protestant book. There is no doubt that he took notable liberties with ecclesiastical tradition; for him, faith determined the efficacy of the sacraments. Although he energetically asserted the Pauline doctrine of grace, he did not draw predestination from it; and while he based justification on faith and not on works, he did not reject any of the practices of the Church, nor the rules of the monastic life. His critical observations, always rather timid, continued to give acceptance to too many apocryphal works. His reading of St. Paul was that of a mystic concerned with the interior life, and he was ever ready to use images and symbols to justify everything in the Church of his time which was not in harmony with the spirit of the apostolic age. His *Epistles* is the work of a spiritual writer, not a reformer. It will be sufficient to recall that, on August 3, 1512, Lefèvre had just published Ruysbroeck's *Adornment of the Spiritual Marriage* in the Latin version of Gerard Groote, and that he was to bring out in June, 1513, an edition of the writings of the mystics and visionaries whose revelations he had brought back from Germany. But his Pauline edition sometimes gives vent to bitter disquiet in a highly apocalyptic tone.

Lefèvre was aware, just as Rome itself was, that his ideas were unconventional. The case the Dominicans had made out against Johannes Reuchlin, German humanist, Hebraist, and theologian, was to be put in April, 1514, before the Paris faculty of theology, which condemned the defender of the Jewish books on August 2, 1514. Lefèvre was neither a cabalist nor a Talmudist, but it was to Reuchlin that he owed what little Hebrew he knew. He had taken an active part in the discussions in Paris, and intervened with the commission appointed in Rome by Leo X. He resolutely testified to his friendship for Reuchlin. He was conscious of a bond with the great German humanist, for he himself had already been accused by the Parisian scholastics of trying to correct the Vulgate. He had had scarcely anything to do with the writings of Erasmus, but now the attacks of the "Goths" brought together two men of very different education and mentality.

In October, 1495, Erasmus of Rotterdam came to Paris; he was probably about twenty-nine years old at the time. Educated by the Brethren of the Common Life at Deventer, near 's Hertogen-bosch, he had been a canon regular at the monastery of Steyn. Although he had lost all taste for the monastic life he was always to keep sincerely faithful to the spirit of the *Imitation of Christ*. He was familiar with Latin antiquity, and among the Italian humanists he took as his guide the one whose work had been the most outspokenly critical—Lorenzo Valla. We have the correspondence on that Italian humanist which he exchanged at this time with Cornelius Geerd, the Windesheim canon who was later, in Paris, to make the fruitless attempt at reforming Saint-Victor. After being ordained to the priesthood in 1492, Erasmus became secretary to the archbishop of Cambrai, Henry of Bergen, and dreamed of journeying to Rome with this candidate for the cardinal's hat. He had to content himself with attending the Collège de Montaigu for the purpose of furthering his theological studies.

He did not see eye to eye with Standonck, and was not long in joining Fausto Andrelini and Robert Gaguin, who that year published his history of France. In 1496 he made his first appearance as a humanist with a little collection of Latin verses. He had turned his back on Montaigu. After several years of struggling and poverty, during which his encounter with Cornelius Geerd and John Mauburnus appeared to be leading him back to the Windesheim ideal of mortification, he finally had a chance to leave for England in the summer of 1499.

He was only an insignificant humanist poet when, both in

London and in Oxford, he had the good fortune to come to know John Colet. The English scholar, who had returned from Italy in 1496, gave lectures on St. Paul's *Epistles* at Magdalen College, and in these Erasmus was able to detect the methods of Lorenzo Valla. Colet practised a religion which had been refined by the discourses of Pico della Mirandola and perhaps also the sermons of Savonarola. This very simple religion, with its indifference to sacerdotal activity, went hand in hand with an ill-disguised sympathy for the Lollards. Erasmus returned to France, and later to the Low Countries; in Saint-Omer in 1502 he came to know the Franciscan Jean Vitrier, whose highly unconventional ideas on St. Paul had been censured by the Sorbonne in 1498 for their suspected resemblance to Bohemian doctrines. Thus, through the influence of Valla, as well as the indirect but very real influence of a combination of unacknowledged Wycliffite and Hussite ideas, Erasmus completed his education as a dissident almost without knowing it.

Ever since writing his *Adages*, which were published in Paris in 1500, he had wished to reconcile Christian beliefs with the Greco-Roman culture. The *Enchiridion militis christiani*, printed in Antwerp in February, 1504, summed up the methods of a new theology, based entirely on Scripture. The book may have had only a middling degree of success in Paris, but Guillaume Budé immediately sensed its importance. Less than fifteen years later the *Enchiridion* was to be a very effective help in spreading the Reformation.

In Paris, on April 13, 1505, Erasmus published the *Annotationes in Novum Testamentum*, the as yet unedited work in which Lorenzo Valla had applied himself to critical exegesis. In 1506 he spent several months in England with Thomas More. The young London lawyer was then actively engaged in the political life of the realm. Together, the two friends read a number of Lucian's dialogues; this was doubtless a humanist labor, but a preface to their combined effort written in November, 1506, by Thomas More brought out very clearly the religious audacity of the translators.

A long journey through Italy, taking in Bologna, Venice, and Rome (where he came to know the pontifical court) kept Erasmus away from his biblical projects for some time. It was now that he became the leading man of letters in Europe and the genial continuator of the *Quattrocento* humanists. His *Adages* appeared in 1508, published by Aldus Manutius. The tiny collection of his Paris days had swelled to a heavy volume into which were condensed all the wisdom and moral nobility of the ancient world. Erasmian irony, under the influence of Lucian, was already venturing into criticism of the social order and the institutions on which it was based.

On his return to England before the end of August, 1509, he brought with him a preliminary draft of his celebrated work, *The Praise of Folly*. However, there is a two-year break in his correspondence which makes it impossible to follow his work exactly. The fantasy of Aristophanes and the satire of Lucian contained in these first pages gave great pleasure to Thomas More. During those months the violent politics of Julius II scandalized the consciences of Christians and drew forth a lively reaction on the part of the French monarchy; it was no doubt then that he wrote his passionate indictment of the heedlessness of prelates, the corruption of the Roman court and the ambitions of the popes. Coming as it did just before the Council of Pisa, *The Praise of Folly* took on a topical character from the actual events of the time. The book, published by Josse Bade in June, 1511, had a success hitherto unequaled in the annals of printing. Erasmus had just left Paris after a short visit; he was never to return.

Five years went by, however, before he completed his first edition of the New Testament; these years, from 1511 to 1514, were spent in comparative obscurity as a professor of Greek at Cambridge.

The trial of Reuchlin, which had deeply disturbed Lefèvre d'Étaples, also affected Colet and other English friends of Erasmus. A letter from Reuchlin, dated Frankfurt, April, 1514, reached Erasmus in Cambridge, and he sided with him warmly. In August he settled in Basle in order to complete his work.

The New Testament appeared in February, 1516. The introductions and various prefaces to the book, which was dedicated to Leo X, formed a thorough treatise on the methods to be followed in biblical exegesis. Erasmus set aside the scholastic commentators and put his trust in the Fathers alone, though with a number of prudent reservations. Satisfied that he had drawn the underlying thought from the text, he was prepared to accept it to the full, even if it went against established dogmas and hallowed practices. Since the divine word was addressed to all men, and because, in spite of what the scholastics said, he considered it at the time to be easy and uncomplicated, he wished to see it translated into the vernacular and allowed to spread freely.

It matters little that the first edition of the New Testament fails to meet the requirements of modern scholarship and that it shows signs of haste. The contemporaries of Erasmus were aware of its greatness and its value. His commentary, broken up by long digressions, expresses a religious thought stripped of all reminiscences of theological and mystical notions from the Middle Ages, as well as of the scholarly speculations of Italian humanism; it reduced itself to the "philosophy of Christ," a summary of the religious and moral propositions to be drawn from the Gospel and St. Paul, and sufficient to form a basis for that worshiping in spirit which he had proclaimed in the *Enchiridion* and which he thought could be reconciled easily with the fundamental spiritual principles of the ancient world. Thus, although Erasmus avoided any discussion of the Roman tradition, he took up again in a new form, and vindicated, the propositions which John Colet and Jean Vitrier had risked pushing to the point of heresy.

In the edition of the New Testament Lefèvre admired the abundance of scholarship, the clarity of thought, and the firmness and sureness of method; yet he remained the disciple of Nicholas of Cusa, whom Erasmus scarcely knew at all. In the course of a dispute which was to arise in 1517 between these two men concerning the interpretation of a passage from the Epistle to the Hebrews, it became evident that, for the Dutchman, Christ remained the crucified figure crowned with bloody thorns, the God of pity of the Flemish and Burgundian studios; while for Lefèvre he remained the metaphysical God of Nicholas of Cusa and Marsilio Ficino.

The two schools worked in collaboration. There was a Fabrist school, which included Josse Clichtove, the faithful and modest interpreter, Charles de Bovelles, the inspired disciple, and Guillaume Farel, to whom the master had said in 1512: "God will change the world and you will be there to witness it." At the same time there was also a Parisian Erasmianism. Jerome Aléandre, introduced by Erasmus to the faculty of arts, and one of the group of friends who had used to meet in the evenings in Venice, had been the reviver of Greek teaching there since 1508; but he felt drawn toward Church diplomacy, and was later to set out on the brilliant career which would one day bring him in opposition to both Erasmus and Luther. Fausto Andrelini continued to extol the greatness of the classics and to compose Latin verses. Guillaume Budé, who, in 1508 and 1514, in the *Annotationes in Pandectas* and the *De Asse*, had revived the study of imperial law, the science of Roman numismatics, and the economics of the ancient world by means of philology, admired Erasmus as a moralist and theologian. In the Paris of those days elements borrowed from the different labors of Erasmus and Lefèvre were to come together to form a doctrine of expectation and hope. The appearance of Luther on October 31, 1517, was to open a new chapter in the history of Christianity.

5 Lyons and Cosmopolitanism at the Beginning of the French Renaissance

LUCIEN ROMIER

THE intellectual, literary, economic, and political history of Lyons at the close of the fifteenth century and through the first half of the sixteenth has for a long time remained little known; yet it is extremely important for any proper understanding of the origins and development of the Renaissance in France.

Some of the original sixteenth-century architecture of Lyons is still to be found between Fourvière and the Saône: mansions whose symmetrical frontages, spacious entrances, and high ceilings have sometimes been compared to Florentine palaces. These were the dwellings of a society in love with "air, light and liberty."[1] What were the circumstances which enabled this civilization, wealthier and more refined than that of any other city in France at that time, to establish itself at the confluence of the Rhône and the Saône?

Behind this material opulence lay a great economic factor. The city of Lyons, situated near the French borders, the "emboucheure de toutes nouvelles,"[2] enjoyed an incomparable geographical situation. The valleys of the Rhône and the Saône gave it direct contact with the Mediterranean, the Seine basin, the Swiss cantons, Germany, and Italy. At the end of the fifteenth century and during the sixteenth the most frequented routes were to the east of the kingdom, and the reasons for this are not difficult to find. First of all, the endless movements of royal troops and the court itself on their way to Italy gave rise to a great deal of traffic; at the same time, travelers were not exposed to any dangers of

[1] Albert Baur, *Maurice Scève et la Renaissance lyonnaise, étude d'histoire littéraire* (Paris, 1906).
[2] Étienne Pasquier, *Lettres*, in collected works.

war, which was fought on the other side of the mountains or in northern France. It is certain too that this border country between the kingdom and the Holy Roman Empire, open as it was to different influences and nationalities, offered much more commercial freedom and even intellectual tolerance than any other region. It might be said that Lotharingia of old had become a neutral territory in the struggles of the spirit just as much as in armed undertakings.

There were three main roads in this region. The first was the traditional road of the Bourbons, along which for several centuries the kings had passed on their way to Lyons, Italy, or the southeast. It went through Montargis, Gien, Nevers, Moulins, and Roanne, and ended in Lyons after crossing the mountains of the Beaujolais. As it did not serve any particularly prosperous region it can be described as an official route. More traffic was to be found on the Burgundy road, which took travelers from the roads of Champagne and Lorraine along the valley of the Saône, and then turned south. It was above all the great thoroughfare for merchants, workers, and humanists from the Low Countries and Germany; the rich province of Burgundy had a number of materially prosperous refuges to offer. Both these roads went from north to south. The Geneva road through the Rhône valley, used not only by the Swiss but also by the Germans from the east, went from east to west.

These three great highways of communications met in Lyons, from which a very important road following the course of the Rhône enabled travelers to reach the Languedoc, Beaucaire, Aiguesmortes, and Spain.[3]

The city of Lyons was thus the principal gateway for Italian trade with the north of France, the Low Countries and the German cities, and as such was destined for considerable economic expansion.

Conditions for growth were favorable. During that long

[3] *Félix et Thomas Platter à Montpellier. Notes de voyage de deux étudiants bâlois,* trans. L. Kieffer (Montpellier, 1892); Ch. Estienne, *Guide des Chemins,* 1553, ed. Jean Bonnerot (Paris, 1936); Th. de Mayerne-Turquet, *Guide des Chemins,* ed. 1603; Thevet, *Cosmographie,* ed. 1575.

period stretching from the Hundred Years' War to the Wars of Religion, thanks to the support of an increasingly absolute monarchy, the middle class added to its wealth and France became dotted with those merchants "who were always seeking immunities."[4] Maritime discoveries transformed commercial routes and conditions alike, and the industry of the realm was given fresh impetus by a new abundance of raw materials and new outlets for its products. Progress was rapid and enormous.[5] The kings of France at that time were singularly eager to see that the country profited from these new conditions. Louis XI was notably persistent. His remarkable efforts are well-known: from 1451 to 1483 a series of ordinances encouraged the economic expansion of the cities.

Throughout the Middle Ages trade was exposed to great dangers whenever it ventured beyond the safety of the city walls, so it had sought refuges where the merchants could find security, immunities, and privileges. These refuges were the fairs. Consignments were assured by safe-conducts, disputes settled by a special summary jurisdiction, and recoveries of debts facilitated by a rigorous administrative machinery. The safeguards were very real and substantial. At the beginning of the French Renaissance the exempt fairs made a considerable contribution to human progress. Set up for the most part in the fifteenth century, they would reach their peak a century later.[6]

At the end of the fifteenth century and during the sixteenth the leading fairs of the realm were those at Lyons. This period of good fortune began under Charles VII. On February 9, 1420, while still Dauphin, Charles granted Lyons two exempt annual fairs, each to last six days;[7] in 1444, as king, he added a third fair,

[4] P. Imbart de la Tour, "La Renaissance économique," Les origines de la Réforme, Vol. I.

[5] O. Noël, Histoire du commerce du monde, II (Paris, 1898), 60–6. Cf. Ch. de la Roncière, Histoire de la marine française, Vol. III (Paris, 1906).

[6] F. Aubert, "Le Parlement au XVIe siècle," in Nouvelle revue historique du droit français et étranger, XXIX, 787; P. Huvelin, Essai historique sur le droit des marchés et des foires (Paris, 1897).

[7] Laurière, Ordonnances, XI, 45–6.

extended all of them to twenty days each, and bestowed on them
the same privileges as those given the fairs of Champagne and
Brie. At that time Geneva attracted all the international trade. A
deadly rivalry started up between the two cities, and Geneva was
to lose out, thanks to the energetic protection which the kings
gave the market of Lyons. On July 7, 1445, Charles VII prohibited the conveyance of merchandise to Geneva, a prohibition
designed especially for the benefit of the Lyons fairs;[8] and on
October 20, 1462, French and foreign merchants alike were forbidden to frequent the fairs at Geneva. Louis XI, on March 8,
1463, increased the number of fairs at Lyons yet further and
arranged for their dates to coincide with those of their rivals.[9]
In 1494 the Lyons fairs were confirmed by Charles VIII, who in
1496 granted them a veritable commercial monopoly for the
time they were in progress. Louis XII,[10] and after him Francis I,
renewed their privileges.[11] In his ordinance of February, 1515,
Francis I set forth the following considerations, which throw some
light on the international character of the Lyons market:

> The good and utility accruing to our country and subjects
> through the well-being of these fairs in the said city of Lyons,
> which is more suited for this purpose than any other, because
> foreign merchants, seeing that it is at the extremities of our said
> realm and near to several great countries, bring both themselves
> and their merchandise all the more willingly and easily, declining
> to go to other places as they might do, were they obliged to
> enter further into our said realm.[12]

The fortune of Lyons was thus solidly established, and Geneva
became a place of transit.

The four fairs at Lyons, which were held on Low Monday,
August 4, November 3, and the first Monday after the Epiphany,[13]
enjoyed considerable privileges: the abolition of the right of

[8] *Ibid.*, XIII, pp. 399 ff.
[9] *Ibid.*, XV, 644. On the struggle between these two cities, cf. F. Borel, *Les
Foires de Genève au XVe siècle.*
[10] Laurière, *Ordonnances*, XXI, 47.
[11] *Privilèges des foires de Lyon*, published by Guillaume Barbier, ed. 1649.
[12] *Ordonnances de François Ier*, Vol. 1.   [13] Huvelin, *op. cit.*, pp. 286 ff.

escheat and reprisal, and exemption from bans and retainers, from the control of overseers, and from the laws governing entry and departure from the kingdom. A special jurisdiction had been set up in the city. In 1462 Louis XI had withdrawn from ordinary jurisdiction all difficulties which might arise during the free fairs or as a result of them; by an edict of February, 1532, Francis I set up the famous tribunal of Conservation, which settled disputes, "sans longs procès et figures de plaids," between all persons, native and foreign, in all commercial matters, whether civil or criminal, connected with the fairs.[14]

Free from all temporal lords and exempt from clerical interference, this city, in which the legal profession was not dominant, secured for itself an economic situation unique in western Europe: at its fairs men from Germany, Switzerland, Florence, Lucca, Genoa, Milan, Flanders, and Spain met and mingled.

The birth of new industries and the impetus given to business occasioned the development of that most cosmopolitan form of commerce—banking. As intermediaries between capital and labor the corporation of bankers were in future to play a dominant part in international relations. These financiers, who provided everyone—especially kings—with the wherewithal for action, tied up the trade of central and western Europe in a network of branch banks; and they frequently mixed politics with their commercial affairs. The Lombards and Genoese had been the principal money-changers during the Middle Ages; at the beginning of the sixteenth century they were supplanted by the Florentines, who had establishments in all the larger cities. In France they had set up in Montpellier, Marseilles, Toulouse, Bordeaux, Cahors, Nantes, Paris, and Rouen.[15]

Lyons became the center of European exchange, "in such wise that Lyons is the monetary foundation for all Italy and a good part of Spain and Flanders," as Navagero wrote.[16] Through

[14] J. Vaesen, *La juridiction commerciale à Lyon.*
[15] E. Picot, "Les Italiens en France au XVIe siècle," *Bulletin italien*, II, 23 ff.
[16] Written in 1528. *Il viaggio fatto in Spagna et in Francia dal magnifico M. Andrea Navagero* (Vinegia, 1563), fol. 58.

banking it became the greatest cosmopolitan center in Christendom.[17] It was the seat of an international syndicate of Italian and German bankers, and was thus directly connected with all the branch banks of continental Europe—in Antwerp, Brussels, Nürnberg, London, Venice, and Florence—and, so long as the Fuggers held the destiny of Germany in their hands, the "bank of Saône" in Lyons had the French crown very heavily in its debt.[18] The kings contracted perpetual loans there, and the financial inducements were so great that the capital of the kingdom would have been transferred to Lyons if the conquests in Italy had been kept up.[19]

The bank in Lyons did occasionally have to undergo some trials, but it only emerged the stronger for them. Most of the money-changers were Florentines. As early a ruler as Charles VIII, in a moment of anger, had once driven out the employees of the Medici banks.[20] Then in 1521 their prosperity was once more rudely interrupted as a result of French political setbacks in Italy: the king had the most prominent Florentines thrown into prison. But these violent reprisals were short-lived, and on May 1, 1535, an edict revoked all the vexatious measures taken against the bank. The importance of banking continued to grow without any break until the civil wars.

The foreign merchants formed into separate national groups, each with its own consul and guard, and turned Lyons into the great emporium of western Europe—Italy, France, Spain, the Low Countries, and Germany—quite apart from the Middle Eastern trade, of which Lyons was also the center.

The fact that foreign merchants in Lyons enjoyed special exemptions caused them to spread abroad very good accounts

[17] R. Doucet, *Finances municipales et crédit public à Lyon au XVIe siècle* (Paris, 1937).

[18] *Catalogue des actes de François Ier*, *passim*. For international banking, see the comprehensive work of R. Ehrenberg, *Das Zeitalter der Fugger*, 1912.

[19] A. Spont, *Semblançay, la bourgeoisie financière au début du XVIe siècle*, Paris, 1896.

[20] A. Desjardins, *Négociations diplomatiques de la France avec la Toscane*, I, 408. Cf. E. Picot, *Bulletin italien*, I, 93–4.

of Francis I; and when Francis struck a blow at the Protestants in France the traders assured their coreligionists in Germany that there was no truth in the reports.[21]

Favored by this happy freedom, the spirit of initiative in Lyons extended to all branches of commerce. Sharing as they did with Marseilles and the Rumanians a monopoly in the import of spices, the people of the city concerned themselves with the discoveries in the New World and took a great interest in access routes to China and the Indies. It was a syndicate of Lyons businessmen which in 1523 provided Verrazano with the means necessary for his explorations.[22]

Economic expansion of this sort attracted to Lyons a host of artisans and common people of all nationalities. The city, in fact, was a refuge of industrial as well as commercial liberty. Only four trades had to be carried out in guilds; all the others were free, without masters or wardens. In this way, industry in Lyons escaped both the tax authorities and the restrictions of royal regulations, and the municipality jealously defended this independence. Since anyone who possessed capital could set up as master in his own right, Lyons attracted all kinds of foreign artisans, printers from Germany, silk manufacturers from Italy, and bankers, money-changers, and traders of all sorts. Letters patent issued by Louis XI on April 17, 1476, and renewed in 1486 had set the official seal on this arrangement. It has been said, quite rightly, that Lyons had become a new town in the modern sense, a sort of industrial "free city," benefiting from privileges and tax exemptions, where foreigners enjoyed a hospitality very much to their advantage.[23]

The life of the workers in Lyons in the sixteenth century had something of the restlessness of modern city life. There were

[21] Guillaume Du Bellay, *Mémoires* (collected by Michaud and Poujoulat); *Catalogue des actes de François Ier* (August 31, 1536). Cf. V. L. Bourrilly, *Guillaume Du Bellay.*

[22] C. de la Roncière, *Histoire de la marine française*, III, 258–60, 349–51.

[23] H. Hauser, *Ouvriers du temps passé*, 5th ed., 1927; also his retrospective considerations in "La Liberté du commerce et du travail sous Henri IV," *Revue historique*, LXXX, 275.

popular uprisings, strikes, food shortages, and all the troubles attendant on industrial development. One of the most notable disturbances of this nature was the celebrated *Rebeine* of 1529, which resulted in the looting of a convent, the smashing of sacred images, and the invasion of an abbey.[24] The bands of revolters were made up of "serviteurs de mestier," the loom-workers. The riot had been stirred up under the pretext of starvation and at the instigation of the tavern-keepers. According to a highly indignant chronicler named Symphorien Champier, this disturbance had its roots far back in the past. In 1505 "a set of vulgar folk arose and called themselves artisans, just as though others a little more important were gentlemen, and not artisans or merchants." And the reasons given by Champier for this invasion on the part of the "artisan sect" are very worthy of note: Lyons had become a city of perdition since it had become a city of wealth. The origin of the evils was to be sought in the creation of the fairs. "Thus nobility was transfigured into merchandise, in that place where people of all nations lived, such as Italians, Florentines, Genoese, Luccans, Swiss, Germans, and Spaniards." The fairs, he said, had peopled Lyons with foreign workers who had no special attachment to the city and who often brought subversive ideas with them. At the sight of these changes Champier could not restrain his anger:

> The people have taken on airs and entertained evil ideas, and will not be corrected either by master or lord or prince, except by force, and the servants, who once were humble in the presence of their masters and were sober and poured much water into their wine . . . now wish to drink better wine, like their masters, without water or any admixture whatever, which is a thing against all reason.

Another historian from Lyons, Guillaume Paradin, compared his city to a great park in which were enclosed all the animals of creation. As for the 1529 riot, he sprang to the defense of the natives of Lyons: "Those who read these memorials," he wrote,

[24] Hauser, "Étude critique sur la Rebeine de Lyon," *Revue historique*, Vol. LXI, 1896.

may charge the people of Lyons with being easily aroused and liable to sedition: but anyone who considers that the city of Lyons is made up of several different elements and that, among these small artisans and lowest of the populace, there are scarcely any natives of Lyons, but only those who have come from many different countries, will not accuse the people of Lyons of being like this by nature, since by nature they are peaceable and obedient." He went on to say that, with a population as cosmopolitan as this, "it could not be otherwise than that minds, customs, humors, intentions, inclinations, conditions, temperaments, passions, affections, dispositions and other natural properties should be all different, opposite and mixed up together."[25]

The cosmopolitan character of the population accounts for the conditions which at that time so often disturbed this great trading city, where "a common refuge of all foreigners, and strange people, who come there from all directions under pretext of trade, can easily set up in business."[26] The number of noblemen and burghers who were actually natives of Lyons had declined to such an extent that it was difficult to find enough of them to fill the twelve aldermen's chairs.[27] The crowd of workers harbored by Lyons can be imagined: it is known that, under Henry II, silk-weaving alone kept seven thousand looms busy.[28]

In the sixteenth century this enormous concentration of people suffered from a great food shortage. By 1530 the soaring price of food "forced the neighboring districts to send there a numberless multitude of poor people, and there descended upon Lyons such a great number that they caused the city of Lyons to be overwhelmed as never before at the sight of the pitiable state of so many poor persons, who were arriving there from one hour to the next in great bands and in full boat-loads, without anyone to govern them."[29] In 1531, in order to relieve the needs of this constantly growing mass of workers, the city councilors founded that admirable institution, the *Aumône générale*.[30]

[25] Guillaume Paradin, *Histoyre de Lyon* (Lyons, 1573).
[26] Cl. de Rubys, *Histoire de Lyon*.   [27] *Ibid.*
[28] Hauser, *op. cit.*   [29] Paradin, *op. cit.*   [30] *Ibid.*

Of all the major industries that helped swell the numbers of this motley crowd the most important was printing, which developed to a remarkable extent in Lyons. In the age of the Renaissance the printing press did much to encourage cosmopolitanism. For one thing, it enabled ideas and discoveries to spread without any limit; for another, the master printers and workers scattered throughout all the major cities of France propagated the intellectual novelties they had picked up, either in their native countries or in the course of their travels.

Because of its geographical situation, Lyons was a great center of attraction for the itinerant printers from Germany or the Low Countries, who introduced the art of typography into France. The industry had been established in Lyons in 1473 and had made such progress there that by the beginning of the sixteenth century eighty printing works were turning out a considerable number of books, with a circulation in Italy, France, Spain, and even Germany itself. Lyons rivaled Venice in the publications it produced. Recent studies have shown that the lists of printers, booksellers, binders, and type founders in the sixteenth century contained no fewer than three thousand names.[31] Such a figure suggests an unparalleled degree of activity.

The printers, masters and workers alike, were mainly from Germany, which also provided Lyons with a constantly shifting succession of illuminators, writers, and even painters. Besides the Germans from the Rhineland, Swabia, and neighboring regions, it is highly possible that the Flemings played at least some part in the development of printing in Lyons. Some of these printers set up permanent establishments, while others returned to their native countries after working in Lyons for ten or twenty years. This constant movement, as well as the translation of books which had already appeared in Germany, caused the commercial market of Lyons to be joined by a sort of intellectual market abounding in new books and ideas. It can be assumed, in fact, that the printing industry enjoyed an unusual measure of freedom

[31] Baudrier, *Bibliographie lyonnaise*; K. Haebler, *Die deutschen Buchdrucker des XV. Jahrhunderts im Auslande* (Munich, 1924).

from the very outset: the printing of numerous works, even books of devotion, in the French language affords evidence of this.

Thus Lyons gained an illustrious reputation in the history of printing; masters like Gryphius, De Tournes and Roville, among many others, are sufficient to show what the intellectual progress of the Renaissance owes to the city. The expansion was not always smooth and unbroken: in 1539 the workers went on strike, complaining of insufficient food and wages, and royal intervention became necessary.[32]

This popular and cosmopolitan environment was extremely favorable for the birth and development of new ideas, and it was hardly surprising "if a great number of people were led astray from the path of true and sound doctrine."[33] The Reformation was to gain a very early foothold there. Lyons, once the cradle of the Waldenses, had always harbored unorthodox ideas in religious matters. The close of the fifteenth century and the beginning of the sixteenth saw even further manifestations of this sort.[34] From the very outset of the religious revolution the "marauders and heretics" showed up in Lyons; as early as January 15, 1520, an inquisitor was sent there to eliminate them, and on September 4, 1524, Francis I put on record in an ordinance "that for five years the Lutheran sect has been breeding rapidly in the city of Lyons and the region and diocese of Lyons and various false doctrines have been disseminated and blazed abroad both through pernicious sermons directed against the Catholic faith and through certain reprehensible books . . . ."

With Geneva, Montbéliard; Switzerland, and the Vaudois cantons as its neighbors, Lyons soon became the center of independent thinkers in France. In 1524, Margaret of Angoulême took up residence at Saint-Just-lès-Lyon, with a whole household of

[32] Hauser, *Ouvriers du temps passé.*

[33] Edict of Francis I (1524), quoted by H. Hauser, *Revue historique,* 1896.

[34] Information laid against Simon de Phares, imprisoned in Lyons for devoting himself to the occult sciences (Arch. Nat., X¹ª 128, fol. 113). See also *Le Tableau historique de la royale abbaye de Saint-Pierre* (quoted by A. Coville in *Revue historique,* 1904, Vol. II).

preachers and proselytes, such as D'Arande, Du Blet, Papillon, Sebville, and Maigret.[35] From the beginning the Reformation held a very strong position in the city, and it continued to do so until the civil wars. This was made all the easier by the determination of the municipality to defend its own material and moral independence against all royal or inquisitorial intervention. With a tolerance born of prudence, the consular corps, even at the most critical moments, was careful to deny any news which might call down repressive measures on the part of royal authority.[36] In 1524, after Francis I had wanted the Spanish and German merchants established in the city arrested as "usurers and heretics," the consuls demanded that all of them should be given their freedom, "even those who have been charged on suspicion of heresy."[37] Far from the theologians of the Sorbonne and the inquisitors of Toulouse, the Reformed enjoyed a measure of security. The main concern of Lyons was for its liberty, and the autonomy of Geneva may well have awakened a desire for similar independence in the minds of a number of its citizens.[38]

All the same, it is doubtful whether the people of Lyons at the time of the Renaissance were attached to any particular form of religion; the reason for this is simply that the ceaseless movements of men and ideas made tolerance and liberalism the only possible *modus vivendi*. This city was a privileged center of a Pre-Reformation outlook, a survival from happier times when the two churches, Protestant and Catholic, had not yet set up as rivals.

The civilization of Lyons, therefore, was to be more favorable to humanism than to the Reformation. Any detailed, scholarly analysis of the works bequeathed by the Renaissance is liable to reveal nothing but the renewal of classical studies; on the other hand, an attempt to grasp the general features of the humanist spirit will show how right Michelet was when he defined the

[35] See Hauser's article, p. 300, referred to in footnote 23 above.
[36] Le Romier, *Jacques d'Albon de Saint-André* (Paris, 1909), p. 310.
[37] Hauser, work cited in note 23.
[38] This is mentioned by C. de Rubys in *Histoire de Lyon* in highly malevolent terms.

Renaissance as *the discovery of the world and the discovery of man.*
There was a widening of the moral horizon. New ways of thinking came to break down the solid front of intellectual unity;
people began to realize that customs and ideas differed from
place to place. The foreigner ceased to be simply an enemy
and became an interesting friend: the notion of humanity had
appeared.

Humanism was essentially a moral cosmopolitanism, an
attempt to break out of the confines of particular times and places;
and since this attempt was exclusively literary and existed through
the medium of books, it created a state of mind which did not
lend itself very easily to national allegiances.[39] For this reason
humanism contributed to the growth of individualism: soli-
darity and close social cohesion are only possible among members
of a restricted and clearly defined group, and the substitution
of general, universal tendencies for immediate and tangible social
relationships leads to the development of individualism. It has
been rightly said that this is one of the most disturbing problems:
if the individual has, in theory, a right to make laws for himself,
then how far does this right extend, and how far do the demands
of groups and masses allow him to exercise it?[40] Humanism,
in fact, resolved the problem, to the detriment of national
allegiances; the thirst for intellectual and artistic delights, the love
of pleasure, and the importance of the human personality stifled
patriotic sentiment.[41]

It is hardly possible to mention a single humanist who did not
travel widely throughout Europe, moving from one city to
another. The humanist did not bear any distinctive national
characteristics, but reflected the intellectual development of the
Renaissance in its most universal aspect. He was a citizen only of
the ideal republic of letters, which knew no frontiers and had no

[39] E. Faguet, *Le seizième siècle, études d'histoire littéraire*, p. xvii.
[40] F. Baldensperger, "Le procès de l'individualisme," *Mercure de France*,
LXXVII, 27.
[41] Jacob Burckhardt, *La civilisation en Italie au temps de la Renaissance*, I, French
trans. by M. Schmitt, 2nd ed. (Paris, 1906), 161.

center. Erasmus was a classic example of this, a true cosmopolitan even linguistically, whose journeys took him from the Low Countries to Italy, from Italy to England, and from England to France, Switzerland, and Germany.

Lyons was the favorite stopping place for traveling humanists, since they found its material and moral circumstances extremely congenial. In fact, the merchants who had become rich there also felt the desire for exquisite and refined delights. Out of this was born a form of the Renaissance peculiar to Lyons, owing its formation, not to books or scholars, but to the social life of the city itself. It was based on the intercourse of bankers, merchants, scholars, and literary men of all countries, and influenced by Italian art and luxury; there was a constant round of pleasures and entertainments, and cultivated ladies of fashion made a contribution of their own. Thus, in these surroundings, where German influence had sown the seeds of religious reform, Italian influence led to the appearance and growth of a local literature, helped along by the intellectual freedom enjoyed by Lyons. But we must restrict ourselves here to the first Renaissance in Lyons. The names of the literary personalities of this period are fairly well known, such as Symphorien Champier, bombastic moralizer and an ardent proponent of public order; Jehan Perréal, painter and poet; and Pierre Sala, a wealthy dilettante and author of the book *Friendship*, who used to gather his literary friends together in the hospitality of his house in the Anticaille, on the slopes of Fourvière.

No idea of the intellectual developments then taking shape in Lyons could be complete without reference to some of the many institutions founded in the city under Francis I: the College of Medicine, for example, where François Rabelais taught, and especially the Collège de la Trinité, an exclusively municipal foundation independent of ecclesiastical authority, instituted by a sort of lay confraternity of Lyons citizens. One of the teachers at this college was Barthélemy Aneau, the pupil of Wolmar, the friend of Amyot and the close supporter of Beza and Calvin.

And so Lyons became a center for all scholars and for all the latest ideas. Neoplatonism found, as it were, a natural habitat there, thanks to Margaret of Navarre, Bonaventure Despériers, Étienne Dolet, and Rabelais,[42] and even found its way into the intimacy of the salons through cultivated ladies like Madame du Penon[43] and poets like Eustorg de Beaulieu. Lyons became the "Florence françoyse." It is quite possible that there was a coterie which gathered together all the traveling humanists who were passing through—the *sodalitium amicorum lugdunensium* mentioned by Nicolas Bourbon and so often extolled by Voulté in his verses.[44] It is sufficient simply to mention that incomparable group in which Rabelais, Marot, Dolet, Scève, Champier, Salmon Macrin, Sainte-Marthe, Charles Fontaine, Gilbert Dûcher, Jean Voulté, and Bicolas Bourbon all met together at one and the same time.[45]

In this environment there flourished what has already been described as moral cosmopolitanism, or, more simply, intellectual liberalism. This makes it possible to account for the attitude toward the Reformation taken by the humanist group in Lyons: although their sympathies were based entirely on the ideas of Lefèvre d'Étaples and the first French Reformation, the temper of their minds hardly suited them to the narrow religious discipline held out by Calvin. "It was precisely because of their breadth of mind that educated circles in Lyons had little sympathy for Luther, that rebellious monk, and all his brutal commotion. They were neither revolutionaries nor innovators, but, as they themselves said, devout restorers."[46]

Something must now be said about the various foreign centers from which Lyons borrowed the elements of its cosmopolitanism.

[42] Abel Lefranc, "Le platonisme et la littérature en France à l'époque de la Renaissance," *Revue d'histoire littéraire de la France*, 1896; *Histoire du Collège de France* (Paris, 1893), pp. 97–8.

[43] E. Picot, *Bulletin italien*, I, 125.

[44] "Lettres inédites de Jean de Boyssonné et de ses amis," published by J. Buché, *Revue des langues romanes*, 1894 *et seq.* Cf. "Un dîner littéraire chez Mellin de Saint-Gelais," by L. Delaruelle, *Revue d'histoire littéraire de la France*, 1897.

[45] A. Baur, *Maurice Scève et la Renaissance lyonnaise*, pp. 53 ff.

[46] Ferdinand Buisson, *Sébastien Castellion* (Paris, 1891), pp. 53–9.

Since Lyons was so near Italy, Italian influence could hardly fail to be considerable, even preponderant. As Alfieri said, "in no country does that plant called man grow as strongly as in Italy." This observation, which so perfectly fitted the race of *condottieri* and potentates who controlled the internal life of the peninsula in the fifteenth century, can also be used to describe the intellectual and material expansiveness of Italy during the Renaissance. Whether as bankers, politicians, merchants, philosophers, warriors, scholars, or artists, the Italians were amazing travelers, who went up and down western Europe scattering not only the intellectual and material riches of their own land but also the elements they had picked up in the course of their wanderings. It has been said so often that Italy was the cradle of the Renaissance both in literature and in art that it has come to be thought that the whole glory of this country was to have rediscovered and brought to light the great intellectual and artistic achievements of the ancient world. The truth is that Italy also provided Europe with those indefatigable pioneers of cosmopolitanism, the merchants and humanists who, precisely because they were constantly on the move and making contacts wherever they went, introduced the most vital and up-to-date elements of the new civilization.

In the convulsions which Italy underwent during the sixteenth century, exile was the main reason for emigration. Jovianus Pontanus wrote: "In our populous cities we see a mass of people who of their own free will have left their homeland, and wherever they go they take with them their qualities and their virtues."[47] Whether by choice or by necessity, thousands of individuals left their native soil because the political or economic situation had become unbearable.

It has been well said that the history of the Italian Renaissance, right up to the end of the fifteenth century, is the history of Florence. Florence did not owe its primacy to the force of its intellectual civilization alone. It was the most vigorous center of Italian expansion: the ceaseless spur of competition made it the

[47] "De tolerando exilio," *De fortitudine*, I, II, Ch. iv.

home of individual energy and the spirit of enterprise. Florence had merchant colonies in all the major cities, from Constantinople to London. Of all the great European cities, Lyons was the favorite abode of Florentine emigrants; and they brought with them the manners and tastes of Tuscany, as well as its intellectual and artistic riches. The economic role they played there has already been seen, and it is sufficient to recall the success of Neoplatonism in Lyons in order to sense their intellectual influence also. Besides Florence there were also Milan, Lucca, and Genoa, all of which added their own considerable quotas to the population of Lyons.[48]

The contribution of Spain and Portugal to the cosmopolitanism of Lyons was purely economic. The strongest foreign counterbalance to Italian influence came from the north—from Germany and the Low Countries.

France, at the beginning of the Renaissance, owed a great deal to Germany: the printing press, the philosophy of Nicholas of Cusa, and even some of the rudiments of classical culture. Under Francis I large numbers of German merchants and printers spread throughout the cities of France and exercised a very far-reaching influence.[49] One has only to read the historical records of Lyons to realize the fruitful role they played there. They brought with them the distinctive characteristics of their own civilization: the spirit of inventiveness and the love of practical achievements, as well as the taste for philosophy and research. It is no exaggeration to say that the whole of the printing industry in Lyons at the beginning of the Renaissance was controlled by the Germans; hence the deep and lasting imprint they left on intellectual life there.

A long account could well be drawn up of the intellectual and economic life of that Renaissance Germany which filled the Lyons fairs with its merchants, and at the same time sent its

[48] E. Picot, "Les Italiens en France au XVIe siècle," in *Bulletin italien*, Vol. I et seq.; see also Charpin-Feugerolles, *Les Florentins à Lyon* (Lyons, 1894).

[49] *Ordonnances de François Ier*, Vol. I, and *Catalogue des actes de François Ier*, passim.

students to the French universities. Two cities bordering on France kept up unbroken contacts with Lyons—Basle and Strasbourg. Basle, controlling both the plateau of northwest Switzerland and the plain of southern Alsace, had outlets to the north and east through the Rhine valley and into France through the Belfort gap.[50] Once an episcopal city, then a free city of the Empire, it had been the setting for a great council in the fifteenth century. This city dominated the whole of the Upper Rhine and was constantly increasing its trade and wealth: Jean Amerbach and Jean Froben had their famous printing works there. Many humanists and reformers loved this city, distinguished by such temporary residents as Erasmus and Calvin, and made it their abode.

Strasbourg, "la ville des routes," had always been resplendent for its letters, arts, and sciences, and especially for its university. Down the Rhine was Cologne, a wealthy city full of printers, made famous by the Brethren of the Common Life; with its lively fairs and its university it was a great source of attraction to foreigners.

But at that time the greatest center in Germany for international contacts was probably Frankfurt, surrounded as it was by Saxony, Lorraine, Franconia, Swabia, and Bavaria; it was a free city, and also the city where the emperors were elected and crowned.[51] Its transactions were mercantile rather than financial, and as a result it kept up very close contact with the exchange in Lyons. At the beginning of the sixteenth century it opened its famous book fair.

There was also Nürnberg, the "pearl of Germany," the "caravanserai of arts and crafts," and the home of Albrecht Dürer and Hans Sachs; Augsburg, whose bankers were rivals of those in Lyons and Florence; Mainz; Leipzig, with its famous fairs; Brunswick, Landshut; and Calcar. German civilization gave the life of Lyons, in the midst of it material luxury and

[50] A. Hunly, *Histoire de la formation territoriale de l'Europe centrale*, 2nd ed. (Paris, 1894), I, 356–68.
[51] *Ibid.*, pp. 150–1.

Italian opulence, a character which was at once practical and intellectual.

For a long time the Low Countries had been in very close contact with France. The great centers of attraction and international influence were first Bruges and then Antwerp, "the source of commerce." The French poured into Antwerp in large numbers, either to do business there or to settle permanently; it was a liberal and cosmopolitan city. For a time, Antwerp and Lyons were the twin poles of European trade.

One might also mention England, where Bartholomew Fair and the fair at Stourbridge drew merchants from Lyons; and Switzerland, which, quite apart from its trade, provided France with an abundance of soldiers who, constantly passing through Lyons on their way to Italy, had their own undeniable part to play in the expansion of Protestantism.

Thus Lyons, at the end of the fifteenth century and during the first half of the sixteenth, offered a very favorable atmosphere for the meeting and mingling of influences from north and south alike. Here, far from all the obstructive measures of the *Parlements* or the Sorbonne, these elements could blend harmoniously together, and this was made possible by the simultaneous rise of industry, trade, printing, itinerant humanism, and art—in short, by the rise of civilization.

One can easily imagine the allurements which Lyons held in the fifteenth and sixteenth centuries for travelers of whatever country or condition. In this new Capua, rich and lively, full of entertainments, gaiety, and luxury, the kings forgot their duties, so it was said; and when they finally had to depart, all the ladies and courtesans looked back longingly on this happy, elegant city. The ladies of Lyons could truly say:

> Françoys, Angloys, Lombards et Genevoys
> Par plusieurs fois nous portent du content. [52]

[52] "La Réformation des dames de Paris faicte par les Lyonnaises," in Montaiglon, *Recueil de poésies françaises*, VIII, 244. "Frenchmen, Englishmen, Lombards and Genevans, time and again they have brought us contentment."

Dolet wrote these grateful lines:

Opulente, mère d'une forte race, riche en beaux monuments,
Elle s'ouvre au commerce de tous, étrangers ou citoyens.[53]

And Clément Marot these enthusiastic ones:

C'est un grand cas voir le mont Pélion,
Ou d'avoir veu les ruines de Troye:
Mais qui ne voit la ville de Lyon,
Aucun plaisir à ses yeux il n'octroye.[54]

[53] "Opulent, mother of a mighty race, rich in fine monuments, she opens herself up to trade with all men, foreigners or citizens alike."

[54] "It is a great thing to see Mount Pelion, or to have seen the ruins of Troy: but he who does not see the city of Lyons bestows no pleasure upon his eyes."

PART THREE

French Humanism and
the Printed Book

6 Printing in France and Humanism, 1470–80[1]

RUDOLF HIRSCH

INTRODUCTION

THE early history of printing in France has been amply and well described, thanks to the work of scholars like Delisle, Claudin, Harrisse, and Scholderer.[2] It will therefore be difficult to present important new facts unless hitherto unknown documents come to light, though minor revisions continue to be made. The re-examination of known data may, however, lead to a clearer understanding or new interpretation of the relation between printing and humanism. Throughout this paper humanism is interpreted to mean not only the revival of classical studies but, in a broader sense, the entire movement which was meant to free the human intellect from rigid traditions imposed by church authority and to promote "new learning" which was fashioned after a somewhat hypothetical classical model.

I begin with a brief summary of the historical development of printing in France, up to about the year 1480; but throughout I shall place the main emphasis on the origin and training of printers, their contribution to the spread of classical and humanist writing, to the languages in which books were printed, to types and illustrations which reflect the predilection or taste of printers or their

[1] This paper was presented at the Middle Atlantic Renaissance Conference, held at Ursinus College, Collegeville, Pennsylvania, on October 24, 1959.
[2] L. Delisle, *Essai sur l'imprimerie et la librairie à Caen de 1480 à 1550* (Caen, 1891); A. Claudin, *Histoire de l'imprimerie en France au xve et au xvie siècle* (4 vols.; Paris, 1900–14); H. Harrisse, *Les premiers incunables bâlois et leurs dérivés, Toulouse, Lyons, Vienne-en-Dauphiné* (Paris, 1902); V. Scholderer, in *Catalogue of Books Printed in the XVth Century Now in the British Museum*, Part VIII: *France . . .* (London, 1949).

sponsors and their clientele, and to the geographic distribution of presses.

At about the time when Gutenberg developed a method of casting type and of constructing a press in Strasbourg, and a short time before he returned to his native Mainz to proceed with the actual production of texts with movable type, a curious experiment took place in Avignon. There a goldsmith named Procopius Waldfoghel (a native of Prague), with the assistance of a Trier watchmaker and locksmith and supported by a young jurist from Gascogne, labored between 1444 and 1446 on an "ars artificialiter scribendi," or a method of writing mechanically. No example survives, but it has at times been claimed that Waldfoghel had thus invented printing. Claudin and others have proved satisfactorily that his work could not have involved the casting of large numbers of identical characters, that the few alphabets which he possessed were apparently not used to set long passages in type to be printed on a press, and that he probably attempted only to improve upon the cumbersome method of writing by hand, perhaps somewhat as we do today on a typewriter.

Knowledge of Gutenberg's invention had seemingly spread to France by the later part of the 1450's, if we may trust a sixteenth-century copy of a supposedly fifteenth-century document.[3] According to this source, King Charles VII, having heard of Gutenberg's invention, asked the masters of the mint in 1458 to select an able engraver and to send him to Mainz to learn the art of printing. Nicolas Jenson was chosen and went to Mainz, where he stayed until 1462. Claudin believes that Jenson's failure to return to France was caused by the death of his sponsor, Charles VII, in 1461 and the lack of interest on the part of Louis XI, who was then fully occupied with internal political problems.[4] After leaving Mainz, Nicolas Jenson is believed to have gone to Italy,

---

[3] Bibliothèque Nationale, MS fr. 5524, fols. 152ᵛ–153ʳ.
[4] Claudin, *op. cit.*, I, 11.

perhaps to help Italy's first printers, Sweynheim and Pannartz, in the establishment of their presses at Subiaco and Rome. He later became famous as a printer in Venice, where he started his own press in 1470, using a pure Roman type and producing many classical texts.

LATE START IN FRANCE

Had Charles lived longer, the history of printing in France might have taken quite a different course. Actually, printing was not introduced until 1470, fifteen or sixteen years after the production of the forty-two-line Bible in Mainz, twelve years after its beginning in Strasbourg, five or six years after its beginning in Cologne and Subiaco. Before printing was brought to France, it had also spread to Bamberg (1460), Basle (1468), Augsburg (1468), Eltville (1467), Rome (1467), Venice (1469), and a few other more or less important towns. We are tempted to speculate why to France in general, and to Paris with its renowned university in particular, it came so late. Various reasons have been advanced.

First of all, it is known that Fust and Schoeffer, the Mainz printers, had excellent contacts in Paris and sold printed books there on regular business trips; indeed, Fust died in Paris on one such trip in 1466. It is doubtful that the number of printed books sold in France could have been sufficiently large to discourage the introduction of printing. Second, we hear about the opposition of scribes and illuminators to the new method of producing texts. This is a plausible explanation; the old book-centered trades were strongly organized, and guilds are known to have opposed the infringement of the new competing art in various towns; but we possess no documentary proof of actual interference in Paris. Third, it has been held that the Hundred Years' War and the plague and famine may have been responsible, since warfare and misery had depopulated France and brought ruin to artisans and small merchants from whose ranks printers could have been recruited. True, France in the 1460's was probably not rich in literate, enterprising, and well-trained craftsmen who would have been willing to risk their fortunes in a new craft, but the scarcity of artisans there would hardly have prevented some German printers from starting a press at an earlier date, as they did in Italy, had they believed that a sufficiently broad demand existed. Furthermore, printing was not entirely dependent upon craftsmen. We find among early printers former scribes, booksellers, students, clergymen, and artists; it cannot be claimed that all these professions or occupations were in decline in France, in the 1450's and 1460's. The most plausible explanation is that though the regular purchasers of manuscripts were able to obtain the texts they required, the broader segments of the population—the semiliterate and the poorer clergymen, students, professionals, and civil servants, who were needed to absorb a greatly increased production—had not shown sufficient interest in reading to promise a fair return to enterprising printers.

PRINTING IN PARIS

When the earliest printers, Ulrich Gering, Michael Friburger, and Martin Crantz, came to France to establish the first French press late in 1469 or early in 1470, they did so not upon their own initiative but by invitation from Heynlin de Lapide (or "von Stein," a place probably not far from Basle), professor and at times prior and rector at the Sorbonne; they did not print at their own risk but were apparently financed by Guillaume Fichet, famous teacher at the University of Paris and friend of Cardinal Bessarion, a Savoyard who held high offices at the university and had been to Milan as royal ambassador. Gering, Friburger, and Crantz had all received academic training; we do not know where they had learned the practical aspects of printing, but it is likely that they acquired the necessary skills in Basle. The first Paris press was housed within the Sorbonne, and it is partly for this reason that it has often been called a university press; this is a misnomer. There is no indication that the university made any financial contribution or sponsored the press. We might refer to it with better cause as the private press of Heynlin and Fichet.

The humanist inclinations of Heynlin and Fichet have most recently been investigated by J. Monfrin, who published and interpreted the list of books borrowed by them from the Sorbonne.[5] We are surprised by the contrast between the orthodoxy of their recorded loans and the distinctly classical and humanist production of the Sorbonne press. We can only surmise that Heynlin selected texts to be printed which stationers and libraries could not supply, at least not in sufficient copies to satisfy his, his colleagues', and their students' needs. The early production of our first printers, between 1470 and 1473, was entirely in Roman characters, fashioned after the humanist book hand, copied from the Carolingian minuscule, and thought in the Renaissance to be derived from classical models. They printed about two dozen volumes, mostly small in size. Their work began with Gasparinus Barzizius' *Epistolae*, which contained a prefatory letter from Fichet to Heynlin which has been called the manifesto of the press:

> You [Heynlin] have rendered a significant service by providing sound texts of ancient authors . . . you have illuminated Latin literature which had been clad in the darkness of ignorance. . . . Most of the blame for this barbarism must be placed upon the carelessness of scribes. . . . Now the printers from your native country produce truly correct copies from texts which you have carefully collated.[6]

The second product of the press was Barzizius' *Orthographia*, printed together with Guarini's *On Diphthongs* and Heynlin's own *On Punctuation*. The *Opera* of Sallust (1471) was their third publication and the first classical text to be printed in France. It concludes with a poem in which the printers refer to their products as "weapons of the future." Did the printers, as has been

---

[5] J. Monfrin, "Les lectures de G. Fichet et J. Heynlin," *Bibliothèque d'Humanisme et Renaissance*, XVII (1955), 7–23, 145–53.

[6] Somewhat paraphrased. The full text is printed in A. Claudin, *The First Paris Press* (London, 1898), p. 75.

claimed, dedicate this book to the citizenry of Paris, stress their
fidelity to the king, and use the expression *"arma futura"* to curry
favor with the king, who had just begun his campaign against
Charles of Burgundy? Indeed, the *Bellum Catilinarium* was an
opportune selection, but we are inclined to believe that the poem
concluding a text selected undoubtedly by Heynlin or Fichet
was written by the latter for the printers and designed to serve
his interests as much as theirs. In any case, Louis XI became
interested in the press and showed his favor to the printers four
years later when the three Germans sought French citizenship.
He granted it without formality or the customary charge.

The program of the Sorbonne press continued in the same vein,[7]
except for three theological texts: Rodericus Zamorensis' *Speculum vitae humanae*, Magni's *Sophologium*, and St. Ambrosius' *De
officiis*. Altogether, the production of the first French press is impressive. No other contemporary establishment could at this early
date boast of similar consistency in the production of humanist
texts, but the credit should go not to the printers but to Heynlin
and Fichet. After Fichet had left Paris to follow Cardinal Bessarion
back to Rome after the conclusion of the latter's legation to
France,[8] Heynlin had returned to Basle, and Jean Royer (who had
succeeded Heynlin as prior) had finished his term in 1473, the
three printers left the Sorbonne, moved to the rue Saint Jacques,
and began to work on their own "At the Sign of the Golden
Sun." Their program changed immediately and radically. They
introduced a new, Gothic type, fashioned after a Basle or Mainz
model and produced about thirty titles of which the great majority
were theological, a few were legal, and none was classical.

Late in 1477 Friburger and Crantz left the firm, probably to
return to their native country. Gering continued until 1509, at

[7] We note Florus' *Historia romana*; Bessarion's *Epistolae et orationes*; Fichet's
Rhetorica; Cicero's *De oratore*; Dati's *Eloquentiae praecepta*; Valerius Maximus
(of which no copy has survived); Valla's *Elegantiae*, with an introduction by
Pierre Paul Vieillot recommending Valla to students; two more Ciceros; Plato;
Virgil's *Bucolica*; Juvenal; Persius; Terence; two tracts by Aeneas Sylvius.

[8] Bessarion died during his return trip; Fichet continued alone and never
returned to Paris.

times in association with others, as printer, publisher, and book-seller. Immediately after the dissolution of the partnership he added a Roman type and returned in part to the program of the Sorbonne press by adding classical and humanist texts to the production of theological titles.[9]

A second press was established in Paris in 1473-4 by Petrus Wagner (called Caesaris) and Johannes Stoll,[10] and a third called "Au Soufflet Vert" ("At the Green Bellows") about one year later.[11] These two presses used similar semi-Roman types with ornamented capitals and were both influenced by the program of the Sorbonne press. No wonder they were and are frequently confused. Caesaris and Stoll issued about a dozen books, almost equally divided between theology and law, on the one hand, and classics and humanist writings, on the other. The "Au Soufflet Vert" lasted longer, until 1484, and issued about thirty-three editions, of which the majority were classical or humanist. It is generally assumed that the selection of both presses was in-fluenced by Guillaume Tardif, professor in the College of Navarre.[12] Caesaris and Stoll were German, while the members of the co-operative printing "At the Sign of the Green Bellows" were all French. The nationality of the printers seems not to have influenced the character of their production.

I shall not attempt a listing of all the Parisian presses of the 1470's. There is, however, one more which deserves our attention,

[9] Gering published twelve titles between late 1477 and the fall of 1480, among them Aristotle, Cicero, Sallust, and Virgil, the *Margarita* by Eyb, and the *Roman de la rose*.

[10] Caesaris studied in Paris, was at various times "procureur et receveur des étudiants allemands," and at one time "libraire juré." The origin of Stoll is unknown, but he had been a student either in Erfurt or, more probably, in Basle.

[11] A co-operative to which belonged Louis Simonel, Richard Blandin, Jean Simon, and Gaspar de Russangis. We know practically nothing about them; Claudin believes that they had been employees of Caesaris and Stoll.

[12] Among authors published by these two presses we note the following classical and humanist authors: Cicero, Plutarch, Sallust, Seneca, Valerius Maximus, Aeneas Sylvius, Eyb, Petrarch, Pierre de la Hazardière, Poggio, and Tardif.

the printing shop of Pasquier Bonhomme. He had been "libraire juré" of the Sorbonne and belonged to a Parisian bookseller family which had been active since 1394. With this tradition and experience Pasquier Bonhomme knew perhaps better than his predecessors what kind of book was likely to sell. He published the first book in French printed in Paris (1476), *Les Chroniques de France*, also called *Les Chroniques de St. Denis*, and introduced a typical French type, the Batarde. He specialized in theological and liturgical texts; his son and successor branched out (in 1484) into French belles-lettres and had many of the texts beautifully illustrated. The program of Bonhomme, father and son, is comparable to that of his Lyons colleagues, who will be briefly described in the following paragraphs.

LYONS

Earliest printing in Lyons (which began in 1473) was of a very different nature from that of Paris. This is not surprising. In contrast to Paris, Lyons was then not a center of learning but rather a predominantly commercial city in which wealthy businessmen and the clergy were the most likely customers for books. Lyons had excellent trade connections throughout France and with Italian towns and centers in the Holy Roman Empire. Later, around 1500, the varied production of books in Lyons vied with that of Venice for the European market.

The patron of Lyons printing and the man who presumably brought Guillaume LeRoy, a native of Liège, to Lyons was a rich merchant, Barthélemy Boyer.[13] His was the vision of a businessman, not that of an educator. LeRoy's and Boyer's first type lacked elegance; it was badly cast and poorly set. Some say that it was designed after Costerian faces. Haebler, however, thinks that the type was designed to resemble Lyons manuscript hands, and I agree.[14] LeRoy is supposed to have learned printing in Venice,

[13] Incidentally, most of the books printed by LeRoy carry Boyer's name in the imprint, but it is unlikely that Boyer did any actual printing.

[14] K. Haebler, *Die deutschen Buchdrucker des XV. Jahrhunderts im Ausland* (Munich, 1924), p. 194.

and, indeed, he introduced in 1477 a Gothic type fashioned after a font which had been used in Venice by Wendelin of Speyer. As long as LeRoy worked for Boyer (to about 1481), he produced primarily theological texts of which all but two were in French. At no time did he publish classical or humanist texts. However, the first Lyons press is to be credited with some important innovations: LeRoy is the first printer in France who published a book entirely in French;[15] he is the first to use woodcut initials,[16] and the first to issue a book with an original woodcut illustration,[17] which is to be dated not much later than the *Mirouer de la redemption*, which was published by the German printer Huss in Lyons in 1478 from blocks which had been imported from Basle, and the *Pratique de chirurgie* of Guy de Chauliac, produced with illustrations of surgical instruments by the German printers Nicolaus Philippi and Marcus Reinhard.[18]

The second Lyons press, under the name of Philippi and Reinhard, opened in 1477 with a Gothic type fashioned after Venetian models. Its production was about evenly divided among law, theology, and old learning, but with fewer texts in French than LeRoy's. A third press was started by Martin Huss, from Württemberg, who worked partly with a compatriot, Johann Siber,[19] from 1478 to 1481 and used a type in Basle style. Huss's production is strong in law and medicine. Siber started his own shop in 1478 with a program similar to that of his former partner. The first Frenchmen to print in Lyons were Pierre de Masson, Boniface Jehan, and Jean de Villevieil (1479). Two other minor Lyons printers of the 1470's were Gaspar Ortuin and Sixtus Glockengiesser.

Contrast Lyons with Paris. The Lyons printers of the 1470's did not produce classical or humanist texts, and they did not use Roman type; Frenchmen entered the field late, they were

[15] Voragine's *Golden Legend* (1476).

[16] Vincent de Beauvais, *Mirouer hystorial* (1479).

[17] *Histoire du Chevalier Oben.*

[18] The first illustrated medical book published anywhere (1478).

[19] Siber, or Syber, had studied at Freiburg in Breisgau, and had learned printing in Basle, like several other Lyons printers.

apparently mostly craftsmen (of whom the majority appear to
have been trained in Basle), and only one was university educated.
Lyons printers pioneered in the printing of texts in French and
in the use of illustrations. As Claudin says, "Les typographes
Lyonnais ne s'adréssaient pas à un public aussi raffiné que celui de
Paris," but rather to the "masses crédules."[20] It is fair to say that
Lyonese imprints of the 1470's had wider appeal than most of the
titles published during the same decade in Paris.

THE PROVINCES

Paris and Lyons were the only two really important centers of
printing in France in the 1470's. Printing in France was not so
widely or densely distributed as in the Rhineland, the Low
Countries, southern Germany and Switzerland, or northern Italy.[21]
By 1480 printing had been established within the whole of France
in only nine towns, probably in the following chronological
order: 1470, Paris; 1473, Lyons; 1476, Angers and Toulouse;
1477, Albi; 1478, Chablis and Vienne; 1479, Poitiers; and 1480,
Caen.

The first printer of Albi is not known. Referred to as the "Printer
of Aeneas Sylvius' *Remedy of Love*," he used two types, one
Roman and one Gothic, both resembling types used by printers in
Rome. The same printer reissued Barzizius' *Orthographia* in 1478,
which had been originally published as the second product of the
Sorbonne press. This might indicate a connection between the
anonymous Albi press and the first Paris press, which would
explain the issuing of some humanist texts at Albi. The first
Toulouse printer, the German Heinrich Turner, had studied in
Basle, where he probably acquired his type. His production
includes a number of legal titles, a few theological texts, and the

---

[20] Claudin, *Histoire de l'imprimerie en France*, III, xii–xiii.
[21] Some few figures illustrate this point. By the end of 1480 we count eight
printing presses in the Rhineland between Basle and Cologne, twelve in the
Low Countries, fifteen in the territory now corresponding to Bavaria,
Württemberg, and German-speaking Switzerland, and more than twenty-five
in northern Italy.

popular *De ludo scachorum* by Cessolis. The second printer in Toulouse during the 1470's was Johannes Parix, who used two Gothic fonts similar to Basle and Lyons types and one mixed type which is reminiscent of Italian fonts. More than half of Parix's production was legal, but it included at least one item which may be classified as classical, an exposition of the terms in Terence. The first printer in Angers was Jean de la Tour. His press was an offshoot of one of the Paris printers', and his types seem to derive from those of the "Au Soufflet Vert." His rather unimportant production includes the pseudo-Ciceronian *Rhetorica ad Herennium*. The first printer of Chablis was a Frenchman, Pierre Le Rouge, who published one theological book in French translation. The first printers in Caen were Jacques Durandas and Guy Quijoue. Poitiers produced only one book during our period, a chronicle based on Landolphus de Columna, printed by Jean Bouyer. The production of Vienne was more important. It was undoubtedly inspired by activities in nearby Lyons. The German printer, Johannes Solidi or Hans Schilling, had studied at Basle and at Erfurt. He learned his trade in Basle, from where he fled in 1476 because of debts. His program was largely in Latin, printed in Gothic types; it consisted of about fifteen titles, mainly of popular character, including the *Proverbia* of Aeneas Sylvius.

We conclude from the survey of the book production in France during the ten years following the introduction of printing that the publishing of classical and humanist texts was largely confined to Paris; it was important only where printers had as their advisers influential adherents of the "new learning."

We now proceed to a topically arranged commentary which will, we hope, clarify the relationship between printing and humanism during the seventh decade of the fifteenth century.

THE PRINTERS AND THEIR PRODUCTION

It is not surprising that so many of France's earliest printers were of German origin. The most likely places in which apprentices might receive training in the "*ars nova*" were Mainz, Strasbourg,

Basle, and a few other towns in Central Europe. Only after printing had been well established in Italy and France could printers be trained in their native countries, as the companions of the "Au Soufflet Vert" probably were. Unfortunately, we have only incomplete information on the background of French printers, but we noted the comparatively large number of university men in the Paris shops, while to the best of our knowledge only one of the earliest Lyons printers had attended a university—as had the first printer in nearby Vienne and Turner in Toulouse. We could not discover among printers in France, in contrast to those of contemporary Germany, men who had originally been trained as professional writers or painters of letters (*Briefmaler*), artists, bookbinders, metalworkers, or clergymen. Two of the earliest printers (a German and a Frenchman) had been "libraires jurés" of the University of Paris.

It is generally assumed that the earliest products of the Paris presses of Gering, Friburger, and Crantz, of Caesaris and Stoll, and of the "Au Soufflet Vert" were issued in small number. Almost all are extremely rare, and in some cases no copy has survived. At the Sorbonne press the printers were granted subventions, and editions were probably calculated closely to supply primarily the needs of Heynlin, Fichet, and their friends, who used these texts for study and teaching. In addition, Fichet had copies of some of the texts printed for private circulation, adorned with printed or manuscript dedications, all different in text. In one particular case, the *Letters and Speeches* of Cardinal Bessarion, we know that within a little more than a year Fichet distributed 46 copies to exhort the powers in France and elsewhere to unite in a crusade against the Turks. During the period under discussion editions of printed books in Paris and elsewhere varied probably between 100 for small editions and 250 for large editions. The latter figure would apply primarily to standard theological texts like Nider's *Manuale* or the apparently popular *Manipulus curatorum* of Guido de Monte Rochen, and perhaps to such classical texts as Cicero's *Epistolae familiares*, which may have been used as textbooks.

In the discussion of individual presses we named occasionally one or another among classical and humanist texts. Their total number in the 1470's is impressive. But how does French production compare with that of other countries? We choose Cicero as a useful example.

During the years 1465 to 1479, 126 Ciceronian books or booklets were published. By far the largest number of these was produced in Venice (32 titles, or 26 per cent). Rome and nearby Subiaco follow with 22 titles (or 17 per cent), Milan with 20 (or about 16 per cent), and Paris with 13 (or slightly more than 10 per cent); next comes Cologne (with 11 titles), and Naples (with 10 titles), and then thirteen other towns with three or fewer titles to their credit during this period. When we examine first printings, which require more initiative and daring, Rome leads with nine (beginning in 1465), Cologne follows with five (its first venture dating from the same year, 1465), Venice with three, Paris and Milan with two each, and Bologna and Naples with only one.[22] The only French town besides Paris which produced a Ciceronian title was Angers.

Sallust and Valerius Maximus were among the most popular ancient writers; among other classical texts we note Plato, Martial, Plutarch, Terence, Vergil, and Horace. When we turn to humanist authors, we find that only three Bessarion items were published anywhere during the fifteenth century, of which one appeared in Paris, namely, the first edition of the *Letters and Orations*; Gering published Beroaldus in 1478; the *Elegantiolae* of Agostino Dati was published at the Sorbonne in 1471–2, by the "Au Soufflet Vert" in 1476, by Gering alone in 1479, and again in 1480, and reprinted in Toulouse about the same time; various writings of Aeneas

[22] To be more specific about the French editions produced between 1472 and 1479, we count four editions of the *Rhetorica ad Herennium*, three in Paris and one in Angers. This was the most frequently printed title. It is followed by *De officiis* with two editions; *In Catilinam*, two editions; and the *Tusculanae disputationes*, also with two editions. The one and only edition of the *Orator* and of *Pro Ligario* was published in Paris. Surprisingly enough, we find only one edition of the otherwise immensely popular *Epistolae familiares*. Finally, there was one edition of the *De finibus bonorum*.

Sylvius were popular in Paris and the provinces; Albrecht von Eyb's *Margarita*, with its extracts from classics and humanists, appeared first in Nürnberg in 1472; Part I alone appeared at the "Au Soufflet Vert" in 1476, again in 1477, and was reprinted by Gering in 1478 and twice in Toulouse in the 1490's. Also printed before 1480 were Valla and Poggio and the three French humanists Fichet, Tardif, and Gaguin. This record may not compare favorably with Italy in mere number, but when we consider that France started late and produced many fewer titles than Italy, the production of classical and humanist texts is impressive. It probably compares favorably with Italy and undoubtedly surpasses that of Germany.

LANGUAGE

Ciceronian Latin was the goal of humanists; vernacular languages did not stand high in their esteem. It is doubtful whether we can consider translations of classical authors an indication of humanist activity or interest. A cursory examination also shows that, apart from authors who may almost be considered within the medieval tradition, like Aesop and Cato, few classical authors were translated into any vernacular tongue during our period. Some exceptions may be mentioned: Livy appeared in Italian in 1476; the first French edition came in 1486–7. The first Valerius Maximus in a vernacular language was a French edition, published probably in 1476. An Italian paraphrase of Vergil's *Aeneid* appeared in 1476; a similar free version in French was published in 1483. In passing, we may add the obvious, namely, that French was not limited to France. A good number of important texts in French were published in Bruges and in Geneva.

As stated earlier, printing in the vernacular had a slow start in France. The first book in French appeared in Lyons in 1476. The first book in German had been published in 1461 and in Italian in 1467, and the first book in English was printed at Bruges perhaps as early as 1473.

TYPOGRAPHY

Most of the earliest printers in Europe cast their own type and fashioned letters after those used in manuscripts produced in their region. Neither observation applies widely in France. That none of the printers active in the 1470's is known to have been a metal worker (though one of the partners of the press "Au Soufflet Vert" probably belonged to a family of Parisian goldsmiths) makes us believe that in most cases the type was cut for them and not by them. Except for the "lettre batarde," and possibly the first Lyons font of LeRoy, types used by these printers are not typically French.[23] The Sorbonne printers used a type which had as its model one of the early Rome types.[24] The Gothic type, developed when they moved to the rue Saint-Jacques, resembled Basle and Mainz types. When Gering continued alone, he chose a type which is somewhat like the Roman type used at the original Sorbonne press. The first Lyons printer, LeRoy, used, besides the font which may be of local character, a Venetian type. Other Lyons types show primarily the influence of Basle and Venetian fonts. The true "national" French script was not used in Lyons during our period but only in Paris. The anonymous printer in Albi used types fashioned, it seems, after Rome fonts. Turner, in Toulouse, used a Basle-style Gothic, while Parix, after he became independent, used a mixed type which shows Italian influence. Angers and Poitiers types are in Parisian style, though one Gothic type used in Poitiers is said to be in the style of Jenson. The Vienne type of Solidi is of Basle origin.

French type of the period shows varied influences; those of Rome, Venice, Basle, Strasbourg, and Mainz seem strongest. Whether the origin of type used in France (e.g., the types fashioned after those of Rome or Venice) reflects an intellectual influence we dare not say. A very careful and complete study of the provenience

[23] This changes in the 1480's, when types and illustrations develop a specifically French genre, probably caused by the appeal of printed books to a widening circle of readers.

[24] Sweynheim and Pannartz, Lignamine, or Lauer.

of types, together with a full listing of models from which printers in France actually reissued texts, may permit conclusions which we cannot now make on the basis of presently available data. As it stands, we can consider only the Roman or "antiqua" type proof of humanist influence. In Paris the Sorbonne press, Caesaris and Stoll, the "Au Soufflet Vert," and the "anonymous printer of the Ockam, 1476" all used pure or mixed Roman type. Outside Paris, printers in only three towns made use of humanist-style fonts: in Albi, Angers, and Toulouse, of which the last may have to be dated later than 1479–80.

BOOK ILLUSTRATION

While Roman fonts can be considered the outward sign of humanist influence and interest, no such parallel can be found in the field of book illustration. No Renaissance-style illustration appeared in a printed book during our period. This is not surprising; illustrations frequently served to promote the sale of books to broader groups of readers. Classical and humanist texts did not lend themselves easily to this type of treatment; they neither appealed to nor were meant for the casual buyer of printed books.

All types of illustrations were slow in developing in France. While the first illustrated book in Germany was published in 1461 and in Italy in 1467, the first illustrated book in France appeared in 1478, when Huss imported the blocks used in Basle in a Latin edition of the *Speculum humanae salvationis* for his French edition. The first woodcut illustration actually drawn and cut in France also appeared in Lyons, probably before 1480, in the *Histoire du Chevalier Oben*. The late use of illustrations in printed books in France is not surprising. We recall that the single woodcut also appears to have been less popular in France than in Germany or the Low Countries.[25] The taste of book-loving patrons in France

[25] This seems true notwithstanding the fact that André Blum in *The Origin and Early History of Engraving in France* (New York and Frankfurt, 1930) lists and illustrates 112 woodcuts and engravings supposedly produced in France between the late fourteenth and the late fifteenth century (see also B. A. Lemoisne, *Les*

ran toward sumptuous illuminations. This technique was simply lifted from the manuscript and applied to the printed book. In several instances printers left spaces blank which were to be filled in with pictures painted by hand; examples are the *Chroniques de France* and the French edition of Valerius Maximus. The love for luxurious illustrations survived tenaciously and somewhat anachronistically, while the graphic methods of reproduction started late and developed along traditional Gothic lines before they changed to a Renaissance style, which found its perfection in the work of Geoffroy Tory.

CONCLUSION

New learning was stimulated in Paris through the production of classical and humanist texts and the use of Roman type, which reflected the taste of the modernists; however, the use of the press to promote classical studies did not represent an organized movement but reflected the attitude of a small though important coterie, chiefly Heynlin, Fichet, Tardif, Gaguin, and a few others. France, because of its geographical location, absorbed Italian and German influences and elements. French presses frequently reprinted texts first produced in Italy or Germany, and they used or copied types originally fashioned in these countries; they gradually adjusted their program and style to meet typically French needs and interests. Whether the humanist production of several Parisian presses had an immediate effect on the intellectual life of France is almost impossible to say; we rather doubt it. Their effort was unique and almost heroic, but their influence was less immediate than that of their less progressive colleagues in Paris or of the Lyonese and provincial presses, which in this early period catered more directly to the broader and basically conservative groups of readers.

An interesting letter from Royal Secretary Pierre Paul Vieillot

Xylographies du XIVᵉ et XVᵉ siècle au Cabinet des estampes de la Bibl. Nat. [Paris and Brussels, 1930], and A. M. Hind, *An Introduction to a History of Woodcut*, 2 vols. [London, 1935]).

F.H.

to Heynlin is printed in Valla's *Elegantiae* (Paris, 1472). Besides bemoaning the low state of copying and the poor quality of Latin and exhorting students to make good use of Valla, Vieillot laments that "the courts of great princes do not make learned men out of the ignorant, but ignorant men out of the learned. In these troubled times it is not necessary to know how to handle pen and paper, but horses and the sword." Ten years later these conditions had changed. The internal political strife had ended, and France was on the way to a spectacular recovery. It was then that the efforts of Heynlin, Fichet, and Tardif, and of printers connected with them, came to fruition, with the sharp increase in the production of classical and humanist writings and the spread of the study of Greek, Latin, and Hebrew.

7 What Parisians Read in the Sixteenth Century

H.-J. MARTIN

IT has been pointed out often enough that there are many interesting things to be discovered in the inventories of privately owned libraries, and particularly in inventories of estates; and there could certainly be no better means of finding out what people read during a given period. Yet hitherto no systematic study has been undertaken in this field.

Two works, however, have been published on the subject by R. Doucet[1] and A. H. Schutz, who both made use of an inventory carried out at the *Minutier Central* of the Parisian notarial records [in the *Archive Nationale*]. That of Doucet, entitled *Les Bibliothèques parisiennes au XVIe siècle*,[2] is in fact a study based on the examination of 185 inventories of privately owned libraries and nine inventories of booksellers' stocks before 1560. That of Schutz is devoted to the distribution of works in the French language (and exclusively those of the major writers of the time, such as Rabelais, Marot, the authors of the *Pléiade*, and Montaigne) to be found in sixteenth-century private libraries.[3]

There is certainly much of value to be found in these two studies, but after reading them, one is left dissatisfied and somewhat

[1] At the time of writing I was unaware of the death of Roger Doucet, and I should like to take the opportunity here of saluting the memory of this historian. The study analyzed here has become his final work. Even at the end of an eminent career, he did not hesitate to undertake a laboriously detailed examination of these unedited documents which no one before him had ventured on; at the same time he also established a method of research.

[2] R. Doucet, *Les Bibliothèques parisiennes au XVIe siècle* (Paris, A. & J. Picard, 1956)

[3] A. H. Schutz, *Vernacular Books in Parisian Private Libraries of the Sixteenth Century* (Chapel Hill, University of North Carolina Press; and Geneva, Librairie Droz, 1955).

in the dark; this is probably because the documents examined were insufficient of themselves to give the information which was expected of them. The most interesting thing, perhaps, about documents of this sort is the "photograph" they provide of the library of some particular person or another, especially of the run-of-the-mill lawyers, notaries, clerics, and merchants. Now, Doucet published, certainly with very great care, only four large inventories (it was no doubt impossible for him to do more without swelling his book to a disproportionate size); but he did not really counterbalance this with sufficient reference to the others. Before the inventory lists he gave a copious introduction of about eighty pages in which he named the most frequently encountered works and classified them into certain categories (law, religion, literature, history, and science), but he provided no system of reference to show which inventories these works were to be found in or to establish how many times they had been mentioned. It would really have been better to have a table giving a list of the most frequently encountered books, together with references to the documents in which they are to be found. Schutz attempted in his study to provide such indications for books in the French language, but the headings are often lacking in clarity, and the books in question are placed in alphabetical order either by name of author or by title, as was often the practice in the past.[4] In effect, the impression is that of a sort of card catalogue, though admittedly a very accurate one, rather than of a systematically arranged exposition.

The interpretation of the documents poses some very delicate problems which could provide endless topics for discussion. For instance, Roger Doucet was most surprised to see that several best-selling books did not appear in the libraries he studied until fifteen or twenty years (and sometimes more) after their date of publica-

[4] Guevara's *Orloge des princes*, for example, is to be found as *Orloge*, while Ariosto's *Orlando furioso* is there in its Italian form; Giacomo Caviceo's *Pilgrim* is classified as *Peregryn*, but the works of Petrarch or Boccaccio are by names of author. [Antonio de Guevara (1480–1545), Spanish bishop, wrote the *Libro llamado relox de principes*, translated into French as the popular *Orloge des princes*.

tion. In particular, no work of Lefèvre d'Étaples is to be found before 1525. The Latin classics did not appear to any notable extent until the second quarter of the century, nor the Greek classics until 1550 and after. But surely the reason for this is that sixteenth-century readers, just like their modern counterparts, tended to remain faithful to the books which they knew in their youth. There is, for example, no cause for surprise if the books mentioned in the inventory of a person who died between 1520 and 1530 were mainly best-sellers from the end of the fifteenth century. This is simply a "time lag," and it goes some way toward explaining why Roger Doucet (whose research stopped at 1560) pronounced a judgment on Rabelais which amounted more or less to a declaration of insolvency, and why he seemed to think that Ronsard enjoyed only a "limited" popularity; while Schutz frequently found the names of both Ronsard and Rabelais in later libraries. This was probably the reason, too, why Roger Doucet found relatively few books in Greek among the libraries he studied, even though there were as many Greek texts in Greek published in France between 1530 and 1560 as there were Latin ones in Latin. And a further criticism, while we are about it, is that Doucet and Schutz, both of whom had extremely interesting inventories of booksellers' stocks in their hands—particularly those of Jean Janot and Galliot Du Pré—were equally of the opinion that there is a relation between the number of copies of a given work in stock and the number of copies actually printed. Despite what Roger Doucet wrote in defense of this viewpoint, it should not be forgotten that there was a fairly definite limit at the time to the total number of copies possible from one printing. For technical reasons this ranged from about 1,000 to 1,500 copies. If a considerable number of copies of a book were to be found in stock, then either the book had been recently printed or it had not sold very well. For instance, the fact that Janot was listed as having only twenty-five copies of *Pathelin* does not necessarily mean that this work met with little success.

It is evident, therefore, that a great deal can be drawn from the studies of Doucet and Schutz. Admittedly, they do not give a

complete picture of what interested Parisian readers, since most of
the libraries in question were important ones belonging to members
of the legal profession or to wealthy merchants; and precisely
because these men were rich, care was more often taken to draw
up an inventory of their possessions after their deaths.[5] All the
same, these two studies do give a valuable picture of interests and
tastes among cultivated circles in the French capital during the age
of humanism and the Reformation, and a reading of the inventories
reveals the preoccupations of these men. There were many books
on law—not merely among the specialists but also among
wealthy merchants; and that they were books on Roman law
rather than customary law suggests that their readers were mainly
interested in studying a cultural form. Bibles, of course, were very
numerous; from the beginning of the century these included a
large number of French translations and more easily digestible
summaries, such as biblical expositions or books on various biblical
figures. Among those on the Fathers of the Church were most of
the better-known texts: St. Augustine's *City of God*, St. Gregory's
Homilies, and St. Bernard's *Meditations*, which were so frequently
brought out in the fifteenth century. And then there were any
number of books on mystics—Gerson, Nider, Suso, and many
others—among which one is surprised, just as Doucet was, not to
find the *Imitation of Christ*. To make up for this, as might be
expected, there were lives of the saints, lives of the Virgin Mary

[5] The owners of the libraries studied by Doucet are distributed as follows:
Lawyers, 109 (comprising 20 presidents and counselors of the *Parlement*;
35 advocates of the *Parlement* and the Paris law courts, officers of the Grand
Conseil, and members of the chambers of exchequer, forests, and waterways,
and the mint); 10 seigneurial libraries; 29 belonging to ecclesiastics; 16 to
prominent citizens (drapers, shearers, dyers, goldsmiths, haberdashers, grocers,
chandlers, tailors, etc.); 25 to physicians and others.

The 220 or so documents studied by Schutz (who combined with the Paris
estate inventories a certain number of inventories of provincial libraries) are
distributed as follows: Lawyers and officers, 105; citizens, merchants, and
artisans, 23; physicians and surgeons, etc., 17; ecclesiastics, 11; professors, 2;
booksellers' stocks, 15.

It should be added that, since the libraries belonging to lawyers and officers
were much more important than the rest, the totals provided by the studies
are mainly a reflection of the contents of these big libraries.

and, above all, Jacob of Voragine's *Golden Legend*, which was probably the best-selling book of the fifteenth century, having been printed hundreds of times before 1500 in all languages. Finally, there was all the edifying literature, comprising a great variety of books with *Speculum* or *Doctrinale* in their titles, as well as moralized versions of Dionysius Cato.

At the same time, the major scholastic texts were read in these circles: not so much the "Sentences" (which in any case were not very frequently reprinted during the fifteenth and sixteenth centuries) as commentators on Peter Lombard, as well as more easily accessible works. Among the names most frequently encountered were Occam, Pierre d'Ailly, St. Bonaventure, Buridan, Duns Scotus, Gabriel Biel, and Tateret. These works seem to have been constantly sought after throughout the period studied by Roger Doucet, and the fact that they persisted right up to 1560 may perhaps be partly explained by the "time-lag" phenomenon. Nonetheless, it does give the impression that parliamentary circles in Paris were singularly conservative. Yet, side by side with these works, Roger Doucet saw the appearance of a whole literature of critical works on the sacred texts from which the Reformation was to take its rise; in particular, St. Paul's *Epistles* and commentaries on them were increasingly sought after. Then again, the names of Lefèvre d'Étaples and Erasmus seem to be especially frequent in inventories from 1525 to 1530 and onward. All this might have been expected; but on the other hand it is surprising to note that scarcely any echo of Lutheran polemics is to be found in these inventories, that the name of Calvin never figures in them, and that there is, for example, only one solitary trace of the *Cymbalum Mundi* [a crypto-Protestant tract by Bonaventure des Perriers (1537)]. What conclusion is to be drawn from this? Does it mean that in Paris such literature interested only a few theologians or Parliamentarians? In my opinion it seems fairly certain that the experts were none too keen on inventory books which were "tainted" or which had about them a whiff of heresy—and that the inventories do not tell all.

It is evident that there were many works of classical authors in these libraries. We have already seen why there seem to have been comparatively few books in Greek, and there is no need to go into this any further. Latin ones, however, were there in abundance.

There were also many copies of the *Adages*, the *Colloquies*, the *Praise of Folly*, and the *Enchiridion*, which is not surprising. There were many of the works of Budé, especially copies of the *De Asse*, which was probably to be explained by the fact that this was Paris, the home, as it were, of the author's friends. Also to be found were several copies of Thomas More's *Utopia*. But it is worth noting that one frequently comes across the *Remedia utriusque fortunae*, Petrarch's *Trionfi*, and, above all, the various works of Boccaccio—especially the *Decameron*, which Schutz found thirty times. There are also many copies of Lorenzo Valla's *Elegantiae linguae latinae*, Bembo's *Asolani*, Poggio's *Facetiae*, Castiglione's *Courtier*, and, later, Ariosto's *Orlando furioso*, which Schutz came across sixteen times in the second half of the century.

There were, therefore, a large number of Italian works, first in translation, and then occasionally, during the second half of the century, in the original. As against this, the Spanish contribution appears quite insignificant: the only thing Roger Doucet came across at all frequently was the *Vocabularium Nebrissense*, a work of grammar, to which may be added Guevara's *Orloge des princes* (of which twenty-one copies were traced by Schutz). There were hardly any English works apart from Thomas More's *Utopia*. But some German books were represented: a few philological and moral treatises of Melanchthon and Reuchlin, some of Ulrich von Hutten's dialogues, and above all Sebastian Brant's *Ship of Fools*, which enjoyed an enormous success in France.

As for works in French, Schutz and Doucet both emphasized the great popularity of two works at the beginning of the century: Meschinot's *Lunettes des princes*, the edifying and more or less satirical character of which seems to have captivated sixteenth-century readers, and especially the very frequently reprinted *Illustrations de Gaule et singularitez de Troye* of Jean Lemaire de Belges, since this work, filled with reminiscences of antiquity, gave endless pleasure by virtue alike of its romantic features and its historical intentions. Marot was among the best-known authors of the century and enjoyed a good measure of success, which seemed to come to an abrupt end in 1560. Although it is possible that he had merely gone out of favor, it is perhaps more likely that people had ceased to mention his name "for religious reasons." In the case of Rabelais, however, whose name was found so rarely by Roger Doucet, Schutz sets matters right. The name of Rabelais, in fact, is frequently to be seen in the inventories after this date. Schutz, interestingly enough, noted that the works of Rabelais in these libraries were to be found, not among the novels, but side by side with works by Erasmus, Cicero, Machiavelli, Boccaccio, Petrarch, and Martin du Bellay—in other words, among the most highly respected authors of the time. This is evidence that he was starting, during this period, to be ranked among the classics of humanism. Finally, as for the authors of the *Pléiade* and their followers, the names most commonly met with seem to be those of Ronsard and Desportes.

A considerably greater success, however, seems to have been enjoyed by history books and romances. The owners of the libraries in question appear to have had a real infatuation with history (and not only the lawyers, but also the clerics and the prominent citizenry); Livy, Caesar, Josephus, Eusebius, and Valerius Maximus were among the most popular. But the most successful history books remained for a long time the medieval compilations, the histories of Troy, like the *Mer des histoires*, and particularly the works of the contemporary annalists. The *Annales et Chroniques de France* of Nicole Gilles were so common in the libraries that Schutz simply gave up counting them. Together with this, the *Annales d'Aquitaine* of Jean Bouchet and the *Annales de Bretagne* of d'Argentré enjoyed a success which can only be compared with that of the chroniclers: Froissart, whose name was found thirty-five times by Schutz (a record), Monstrelet twenty-nine times, and Commynes twenty-five times. These three authors enjoyed prolonged success, since they were still among the fifteen or twenty most commonly found works in Paris libraries in the seventeenth century. And lastly, it might be added that Bodin's *République* also enjoyed an equally lasting popularity among Parisian readers.

However enthusiastically the owners of these libraries sought after history books, they seemed, especially at the beginning of the century, even more interested in imaginary histories such as novellas, romances, and romantic epics; these formed no less than a tenth of the libraries studied by Schutz. The *Roman de la Rose*, the influence of which during the sixteenth century is well-known, was reprinted seventeen times between 1500 and 1540, and was found by Schutz in seventeen libraries. Sometimes this book was accompanied by the *Petit Jehan de Saintré*, the *Cent Nouvelles*, or Marguerite of Navarre's *Heptaméron*. But far more numerous than all these were the tales of chivalry. Ever since the introduction of printing the presses had never stopped turning out edition after edition of these old medieval romances, often with many hasty overrunnings and adapted to the tastes of the moment; the *Quatre fils Aymon*, for instance, certainly went into eighteen editions before 1536. The educated readers in the capital seemed to appreciate these romances for a long time, and even those who had read the original text of the *Aeneid* did not omit to follow the exploits of *Virgile l'enchanteur*. Among the most popular romances may be mentioned *Lancelot*, *Tristan de Laonois*, *Godefroy de Bouillon*, *Huon de Bordeaux*, and *Giron le Courtois*. But a special place in this literature must be reserved for *Amadis de Gaule* which, at the same time as it nourished the dreams of the *conquistadors* in America, also provided food for the more peaceful musings of the Parliament-arians and leading citizens of Paris.

But the interest in these romances among the educated public of Paris was not to last forever. At the end of the century Schutz found fewer and fewer traces of them; and, as is known, in 1560 Étienne Pasquier confirmed that the popularity of *Amadis* had ended as suddenly as it had begun. Yet the presses continued to turn out as many as ever of these romantic and chivalric tales with their numberless episodes. But the public for them had changed— it was now the less sophisticated public in the country and the small towns. Copies of the *Quatre fils Aymon* were consigned, along with those of the *Calendrier des bergers* and the *Figures de la Bible*, to the peddlers' packs. From the eighteenth to the nineteenth century they formed the basis of the so-called *Bibliothèque bleue* and in this were to enjoy a lasting popularity among a public rather like our present-day lovers of adventure films of the sort often taken from books of this genre.

All the same, the taste for the romantic did persist in more educated circles. At the time when interest in tales of chivalry was diminishing, Ariosto wrote his *Orlando furioso*, then Tasso his *Gerusalemma liberata*. In Spain, Cervantes composed *Don Quixote*, the picaresque novel was born, and at the same time the sentimental and pastoral novel, descended from Boccaccio's *Fiammetta*, began to develop; before the appearance of *Astrée* the French read Diego de San Pedro's *Carcel de Amor* (fifteen Spanish editions during the sixteenth century, together with a dozen in French, ten in Italian, and one in English), or the *Tratado de amores de Arnalte y Lucenda* (three Spanish editions from 1522 to 1527, seventeen in French after 1537, and four in English). Surprisingly enough, the libraries studied by Doucet and Schutz give only a partial reflection of movement: Ariosto and Tasso, certainly, were to be found this frequently. On the other hand, there were very few traces of the Spanish novels: Schutz discovered only two references each to the *Carcel de Amor* and to Montemayor's *Diana*. Furthermore, if one turns from the novel to the theater, one finds again that the *Celestine* of Rojas (sixty-two Spanish editions, eleven Italian, twelve French, three German, three Dutch, and two English) is likewise mentioned only twice. How are these gaps to be explained?

One explanation certainly comes to mind, and it is at least to some extent valid: although these books are not mentioned in the inventories, it does not necessarily mean that they did not figure in the libraries. If the assessor did not copy down their titles, it was because they had little market value. These are unquestionably among the whole lots of books which were not given any description and which were only referred to by packets at the ends of the inventories. Furthermore, how far is it possible to rely on the information given by booksellers? Many books, and especially plays, were obviously tied up together in bundles, in which case the bookseller would undoubtedly content himself with giving only the title of the work on the top of the pile. These very tempting hypotheses would account for many such absences— that of *Pathelin*, Villon, and the farces and mystery plays at the beginning of the sixteenth century, and the plays at the end of the sixteenth and during the seventeenth century. I myself studied the seventeenth-century Paris inventories and found no mention of *Astrée* or *Grand Cyre*, nor of Corneille, Racine, or Molière; this suggests to me that the owners of these big libraries, after 1560, being mostly lawyers, part humanist and part scholar, considered themselves much too serious-minded to bother with trivia of this nature.

To what extent, though, did these lawyers and citizens of Paris, with all their appreciation of historical works, keep in touch with the current events of their own times? This is a very big question, and Doucet very rightly asked it. As regards the political events then taking place in Europe, Doucet found references to a small number of books and occasional pieces of a more or less official nature. There was virtually nothing about the wars in Italy, and very little on the history of the struggle waged by Francis I and Henry II against Charles V; there were, however, rather more texts on the wars waged against the Turks (notably the siege of Rhodes), which will not surprise anyone who has read [Geoffroy] Atkinson's works on the subject. From the comparative rarity of such literature Doucet thought it possible to conclude that even the most enlightened public was kept inadequately informed. This, however, is probably going too far: for example, it is known that the wars in Italy led to the publication of a considerable number of descriptive pieces, letters, accounts, and works commemorating ceremonial entries into cities; on the other hand, the royal entries were the subject of many publications. But such works, now scarcely to be found at all, were probably not kept very long; they would in all likelihood have suffered the same fate as modern magazines and reviews.

There were, in any case, certain events which seem to have aroused an enormous amount of curiosity among the educated public; and this curiosity was perfectly legitimate, since it concerned the great new discoveries. There seems to have been a very powerful interest in these and the prospects they opened up. People would read the *De Orbo novo decades* of Peter Martyr, the *Novus Orbis* of Grynaeus, or the *De Nova hispaniorum navigatione*. At the same time, there was a considerable interest in geography and things to do with the sea; in particular, several libraries had books entitled *L'Art de naviguer* or *L'Art de pilotage*. Often these lawyers and merchants would possess treatises on methods of measuring the globe or of calculating latitude and longitude. Very numerous, too, were works on astronomy and the use of the astrolabe—but in this particular field it can easily be seen that their owners' interests were primarily astrological. Volumes on astrology were particularly numerous in these libraries, and even the most informed people were impassioned students of heavenly signs, meteors, and portents. In scientific matters these men of the sixteenth century had a taste for the mysterious, the strange, and the prodigious, a fact which will be of no surprise to those who have read Lucien Febvre on the subject.[6]

There is, however, a third study which remains to be considered, and it serves to complement those of Doucet and Schutz. This is the work of Mlle. Françoise Lehoux, who was also attracted by the documentation provided by the post-mortem inventories in the *Minutier Central*. She too realized the importance of the inventories of libraries preserved there. As a result she published a work entitled *Gaston Olivier, aumônier du roi Henri II, Bibliothèque parisienne et mobilier du XVIe siècle*.[7] This contains a forty-six-page introduction and the inventory of Gaston Olivier's estate, together with a number of connected documents (about sixty pages). These

---

[6] Cf. L. Febvre, "Le Problème de l'incroyance au XVIe siècle," in *La religion de Rabelais* (Paris, 1947), pp. 478 ff.

[7] Françoise Lehoux, *Gaston Olivier, aumônier du roi Henri II, Bibliothèque parisienne et mobilier du XVIe siècle* (Paris, the author, 1957).

are followed by a hundred and fifty pages of notes as an aid to identifying the eight hundred or so works in the library.

It can be seen, then, that the book in which Roger Doucet studied some two hundred inventories is smaller than that of Mlle. Lehoux, which is devoted exhaustively to only one inventory. It was unfortunate, though probably unavoidable, that the studies of Doucet and Schutz were so inconclusive and thus left the reader feeling unsatisfied. But this cannot be said of Mlle. Lehoux's work; the notes identifying the books give extremely valuable information about editions and authors. This study could hardly fail to be enormously useful to anyone interested in humanism in Paris. At the same time it cannot be denied that, for our present purposes—which are in any case different from those of Mlle. Lehoux—the only way to come to any general conclusions is to have a study covering a large number of libraries. But two extreme approaches are represented here, and some compromise would have to be struck when it came to finding a systematic method. This is, of course, an important question, about which much more could be said.

Be that as it may, the library of Gaston Olivier probably gives a very good idea of the favorite reading matter of prominent Paris citizens under Henry II. These are clearly set out in Mlle. Lehoux's very welcome introduction. Out of 800 titles, 225 were theological works: the Fathers of the Church, including Origen, St. Gregory of Nazianzus, St. John Damascene, St. Cyril of Alexandria, St. John Chrysostom, St. Basil, St. Augustine, St. Ambrose, St. Jerome, and St. Gregory the Great; medieval theologians such as Aymon of Halberstadt, Rabanus Maurus, St. Anselm of Canterbury, Hugh of Saint-Victor, Peter Lombard, and Pierre Bersuire; there were also fifteenth- and sixteenth-century writers such as Jean Raulin, Jean Quentin, and Guillaume Pépin. Like many of his contemporaries, Gaston Olivier followed the disputes which centered round Reuchlin, was interested in the quarrel of the three Marys, and possessed works of Johann Eck, John Fisher, Josse Clichtove, Jerome of Hangest, and Noël Béda. Very often one gets the impression that, like many Parisians, he followed the rise and development of false doctrines by reading works written to refute them; yet it is quite possible that compromising books of this sort might have been sitting on a shelf which Galiot Du Pré, the bookseller charged with drawing up the list, had prudently decided to ignore. Unlike many of his contemporaries, however, Gaston Olivier took little interest in law. To make up for this there were many literary works: translations of Plato, Aristotle, and Seneca the philosopher; works of Pico della Mirandola; works of Cicero and Seneca the rhetorician; but above all, most of the great Latin poets and their modern imitators, such as Andrelini, Bembo, Baptista [Spagnuol] Mantuanus, and many others.

It is worth noting too that Gaston Olivier possessed about fifty works in Arabic, Hebrew, and Greek—though he probably knew none of these languages—and about a hundred scientific works, among which were a fair number on the occult sciences. It need only be added that he also possessed the works of Erasmus and those of most of the major humanists, and with this the picture is complete. His library was, in all likelihood, typical of the more cultured among the leading citizens of Paris in the middle of the sixteenth century.

These studies, however, lead up to a big problem which it is worth touching upon in conclusion. These libraries, as we have seen, belonged for the most part to lawyers and rich citizens, and were generally very important ones, comprising hundreds of books toward the middle of the century. Taken in all, their owners constituted small groups, very restricted in number and often conservative in taste, which gravitated mainly around the *Parlement*. But what other readers were there, and how widely were books distributed in Paris in the sixteenth century? To put it more precisely, did books come into the hands of people in much broader social categories, or did they remain essentially the preserve of a limited public?

In answer to these questions, here are a few figures: thirty-five to forty thousand different fifteenth-century impressions have come down to our own day—and there is no knowing how many have been lost—representing a total of fifteen to twenty million copies. In Paris alone there were some twenty-five thousand impressions between 1501 and 1600—say, about twenty-five million copies—of which a good number were sold outright in the shops. These figures hardly need any comment. It is evident that books in the sixteenth century were very widely distributed and were not treated as rare treasures, and that they would have come into the hands of anyone who could read. Out of this enormous mass, the libraries studied by Doucet and Schutz obviously only represented the reading matter of very small groups. Roger Doucet was certainly aware of this problem and even provided a few invaluable suggestions when, at the end of his study, he provided an analysis, not of inventories of libraries, but of inventories of booksellers' stocks (including that of Jean Janot). Thanks to these documents it is possible to catch a glimpse of a much wider readership than the relatively limited circle of cultivated men who formed the main object of the study.

These inventories of booksellers' stocks provide some often surprising indications, and it would be well to conclude by giving some idea of them. Concerning the distribution of liturgical books and Books of Hours, it is known that Guillaume Godard was a powerful publisher (and there is positive proof that he and his associate Merlin had 260 persons working for them). Yet it comes as a shock to find out that in 1545 his stock included 271,420 liturgical books, of which 166,460 were Books of Hours. In 1528, again, there were more than 100,000 works of the same type. The enormous quantity of Books of Hours, breviaries, and devotional books distributed at that time and of which whole editions have disappeared completely may be left to the imagination. One has only to think, in particular, of the books of suffrages, those little collections of prayers addressed to various saints which were to be found in the bookshops by the tens of thousands and of which so few copies have survived to the present day; or of the little manuals of piety like the *Hortulus animae*, the *Lavacrum conscienciae* and the *Abus du monde*, or of the books of pilgrimages and the lives of the saints, some copies of which were decorated with woodcuts worn down by thousands and sometimes maybe tens of thousands of printings. Then again, there are those alphabet books, now almost completely disappeared, which so often served as vehicles for Reformation ideas; and all that pious literature which accounted for most of the 53,475 volumes mentioned in the inventory of Jean Janot. All these will give a clearer idea of the penetrating power of the printed word, which at that time was not simply restricted to small circles but reached the vast bulk of the population. In this way it will be possible to appreciate better the role played by printed books in the spread of the Reformation—especially in the light of that classic study by Henri Hauser[8] in which it is shown how heretical propositions were often inserted into popular works of devotion.

[8] *Études sur la Réforme française* (Paris, 1909), pp. 86–7, 255 ff.

8 Lyons and Geneva in the Sixteenth Century: The Fairs and Printing[1]

PAUL F. GEISENDORF

LYONS and Geneva, since the Renaissance, have developed very differently—there have been extreme fluctuations in the growths of their populations at various times, and their spheres of influence, both economic and spiritual, have been totally dissimilar; yet there can be no doubt that originally they were brought very close to one another by geographical conditions. For one thing, they were both situated at crucial points in the Rhône valley which joins the Alps with the Mediterranean: in the case of Lyons the confluence of the Saône, and in that of Geneva a position commanding Lake Leman and the Jura pass. Then again, right up to the nineteenth century, they were two of the most important crossroads for traffic over the Alps—from the two Saint Bernard passes and from Mont-Cenis and Mont-Genèvre. (It is worth pointing out that the age of rail has not been altogether to the good for either: Geneva lost its access to the Simplon Tunnel in favor of Lausanne, and Lyons its connection to Mont-Cenis in favor of Chambéry—but in recent years road and air transport, in a historically interesting way, have to some extent atoned for this disgrace and restored the ancient balance.) Finally, a study of historical geography reveals a community of origins: both belonged once to the archbishopric of Vienne; then to the kingdom of Burgundy, of which Lyons, Vienne, and Geneva in turn were the capitals; and ultimately to the Holy Roman Empire, until the end of the thirteenth century in the case of Lyons, and until the seventeenth century in the case of Geneva.[2]

[1] This paper was presented at the Colloque International, "Lyon et les Pays de l'Europe centrale et méridionale," Lyons, July 3–5, 1958.
[2] Since the simplest notions are frequently the most misunderstood it may

Since history and geography together offer an explanation of world events, it is only to be expected that such a similarity of interests and geographical situations would cause the development of both cities to run parallel. Sometimes they complemented one another, sometimes they competed with one another, and often they did both at the same time. This can be shown by a few examples.

It is fairly well known that the Geneva fairs during the Middle Ages were among the most important in Europe, and it has become a commonplace to say that it was in order to enable Lyons to profit from the great currents of trade from northern to southern Europe that Louis XI, in 1462, established and fostered markets there, which soon superseded the older ones. But more recent studies[3] make it necessary to revise this judgment, or at least to draw a few distinctions. It is true that after the end of the fifteenth century Geneva lost ground to Lyons, handicapped as it was by its smaller population and by the enormous sacrifices it had had to make in order to defend and secure its political liberty. All the same, its commercial decline was not as drastic as is generally supposed. From about 1480 to 1520 the crisis was serious, and the short-term transfer of the fairs from Lyons to Bourges was not enough to stem the tide. One after another the great Italian merchants from Milan, Genoa, and Florence transferred their accounts from Geneva to Lyons; for a very short time there were hopes that they would come back, and measures were taken to

perhaps be useful at this point to recall that Geneva was an episcopal principality until the sixteenth century and an independent republic after the Reformation, and did not formally become a Swiss canton until 1815, although it had made an alliance with Fribourg and Bern in 1526 and later with Bern and Zürich. For this reason it would be wrong to speak in the present context of any relationship between Lyons and Switzerland. Geneva alone is in question.

[3] What follows is based on the first published results of the interesting research carried out by the archivist and palaeographer Jean-François Bergier: "Recherches sur les foires et le commerce international de Genève principalement de 1480 à 1540," in *École nationale des Chartes. Positions des thèses soutenues par les élèves de la promotion de 1957* (Paris, 1957), pp. 31–6; "Marchands italiens à Genève au début du XVIᵉ siècle," in *Studi in onore di Armando Sapori* (Milan, 1957), pp. 885–96.

make this easier. But in vain. At the end of the fifteenth century only the Germans from Augsburg, Nürnberg, and Nördlingen kept up and extended their branches in Geneva. This was not without importance for the future, since it was they who were later to introduce the Reformation.[4] But after 1520 there were tentative signs of improvement, and the Italian bankers returned. An unexpected but very real effect of the abolition of the Mass in 1535–6 was the development of interest on loans, which had always been prohibited by the Roman Church; Calvinist legislation sanctioned this innovation, providing it was kept in moderation, and Geneva began its career as a banking center and continued to develop right up to the eighteenth and nineteenth centuries. Trade with Lyons, for so long at a standstill, became very active once more. As a result, after fifty years or so of commercial rivalry, during which the advantage had always been on one side, a sort of balance was restored and the two cities seemed to complement one another. The crisis which came about in Lyons at the end of the sixteenth century was to make its ruinous consequences felt until well into the reign of Louis XIV; as it was, the double waves of Protestant refugees to Geneva after St. Bartholomew's Day and the revocation of the Edict of Nantes—especially the former—together with the introduction of clockmaking and the printed-cloth industry in the eighteenth century, were to give a considerable boost to an economy which might have been thought to be in the last stage of collapse.

Printing is a typical case in point, and it is worth giving a few details about it.[5] This new and divine art of the fifteenth century

[4] Cf. H. Ammann, "Oberdeutsche Kaufleute und die Anfänge der Reformation in Genf," in *Zeitschrift für Württemberg. Landesgeschichte*, XIII (1954), 150–93.

[5] As regards the printing trade in Geneva, it is no longer possible to make use of the far too general and all too often inexact account given by E. H. Gaullieur, "Études sur la typographie genevoise du XVe au XIXe s.," in *Bulletin de l'institut national genevois*, II (1855), 33–292. But for the period from the origins up to 1564, the following useful works are available: Mgr. Marius Besson, *L'Église et l'imprimerie dans les anciens diocèses de Lausanne et de Genève jusqu'en 1525* (Geneva, 1937–8), 2 vols.; T. Dufour, "Notice bibliographique sur le catéchisme et la confession de foi de Calvin (1537) et sur les autres livres

appeared in Paris in 1470, in Lyons in 1473, and in Geneva in 1478; between 1473 and 1478 Geneva had been preceded only by Basle in Switzerland and by Toulouse and Angers in France. It developed more quickly and remarkably in Lyons than anywhere else; at the end of the fifteenth century about sixty printers were in business on the banks of the Saône. When allowance is made for the respective importance of the two cities, one of which had about five times as many people as the other, it can be seen that Geneva was not really much behind; it sustained eight printers in the years 1479 to 1525 and six between 1525 and 1550, as against roughly five times as many in Lyons, which makes the numbers proportionately equal.

The very origins of the first printers were similar: there were Bavarians, Franconians, and then Frenchmen in Geneva; and Württembergers, Hessians, Rhinelanders, and, naturally, Frenchmen in Lyons. From this early period on there can be seen an exchange between these rival cities. Gabriel Pomard and Pierre de Vingle went from Lyons to Geneva in 1525 and 1533, Jean Michel moved from Geneva to Lyons in 1544, and Michel Dubois, a Parisian, shuttled to and fro between the two cities. Dubois sought refuge in Geneva in 1537, probably for religious reasons, but in 1542 he left the city of Calvin for Lyons, where he stayed for fifteen years before returning to Geneva; the first thing he had to do after his return was to acknowledge that he had in the meantime allowed himself to become, in the charitable words of the time, "tainted with idolatry."[6]

imprimés à Genève et à Neuchâtel dès les premiers temps de la Réforme," in *Le premier catéchisme français de Calvin* (Geneva, 1878), pp. xcix–cclxxxvii; Alfred Cartier, "Arrêts du conseil de Genève sur le fait de l'imprimerie et de la librairie de 1541 à 1550," in *Mémoires et documents*, published by the Société d'histoire et d'archéologie de Genève, xxiii (1888–94), 361–566; Paul Chaix, *Recherches sur l'imprimerie à Genève de 1550 à 1564* (Geneva, 1954), in *Travaux d'Humanisme et Renaissance*, xvi. For a general conspectus the following are very stimulating and well-informed: Henri Naef, *Les origines de la Réforme à Genève*, i (Geneva, 1936), 299–306; Henri Delarue, "La culture au XVIe s.," in *Histoire de Genève, des origines à 1798* (Geneva, 1951), published by the Société d'histoire et d'archéologie de Genève, pp. 315–34.

[6] T. Dufour, *op. cit.*, p. cxcvi.

Up to this point there is nothing unusual to note. Then from 1550 onward this two-way traffic suddenly became one way and the proportions were reversed. In his excellent *Recherches sur l'imprimerie à Genève*, recently published, Paul Chaix says that of 330 printers (an enormous number) he had been able to trace down from these fifteen years [1550 to 1564] he found no less than thirty-seven natives of Lyons (or at least men who had come from Lyons), while the Genevans, or printers from Geneva, who subsequently set up business in Lyons formed only the merest handful: Pierre Eskrich, known as Cruche or Vase, in 1565, and François Duron and Guillaume Forest, who in 1562 and 1564 requested permission to withdraw to Lyons but failed to obtain it.

What had happened? How is it possible to explain what M. Henri Delarue has so rightly called a "revolution"? It was simply the Reformation and the role of leadership which, under the influence of Calvin, Geneva assumed in the history of French-speaking Protestantism. Even in the days when Geneva was still uncertain about its faith (though very sure about its will to independence) and was struggling with all its might against the Duke of Savoy, who had it surrounded on all sides, the French reinforcements which were brought out in December, 1535, from Lyons and Burgundy by François de Montbel, the Seigneur de Verey, only to be stopped on the way, numbered, if a Genevan contemporary is to be believed, "five hundred men of arms from Lyons, among whom there were as many printers as anything else."[7] In actual fact Verey's force included men from Dauphiné, as well as Italians, and there were more professional cavalry soldiers in it than printers; but it is certainly true that this improvised and ill-fated force was led by a printer from Lyons called Roboam.[8] And it is well known, too, that pretty well everywhere in France the printers were among the first partisans

[7] Text published in Paul F. Geisendorf, "Les annalistes genevois du début du XVIIe s.," in *Mémoires et documents*, published by the Société d'histoire et d'archéologie de Genève, xxxvii (1942), p. 454.

[8] Cf. Baudrier, *Bibliographie Lyonnaise* (Paris, 1895-1950) Vol. i, p. 380, who in this connection mentions, though with certain anachronisms, the relations between Lyons and Geneva.

of the Reformation,[9] that Lyons was the French printers' capital, and that it was mainly printing workers who, in the spring of 1551, awoke the townspeople and annoyed the canons of Saint-Jean by singing the psalms of Marot and Beza at the tops of their voices on the left bank of the Saône.[10]

But at this point a question arises. This flight to Geneva of printers from Lyons was certainly the first from France, and the numbers involved makes it very important; but the most outstanding refugee printers came not from Lyons but from other parts of the Most Christian Kingdom. The cream of contemporary printers came, in fact, from Paris: Conrad Badius, Jean Crespin, and Henri Estienne—and Paris, ever more accustomed to receiving people than to seeing them go, never forgave them for their exile. And there were, of course, towns like Saint-Malo, where the banning of the Reformation meant purely and simply the abolition of all printing works.[11] This was certainly not the case with Lyons. But it may be asked whether this transfer of manpower and energy was as keenly felt in the place of departure as it was at the receiving end; or, in other words, whether Geneva was really gaining at the expense of Lyons.

After reading Vingtrinier,[12] and even Baudrier,[13] one would be tempted to say no. The undeniable decline of printing in Lyons at the end of the sixteenth century seems to allow an explanation in purely internal terms, both economic and political, and there appears to be no need to bring in religious factors or any question of a denominational exodus. In fact, a distinction has to be made between quality and quantity.[14] With four hundred or so printers

[9] Cf. H. Hauser, *Études sur la Réforme française*, 1919, p. 24.

[10] Cf. J. Guéraud, *Chronique lyonnaise*, pp. 54–5; N. Z. Davis, "The Protestant Printing Workers of Lyons in 1551," in *Travaux d'Humanisme et Renaissance*, XXVIII, 247–57.

[11] *Bulletin de la soc. de l'hist. du protestantisme français*, XLIII (1894), p. 665.

[12] A. Vingtrinier, *Histoire de l'imprimerie à Lyon jusqu'à la fin du XVIᵉ s.* (Lyons, 1894).

[13] Baudrier, *Bibliographie lyonnaise* . . . (Lyons–Geneva, 1895–1950), 13 vols.

[14] Here is a good example of how careful one must be when handling historical statistics. Of some three to four thousand Frenchmen who counted as "residents" of Geneva from 1549 to 1560, only eighty were natives of Lyons or

in Lyons at the time, the departure of roughly a tenth of the total force would have passed unnoticed, especially since those in question were only journeymen or owners in a small way. It is, therefore, very significant that, of the thirty-seven printers listed by Chaix as going from Lyons to Geneva between 1550 and 1564, eighty were just unaccounted for or passed over in silence by Baudrier, who also knew nothing about another dozen or so who took refuge in Geneva; almost the only case given is that of Jean Marquorelles of Millau, who, like some of his predecessors, moved regularly between Lyons and Geneva: between 1554 and 1559 in Geneva, from 1560 to 1572 in Lyons, and back once more to Geneva in 1572.[15]

But if attention is paid to the years after 1564, at which date Paul Chaix terminated his research, and above all if attention is paid to quality rather than to quantity, then it becomes evident that Geneva was indeed profiting at the expense of Lyons. A few names will be enough to prove this. For example, that of Antoine Vincent, a merchant and citizen of Lyons, who contrived to remain an alderman of his native city when he moved with the whole of his family to Geneva;[16] at the same time, he kept up important commercial interests in Lyons, where he was to return in 1568, and divided between the two rival cities the burdens and profits of his enormous bookselling venture, "the biggest publishing enterprise of the century": the printing of the Reformed Psalter. Then there were the Senneton, Gabiano, and Honnorat families; these were not converted en bloc, and only the Huguenot

people simply from Lyons, and only about half a dozen printers, which is very few (Livre des habitants de Genève, I, 1549–60, published with introduction and tables by Paul F. Geisendorf [Geneva, 1957], Travaux d'Humanisme et Renaissance, XXVI). But in our introduction to this valuable document we gave the reasons for this tiny percentage; and it should be added that quite a few "residents" did not state their profession and that several "bigwigs" do not appear on this list (cf. E. Droz, "Antoine Vincent, La propagande par le psautier," Travaux d'Humanisme et Renaissance, XXVIII, 1957, 277). Thus even when correctly interpreted, a document of this sort can lead to completely mistaken conclusions unless amended and completed by special studies such as that of Chaix.

[15] Baudrier, op. cit.   [16] Droz, op. cit., XXVIII, 276–93.

members emigrated to Geneva—Claude Senneton in 1568, Barthélemy and Henry de Gabiano in 1571, and Barthélemy and Sébastien Honnorat in 1572. Finally, and most important of all, was the Tournes family, because this time the exile of Jean II de Tournes to Geneva in 1585 was definitive and total; and there is general agreement among historians today that the illustrious printing house which Lyons then lost was the best and most renowned of its day anywhere.

This, moreover, throws a curious light on the only episode in the rivalry between Lyons and Geneva of which the texts have preserved any trace. In 1583 the printers of Lyons requested the consulate to support them in their claim that the booksellers should henceforth be forbidden to have any books published in Geneva under the borrowed name of Lyons. As they said:

> To the great detriment of the city and of the said printers, the booksellers have destroyed the printing-trade of Lyons and removed it to Geneva, and, what is worse, caused to be set on the title-page of works printed in Geneva words to the effect that they have been printed in Lyons, in order that they may have free movement in Italy, Spain, etc., which is a falsehood and a forgery; and printing, which should enjoy full scope and a good repute in this city, will thereby be utterly ruined, and, so long as this continues, the printers' journeymen will be constrained, in order to earn their living, to leave Lyons and go to Geneva where, in the course of time, they will turn heretic.[17]

To this the booksellers replied that the fault really lay with the monopoly run by the journeyman printers of Lyons in order to keep the prices high. All the same, the municipal aldermen could hardly fail to support the claim of the master printers, and so they prohibited the entry into Lyons of all books printed in Geneva under the Lyons imprint. Baudrier considers that this was mere snatching after pennies on the part of the Lyons publishers, since, although it was cheaper for them to have their work done in Geneva where labor costs were lower, the quality was "only

[17] Baudrier, *op. cit.*, VII, 241.

middling as regards type, inking and paper."[18] But this is an improper generalization; it is hard to see how a mere removal from Lyons to Geneva could make it possible to say that work like that of the De Tournes family, for example, had become *ipso facto* only middling.

But this is not the whole story. For just under a century the Edict of Nantes had assured liberty of conscience to the Protestant printers of Lyons, thereby, quite naturally, making it unnecessary for them to flock to Geneva; the revocation would, of course, produce the same effects as St. Bartholomew's Day, though to a lesser extent. The Huguetan family had been great booksellers in Lyons, but they were nothing more than businessmen and bankers when the revocation forced them to transfer their considerable business interests to Geneva, and later to Amsterdam; the precise details of these interests are still a matter of discussion among historians.[19]

A name exclusively attached to the bookselling world of Lyons was that of Philibert Perachon. In 1703, as a citizen of Geneva, he associated with the Cramer brothers, the famous publishers of Voltaire, Jean-Antoine Chouet (who also was French, though a Burgundian), and Gabriel and Samuel II de Tournes, and formed the great company of Chouet, De Tournes, Cramer, Perachon, Ritter and De Tournes (*sic*), which was one of the most important French-language booksellers of the eighteenth century.[20] Also from Lyons was Jacques Barrillot, who in 1706 joined up with the Genevan patricians Jacques Gallatin and Jacques Fabri to found the house of Fabri and Barrillot. This house had the honor of bringing out the original edition of Montesquieu's *Esprit des Lois* (and very badly, too, but that is another story) and Burlamaqui's *Principes du Droit*; it also placed its name—and nothing else, since the address was a made-up one—on the title page of what was, together with

[18] *Ibid.*, p. 469.

[19] Cf. A. E. Sayous, "Le financier J. H. Huguetan à Amsterdam et à Genève," in *Bulletin de la soc. d'hist. et d'arch. de Genève*, VI, 1933–8, 255–74.

[20] Cf. J. R. Kleinschmidt, *Les imprimeurs et libraires de la république de Genève, 1700–1798* (Geneva, 1948), pp. 156–7.

the other two, perhaps the most famous, and in any case the most resounding, book to appear in the eighteenth century: Rousseau's first *Discours*.[21]

And, finally, it must be pointed out that this movement of interchange between Lyons and Geneva, which had been one-way since 1550, tended to become two-way once more in the eighteenth century, just as it had been before the Reformation. For instance, in 1777, the printers Nouffer and Bassompierre[22] worked for Duplain et Cie of Lyons in the printing of the *Dictionnaire encyclopédique*. And, most important, from 1726—and again in 1749 and 1754, nigh on two centuries after their great-great-grandfather's exile in Geneva—the two brothers Jean-Jacques and Jacques de Tournes sought to re-establish a footing in Lyons. In 1726 they had acquired the Latin stock of Anisson and Posuel, booksellers in Lyons, and asked the distrustful authorities for permission to start business in the French city.[23] The matter was taken as high as the Keeper of the Seals at Versailles, who replied that "although the Genevans have all liberty to pursue any other profession in this city, that of bookselling is so delicate and important for religion and the peace of the state that it is not possible to allow it to be practised publicly by subjects who profess the so-called reformed Religion." The most Versailles would agree to do was to authorize an association with "a good Catholic bookseller established in Lyons," in whose name the new concern would be run and who would take "all necessary precautions to prevent the introduction and sale of evil books which the city of Geneva delivers in all too great numbers to every province of the Realm." These fears were, in actual fact, exaggerated. "The business of the Tournes, that is, the share they had acquired in Posuel's stock, was exclusively in Latin Catholic books, and with these their principal trade was with Spain and Italy," says Audin. Moreover, he adds, "this considerable stock

---

[21] Cf. Kleinschmidt, *op. cit.*, pp. 62–4. Paul F. Geisendorf, "Quelques notes sur une maison d'édition genevoise du XVIIIe s.: les Barrillot," in *Geneva*, XXII (1944), 293–10.

[22] Kleinschmidt, *op. cit.*, p. 146.   [23] *Ibid.*, p. 99.

which they were to manage, their concern to avoid infringing the royal regulations and their strict and universally recognized integrity were a sufficient guarantee that their presence in Lyons constituted no danger whatsoever, except perhaps to the comfort and commercial interests of their competitors."[24]

What Audin has to say about this encourages a reference to that very surprising text which I myself found in the notarial archives in Geneva. According to this, just before selling the De Tournes stock (henceforth to be purely secular) to Nouffer and Bassompierre in 1774, the two brothers Samuel and Antoine de Tournes, "preferring a quiet and peaceful life in Geneva to the travels, worries and cares inseparable from a business enterprise" such as theirs, gave as an additional reason for selling out "the great changes which studies in Spain have undergone since the expulsion of the Jesuits, changes which have made a large quantity of the theological books we had made ready of no more value than the paper they were printed on."[25] Although the family remained good Huguenots until it died out two generations later at the beginning of the nineteenth century,[26] the great-grandsons of Jean de Tournes worked mainly, as they themselves admitted, with the Jesuits! Commercial history is full of these contradictions.

And it is not only in the bookselling world that traces can be found of these commercial exchanges, half rivalry, half collaboration, between Lyons and Geneva. This is shown by the very interesting *Observations* drawn up in Lyons by Superintendent d'Herbigny toward the middle of the eighteenth century.[27] In these he states first of all that "as regards its situation Lyons has an infinite advantage over Geneva, and also as regards its more numerous population and labor force; there can scarcely be any

[24] Alfred Cartier, *Bibliographie des éditions des de Tournes, imprimeurs lyonnais*, published by Marius Audin . . . (Paris, 1938), pp. 26–7.
[25] Geneva State Archives, minutes of Mercier and Du..ant, Not. Vol. 11, 643.
[26] Inadequately treated in Vol. III of Galiffe's *Notices généalogiques sur les familles genevoises*, the genealogy of the De Tournes family is considered again in Vol. II of *Généalogies genevoises*.
[27] André E. Sayous, "Observations de l'intendant de Lyons sur le commerce de Genève," in *Bulletin de la soc. d'hist. et d'arch. de Genève*, VII (1939–42), 31–4.

limit to its trade and production, while Geneva, with only a restricted number of tradesmen and craftsmen, is much more limited in the possibilities it offers for work and trade." But, he added, if Lyons was to "ruin" Geneva, its fairs would have to enjoy the tax exemption which, with the exception of export duties, had been taken away from them, because

> it is more for this reason than for any other that the spice trade has been ruined in Lyons . . . and the free transit accorded to the Levantine Company has made it easier for Geneva to profit by it. For the same reason, and helped by their embargo on foreign cloth, their cloth trade has become quite considerable; this is made all the easier for them by the fact that they are in a position to take coarse cloths from France, and therefore, since they already have fine and middle-grade cloths from Holland and England, they have a full assortment. They have the same advantage with linens, even those from the (French) Kingdom, since, bringing them from Burgundy across Picardy, they have infinitely less dues to pay than the dealers of Lyons.

And finally, as to gilding, the advantages of the Genevans were also due to their exemption from taxes.

> Added to all these circumstances, the difficulties in the way of foreign trade during the war have so favored the Genevans' production and trade that not only all the workers, believed to be about four or five thousand in number, whom they have managed to gather together are engaged in this production, but also, since these are not sufficient for all the business they are in a position to carry out, some of them still come to have work done for them in Lyons. This production does not extend to materials but limits itself to thread, lace-work, galloons and similar items; but it is from these that the most is to be gained, because a great quantity of it is sent to the Spanish Indies, and the profit, though casual, is enormous, sometimes reaching fifty per cent in the most successful deals . . . . The Genevans have not by any means attained to the perfection with which gold and silver work is carried out in Lyons, and they are not always scrupulous in their labelling; but quite apart from the fact that they could perfect themselves with the necessary effort,

the people in the Indies do not examine things so closely, and the best things are never sent there.

The superintendent of Lyons did not touch on the subject of clockmaking because his government had no interest in this industry. But it is evident that, one day, when we have the necessary monographs on the textile industry of the eighteenth century, it will be possible to fill out these observations in a very interesting way.

Meanwhile, we could close the economic and geographical considerations brought forward in this study and introduce here a more personal, and thus more human, note. I myself am descended on my mother's side from a family which originated in Saint-Symphorien-sur-Coise, and in the family records I found the memoirs of an ancestor who in the sixteenth century left Lyons to settle in Geneva as a result of religious persecution. This ancestor, Jérôme Des Gouttes, had married in 1559 the daughter of one of the most notable Protestant printers in Lyons, Jean-François de Gabiano. Claire de Gabiano, only thirteen at the time of her marriage(!), bore her husband seven children and followed him into exile, first in Lausanne, then in Geneva; but worn out by so many confinements and successive persecutions, she died in Lausanne, while still very young, on November 21, 1574. And this is the wonderfully moving tribute which ten years later, when compiling his memoirs, the sexagenarian devoted to the memory of the bookseller's daughter from Lyons. In all the literature of family books, ledgers, or genealogies I know very few which are so beautifully simple or so deeply human:[28]

> In the first place she was of good family, as will be seen below.
> She was a slender woman and very beautiful.
> She was very sober in eating and drinking and was in no way a slave to her appetite.
> She was equally sober in her dress, with no concern for novelties.

[28] Paul F. Geisendorf, *Histoire d'une famille du refuge français, les Des Gouttes, de St-Symphorien-le-Chatel en Lyonnais et de Genève* (Geneva, 1943), pp. 71-2.

She was not constantly running here and there, but usually remained at home when she had no business in the town, instructing her children to fear God, and training and educating them in all other things.

She never brought any gossip into the house, and never spoke ill of other people.

She never picked any quarrels with her neighbors, but lived so courteously with them that she was loved and honored for it by everyone.

She was an excellent housekeeper, keeping her tranquillity in the most wonderful way in her own household.

And, as for myself, she was such that we lived together for fifteen years in the greatest peace and friendship which husband and wife could enjoy.

And you, Zacarie, who knew her, could not say that you had ever seen between her and me anything which could have been of bad example to you; I want to put this clearly before you here so that you may do the same, both you and your brothers, if God should call you to the state of matrimony, and that you may point out this same path to your own children, if it should please God to give them to you.

She was always close by my side in all our persecutions and afflictions, in great patience and without any murmur.

And finally, she showed by her death that she had lived as an upright woman, recognizing the miseries of this life and not regretting to have to leave them, especially since she had had great experience of them and could look forward to the enjoyment of that blessed life in heaven.

She was greatly mourned in the city of Lausanne, loved as she was by people of all stations.

And you, therefore, Zacarie, Jerôme, Jehan and Lidie, my children, you will have her all your lives before your eyes as a shining example to follow. And may you, likewise, set her before your own children as a model. And so God will bless you from generation to generation and will grant you all prosperity and eternal life to come.

PART FOUR

French Humanism, Christianity, and the Pagan Past

9 The Humanist Idea of Christian Antiquity: Lefèvre d'Étaples and his Circle[1]

EUGENE F. RICE, JR.

THE major intellectual interests of Jacques Lefèvre d'Étaples and his circle focused in the high ambition of "joining wisdom and piety with eloquence."[2] To this end the group worked to restore a "cleansed and purified Peripatetic philosophy."[3] They studied the Bible in a series of New Testament editions, commentaries, and translations. They printed the medieval mystics: the Victorines, Elizabeth of Schönau, Raymond Lull, Ruysbroeck. Finally, they devoted time, energy, and enthusiasm to the investigation of Christian antiquity and the editing of patristic texts. Lefèvre himself showed them how these separate enterprises meshed in a consistent program: "For knowledge of natural philosophy," he wrote in 1506, "for knowledge of ethics, politics and economics, drink from the fountain of a purified Aristotle. Those who wish to set themselves a higher end and a happier leisure will prepare themselves by studying Aristotle's *Metaphysics*, which deals with first and supramundane philosophy. Turn from this to a reverent reading of Scripture, guided by Cyprian, Hilary, Origen, Jerome,

[1] This paper was read at Harvard University before the New England Conference of Renaissance Studies on April 21, 1961. Much of the research on which it is based was done during a year abroad generously made possible by a Fulbright research grant and a Guggenheim fellowship.
[2] The formula is Beatus Rhenanus'. "Magno dei opt. max. munere fieri arbitror . . . ut complusculi hac tempestate ubique fere nationum sapientiam ac pietatem cum eloquentia coniungant, quod . . . apud Gallos Iacobus Faber Stapulensis, praeceptor meus, Iodocus Clichtoveus, Bovillus et Fortunatus hoc aevi faciunt" (A. Horowitz and K. Hartfelder, *Briefwechsel des Beatus Rhenanus* [Leipzig, 1886], p. 12). Beatus was Lefèvre's student from May, 1503, until the autumn of 1507. The fundamental work on Lefèvre and his circle remains Augustin Renaudet, *Préréforme et humanisme à Paris pendant les premières guerres d'Italie (1494–1517)* (2nd ed., Paris, 1953).
[3] Cono of Nürnberg to Beatus Rhenanus, *Briefwechsel des B. R.*, p. 45.

Augustine, Chrysostom, Athanasius, Nazianzen, John of Damascus, and other Fathers. Once these studies have purified the mind and disciplined the senses (and provided one has extirpated vice and leads a suitable and upright life), then the generous mind may aspire to scale gradually the higher heights of contemplation, instructed by Nicholas of Cusa and the divine Dionysius and others like them."[4] Lefèvre's program thus demanded a graduated ascent from the knowledge of sensible experience to a contemplation of the mind of God. From the beginning the study of the Fathers formed an important and necessary stage in that ascent.

French humanists regarded their study of the Fathers as part of a general rebirth of ancient Christian knowledge after centuries of neglect. We are told that Jan Schilling of Cracow, a pupil of Lefèvre, rescued Hilary's *Commentary on the Psalms* from "dust, filth and neglect";[5] that the works of Cyprian, before their Renaissance editions, had been "rotting away in mouldy obscurity";[6] that Nemesius of Emesa's *De natura hominis* was "a rare work unknown for centuries."[7] Lefèvre, we learn further, from the time of his adolescence traveled widely from library to library looking for the honey of the Fathers,[8] while Guillaume Parvy, the king's confessor, searched for patristic manuscripts as indefatigably as Poggio had hunted the classics. He discovered Hilary's *Commentary on Matthew* in the Dominican house of Saint-Benigne in Dijon and Origen's *Commentary on Leviticus*, "inter blattas et tineas" in the library of Corbie.[9] A letter of Clichtove, occasioned

---

[4] *Politicorum libri octo*, ed. Lefèvre d'Étaples (Paris, H. Estienne, 1506), pp. 123^v–4^r.

[5] VII, aii^v.   [6] x, aii^r.   [7] IX, preface; *Briefwechsel des B. R.*, p. 43.

[8] xv, ai^v: P. Renouard, *Bibliographie des impressions et des œuvres de Josse Badius Ascensius* (Paris, 1908), II, 146: "Jacobus Faber Stapulensis, philosophus sane insignis et omni disciplina laudabili extra invidiae aleam ornatus . . . ubi in adulescentia sua cum experiundi religionis ergo varias regiones peragrasset multasque bibliothecas invisisset, perinde ac apes daedalea solerti indagine tanquam e floribus fragrantissimis optima ac liquidissima mella praestantissima summi cujusque scriptoris opera delegit, eaque honustis alis ad nos usque transvexit. Inter quae superioribus annis divi Hilarii, Aegesippi, Nicolai Cusani et quasdam alias neutiquam poenitendas lucubrationes ipso auctore emisimus."

[9] VII, aii^v; x, aii^v; XIII, 1^v.

by the discovery of Origen's *Commentary*, captures nicely the romance of patristic Renaissance: "They who carefully search libraries for the literary monuments of the ancient [Fathers] and publish them for the use of all deserve the highest praise; for in this way they learnedly benefit the community of scholars by enriching their libraries with the instruments of knowledge. Just as Camillus, because he raised up Rome again after defeating her enemies, was accorded praises almost equal to those of Romulus, the original founder, so also hardly less praise is due to them who find and publish the illustrious works of the ancients (thus freeing them from their long imprisonment in dust and darkness) than to the original authors, since the works themselves can hardly benefit posterity until a watchful vigilance has again made them available to all."[10] French Renaissance scholars knew perfectly well that many of the patristic texts they were discovering and publishing had been available to the high scholastics. They remained convinced, nonetheless, that only in their own age, when the light of the gospel itself was beginning to shine again, were the Fathers properly known, properly read, and properly used.

The time-consuming labor of discovering manuscripts, of transcribing, editing, translating, and publishing them, measures the high value French humanists of the early Renaissance placed on the Fathers. Quoting Pseudo-Chrysostom, Lefèvre called Dionysius "volucris caeli" and found his works "most sacred, so eminent in dignity and excellence that no word of praise is adequate to describe them."[11] Ignatius is a "Dei miles ferventissimus," "filled

[10] XIII, IV.
[11] I, aiii^r: Dom Chevalier and the Benedictines of Solesmes, *Dionysiaca. Recueil donnant l'ensemble des traductions latines des ouvrages attribués au Denys de l'Aréopage* (Brussels, 1937), I, p. CXI: "Inter quae sunt divini Dionysii Areopagitae sacratissima opera, tanta excellentiae dignitate eminentia, ut commendationis eorum nullus unquam verbis valeat assequi summam. Ut enim dilectissimus Deo discipulus Ioannes ob evangelii sui sublimitatem inter evangelistas aquila nominatur, ita et sanctus Ioannes Chrysostomus hunc beatissimum patrem, suorum scriptorum altitudinem demiratus, totus paene effectus attonitus, volucrem caeli exclamat." Lefèvre's source is *Sermo de pseudo prophetis et falsis doctoribus* (Migne, *P.G.* LIX, 560). The sermon is apocryphal and may be very roughly dated between the middle of the sixth century and 876, when Anastasius

with the Holy Spirit," "intoxicated with the love of God."[12] The
Historia Lausiaca of Palladius, which Lefèvre had found "languishing in the squalid prison of an ancient library," is filled with "piety
and doctrine, the two things necessary to raise men's minds to
God."[13] Cyril of Alexandria is *probatissimus*, his works particularly
conducive to "piety and true moral instruction."[14] Nemesius of
Emesa is *divinissimus*.[15] Origen's doctrine is *absolutissima*.[16] Basil
the Great is *sapientissimus, potentissimus, sanctissimus, piissimus*.[17]
The very words suggest what Lefèvre and his followers sought
and found in the Fathers: *pietas, doctrina*, religious and moral
insight; by extension, authorities and models for a profound
reform of theological writing and teaching on the basis of the

Bibliothecarius mentioned it in a letter to Charles the Bald: "Sane quia nonnulli
beatum Dionysium 'pterygion tu uranu' a Graecis appellari commemorant,
notandum quod hunc beatus Iohannes Chrysostomus 'petinon tu uranu,' id est
volucrem caeli, in ultimo sermonum suorum describat" (*Epistolae Karolini aevi*,
v, ed. E. Perels and G. Laehr, *Monumenta Germaniae historica* [Berlin, 1928],
pp. 440–1).

[12] I, 102ᵛ. Cf. note 35 below.

[13] II, aiᵛ: "Heraclidis Alexandrini et Recognitionum Petri apostoli libros, eos
arbitror qui legerint duplicem suae lectionis reportaturos mercedem, pietatis
videlicet atque doctrinae, quae duo praecipua videntur quae hominum mentes
ad Deum elevent, sine etiam quibus ianua vitae semper clausa videtur. Quare
operae pretium me facturum duxi et praesentibus et futuris, si libros illos
vetustate et situ in antiquis bibliothecis marcentes recognoscerem, recognitos
autem quasi de carceris squaloribus exemptos plurimorum (et praesertim eorum
qui religiosa mente sunt) virorum oculis legendos ingererem."

[14] XIII, IV.

[15] IX, preface: *Briefwechsel des B. R.*, p. 43.

[16] Jacques Merlin, a pupil of Girolami Balbi and professor of theology at the
Collège de Navarre, edited the works of Origen in 1512. Prefacing Vol. III is a
fulsome *Apologia pro Origene* maintaining that Origen's doctrine is "probatissima,
absolutissima et ab heretica pravitate prorsus aliena." At the end of Vol. IV is a
Commendatio Origenis by Badius Ascensius, dedicated to Guillaume Parvy
(Renouard, *Badius Ascensius*, III, 94–7). On this edition see the interesting article
by D. P. Walker, "Origène en France," in *Courants religieux et humanisme à la
fin du XVᵉ et au début du XVIᵉ siècle. Colloque de Strasbourg 9–11 mai 1957* (Paris,
1959), pp. 107 ff. Lefèvre had no part in this edition, but his favorable opinion
of Origen is suggested by the passage from his *Commentary on the Politics* quoted
above, p. 126. Cf. Rudolf Pfeiffer, "Erasmus und die Einheit der klassischen
und der christlichen Renaissance," *Historisches Jahrbuch*, LXXIV (1955), 186 ff.

[17] XV, aiᵛ; Renouard, *Badius Ascensius*, II, 146.

cultural program of humanism. For the piety of the Fathers was, in their eyes, of a special and attractive kind: it was eloquent; it was a simple, affective wisdom, not a syllogistic science; it was, finally, peculiarly authoritative, far closer to the primitive source of Christian illumination than the scholastics. Indeed, they found in the Fathers precisely what they missed in high and late medieval scholasticism. A principal aim of their enthusiasm was to undermine the authority of the one by magnifying the authority of the other.

The humanists of Lefèvre's circle were not dogmatic in their demand for eloquence, nor was their ideal of eloquence (to say nothing of their practice) sophisticated by contemporary Italian standards. Lefèvre himself seems to have admired most what he called a "humble Christian style" and he was always ready to defend the "divine rusticity" of the Latin works of Raymond Lull or even Ruysbroeck's vernacular.[18] But the common view was that piety and eloquence united were preferable to either alone. For eloquence, it was argued, preserves a work and an admirable content will disintegrate without the fixative of style. Moreover, eloquence has a positive religious significance. A work which can be read with pleasure and without toil more effectively persuades to religious truth and excites devotion.[19] An initial reason for admiring the Fathers, therefore, was their eloquence: the Laconic

[18] Lefèvre praised the *Lausiac History* of Palladius because it was written "humili Christianoque stilo" (II, ai[v]). Cf. Lull, *Liber de laudibus beatissime virginis marie* ..., ed. Lefèvre d'Étaples (Paris, Guy Marchand for Jean Petit, 1499), ai[v]: "Neque item sermonis eius simplicitas vos avertat; qui enim nimium delicatas aures habent, praesertim in iis quae pertinent ad vitae instituta, timeant ne sint de numero de quibus beatissimus Paulus vaticinatus ait, Erit enim tempus quo sanam doctrinam non sustinebunt, sed ad sua desideria coacervabunt sibi magistros prurientes auribus: et a veritate quidem auditum avertent, ad fabulas autem convertentur [2 Tim. iv. 3–4]"; Ruysbroeck, *De Ornatu spiritualium nuptiarum*, ed. Lefèvre d'Étaples (Paris, H. Estienne, 1512), aii[r]: "At vero quod hic liber primum patrio sermone et vernacula lingua aeditus sit, id argumento sufficienti non est auctorem paucarum fuisse litterarum. Nam et litteratissimus quisque vernaculos aedere potest libros longe forsan melius quam illitteratus. Et grammatici qui hunc legunt iudicabunt auctorem pro illa tempestate apprime elegantem, rhetores copiosum."

[19] VII, ai[v].

brevity or Attic elegance of the Greeks;[20] the Latins' clear sober
concision, for which they were held to merit the praise traditionally
given Sallust—that he offered as many ideas as he used words.[21]
Indeed, the Fathers were themselves considered classical men of
letters. They had often been poets, orators, and the friends of
philosophers; and most of them wrote before "Roman eloquence
began to totter with the tottering Roman Empire."[22] In this
perspective, Basil the Great was used to justify the study of the
pagan classics; verses by Cyprian (unfortunately spurious) and
Paulinus of Nola, the writing of Neolatin poetry; Jerome or
Gregory Nazianzen, the personal cultivation of verbal elegance;
while, for French humanists, Hilary in particular became an
exemplary figure. For as Robert Fortuné, a colleague of Lefèvre
and *primarius* of the Collège du Plessis, pointed out, he had lived at
the beginning of that declining age (ending, Fortuné thought,
only in his own day) when all around him spoke Gothic rather
than Latin. He was an appropriate model, encouragement, and
authority, for he too struggled against the degeneration of his age,
felt ˙no shame in looking back to the ancients, and successfully
studied to imitate them.[23] The contemporary humanist ideal of
eloquence, in short, was considered to reproduce the ideal and
practice of the Fathers; to imitate the Fathers was to imitate
stylists of the great periods of classical letters; to imitate the pagan
classics was to follow the example of the Fathers.

Yet Lefèvre and his circle attached more importance to the piety

[20] In his preface to a translation of two letters of Gregory Nazianzen to
Themistius, Beatus Rhenanus praised the "Attica venustas" and "Laconica
brevitas" of Gregory's style (*Briefwechsel des B. R.*, pp. 52–3).

[21] VII, aii[r]. Cf. Badius Ascensius on Hegesippus, VI, I[v]; Renouard, *Badius
Ascensius*, II, 487: "Ut enim silentio pertranseamus admirabilem eius in narrando
gratiam, quippe qui sub miro compendio sit maxime dilucidus et sub maxima
luce mire compendiosus, tanta rerum gestarum varietate scatet tantoque
sententiarum pondere, ut (quod de Sallustio dici solet) res verbis aequasse
videatur."

[22] VII, aii[r].

[23] *Ibid.* Cf. P. O. Kristeller, "Augustine and the Early Renaissance," in *Studies
in Renaissance Thought and Letters* (Rome, 1956), pp. 361–7. Badius Ascensius
published Bruni's translation of Basil's enormously popular *De legendis anti-
quorum libris* in 1509 (Renouard, II, 145).

of the Fathers than to their eloquence. What particular characteristics did they attribute to ancient Christian piety? We get an
initial hint in a passage from Fortuné's preface to his edition of
Cyprian: "Reading [Cyprian] awakens the sleeping mind, stimu-
lates it, turns men to God, leads them to the theology of the
blessed, ineffably, and not through riddles and enigmas or in-
extricable labyrinths or Gordian difficulties." And he quotes the
Metamorphoses: "The windings of the labyrinth lead into error."[24]
Beatus Rhenanus made the same point in recommending Nemesius
of Emesa to the theological faculty of the University of Paris.
Parisian students, he hoped, would learn from Nemesius "many
excellent things, without contention, without disputation, learn
in simplicity things which are too often made the object of verbal
duels, of pride rather than utility. For, alas, too many are per-
suaded that the holiest theology is impossible without sophistical
argument. 'So hard a thing it is to know what is just,' as
Aristophanes truly says in the *Plutus*."[25]

What the humanists of Lefèvre's circle admired in the piety of
the Fathers, then, was its simplicity and clarity. Instead of emphasizing difficulties, *nodi*, openly opposing authorities *sic et non*,
probing *quaestiones* in disputations, and finally reconciling them by
a subtle dialectic, Hilary, for example, solved knotty points in his
argument "so neatly the unattentive reader may think he has
scarcely dealt with them, so expeditiously he should be compared
with Alexander cutting the Gordian knot."[26] The Fathers'
theological method was simple, it was further believed, because
their conception of theology itself was more "pure," more true,
indeed, than that of the schoolmen. The scholastics answered the
question "Is theology a science?" in the affirmative; the Fathers
answered it negatively. Theology is not a *scientia*, but a *sapientia*,
not a systematically ordered body of true and certain knowledge
derived from the certain but undemonstrable principles of revelation, but a *doctrina sacra* derived from the *pagina sacra* of Scripture,
a holy rhetoric in the humble service of the text, unprofaned by

[24] X, aii^v.   [25] IX, preface: *Briefwechsel des B. R.*, p. 44.   [26] VII, aii^e.

the syllogisms of the *Posterior Analytics*.[27] In the Fathers, as in Hilary, "totus est hilaris religio, totus sanctitas, totus amor, totus sapientia";[28] while patristic doctrine, as Lefèvre put it, teaches simple truth, unobscured by empty sophistry, "simplex veritas absque ullo fuco."[29]

The Fathers wrote no *summas*, therefore, As the most orthodox possible soldiers of Christian truth, they wrote polemics against the heretic or they wrote commentaries on Scripture in which, Clichtove tells us, the blinding illumination of the sacred text becomes accessible to the fragile eyes of the human mind[30]. In

[27] Cf. M.-D. Chenu, *La Théologie comme science au XIIIᵉ siècle* (2nd ed., Paris, 1943), pp. 38–53.

[28] VII, aiᵛ.   [29] II, aiᵛ.

[30] IV, 2ʳ: "Non mediocre praestat hominibus beneficium ... qui solem illis conspicuum reddit qui ob oculorum imbecillitatem validioremque radiorum iactum in suo orbe contueri firma acie haudquaquam possent, in subiectis autem corporibus diffusum et multiformem facile conspiciantur, maxime ubi quippiam accesserit adiumenti quod nebulas caliginesque interceptas dispulerit. Quod ideo dictum velim, quia sacra inter eloquia et potissimum evangelia Ioannes, Deo imprimis dilectus discipulus solari splendore radians, de summa Christi divinitate ceteris tanto sublimius locutus est, quanto ceteris sideribus sol rutilantius emicat. Quo factum est, ut non ab re Dei loquentissimus Dionysius illum evangelii solem nuncupaverit; et Ezechiel in sacra mysteriorum visione eundem aquilae persimilem describit, quod reliquis altiore volatu sese ad caelestia sustulerit irreverberatoque et minime trepidante mentis obtutu illustre caeli hauserit iubar. Verum cum non posset hic eximius divinitatis fulgor a Ioanne depromptus plane comprehendi ob insignem suae claritatis eminentiam, beatissimus pater Cyrillus urbis Alexandrinae patriarcha, divinae sapientiae dux et moderator egregius, nostrae fragilitati consulens, radios illius multiplices lucida suorum commentariorum explicatione nudavit effusosque latius et expansos nobis spectabiles effecit. Quantum vero sincerae divinorum cognitionis lucem omnibus offerat, quotve impietatis hac sua elucidatione tenebras eliminet, cuivis legenti in promptu obviumque protinus erit; ut strenuus enim Christi veritatisque miles in Ebionitas, Sabellianos, Arrianos, Eunomianos, Macedonianos et reliquam patris mendacii catervam classica concinit, arma movet, spicula librat et instructissimam ducit aciem, sacrarum litterarum testimoniis rationibusque acerrimis lucifugos ipsos et errorum magistros omnis invadens, profligans et in fugam agens." Writing to Guillaume Briçonnet in 1514, Clichtove emphasized again the Fathers' orthodoxy and ceaseless struggle against heresy (XII, a2ʳ). "Non parva illis debetur gratia, sacratissime praesul, qui sua industria contra hostiles incursus munimenta parant, quibus adversariorum tela retundantur, irriti fiant eorum conatus et insultus inanes. Unde Archimedes Syracusanus magnopere celebratur auctore Plutarcho, quod cum Marcellus dux

Leviticus they explained allegorically the ceremonies of the law, adapting its teaching to the mysteries of faith and to the ethical problems of human life.[31] They revealed in the Psalms the mystery of our salvation and in the gospels they mystically interpreted for us the deeds and sayings of our Lord and Saviour. We come to them depressed with worldy cares. We leave them hungry and thirsty for the page of Scripture. "Oh, would that I had the power and understanding," exclaimed Fortuné after reading Hilary, "to find support for the rest of my days in reading Hilary and others like him. Then my conversation would be in heaven, the world crucified unto me and I unto the world and Christ would live in me."[32]

Ultimately, the correctness of patristic method, and so the purity and truth of its theological results, was due to the fact that it was based on the techniques of textual criticism. The scriptural page was central, and the Fathers had made every effort to reach its true meaning. Origen and Jerome had read the Bible in its

Romanorum Syracusas obsidione premeret, ipse varia excogitarit machinamenta, ratione geometrica fabricata, quibus hostium navigia tormenta et machinas magno impetu elisit urbemque diutius incolumem ne caperetur servavit. At vero longe maiore gratia et laude cumulandi sunt ii qui suo studio in certamine litterario veritatem licet invincibilem opprimere contendentium spicula contundunt, arma reddunt imbecilla et collatis signis eos in fugam vertunt, ut non prevaleat contra sincerae fidei pietatem demonica cohors et insana impiorum caterva, sed obstruatur os loquentium iniqua et victrix tantem veritas profugatis hostibus gloriosa triumphet. In quorum numero merito inter ceteros habendus est Cyrillus Alexandrinus, inclytus veritatis catholicae satelles, propugnator ac signifer et orthodoxae fidei contra hereticorum rabiem defensator acerrimus." These texts, and others like them, are best understood as humanistic efforts to underline the purity of patristic doctrine. Having cast the Fathers in so important a role, having forged them into rods with which to birch the scholastic doctors, humanists spared no effort to defend their orthodoxy. The humanist rehabilitation of Origen fits into this same pattern.

[31] XIII, 1ᵛ: "Continet enim volumen illud [Cyrilli (Origenis) Commentarium in Leviticum] mysticam explanationem sacrorum veteris legis, allegoricas caerimoniarum rationes et multiformium hostiarum symbolicas significativasque notiones, ut quicquid corporaliter et ad litteram in Levitico observandum statuitur, id omne ad spiritualem vivificantemque transferens intelligentiam aut fidei sacrae mysteriis aut humanae vitae directioni moribusque formandis concinne et decenter adaptet."

[32] VII, aiᵛ: Appendix II (1), ll. 23-8.

original languages; they had developed the critical techniques necessary to maintain an uncontaminated transmission of the sacred text; they had prepared new translations and corrected older ones against the original. The biblical studies of the Fathers thus became a model for an important part of the humanist program: the call for a return to the sources, the learning of Greek and Hebrew, the critical examination and correction of the Vulgate. When Lefèvre, in the first major attempt in France to put this program into practice, began work on his *Quincuplex psalterium* (1509), he turned to the Fathers. He corrected (timidly) the Vulgate of the Psalms from the *Psalterium iuxta Hebraeos*, Jerome's translation direct from the Hebrew. He indicated these corrections by using the Aristarchan signs, those obelisks and asterisks already used by Origen and Jerome to mark departures in the Septuagint or Latin texts from the Hebrew original. He printed a medieval triple Psalter, which gave the texts of Jerome's three versions of the Psalms in parallel columns, in order that "so signal a work of our ancestors should no longer lie neglected among moths and worms." He printed (although he made no critical use of it) an Old Latin Psalter which he had put together from the *lemmata* of Augustine's *Commentary on the Psalms*. And he disarmed his critics in advance with the example of Origen's *Hexapla*, which, "far from exciting censure, is still praised even in our own time."[33]

French humanists, in short, associated the theological learning of the scholastics with dialectical pride, sophistry, arid intellectualism, and an imperfect knowledge of Scripture. They considered the piety of the Fathers more humbly and accurately dependent on the divine text, more personal, more emotional, directed less toward the presumptuous and inevitably disputatious goal of trying to *know* God in His fullness than toward the more human and possible aim of ardently *loving* Him. This was, in reality, their own ideal, as it had been the ideal of Petrarch and the *Imitatio Christi*; but just as the eloquence of the Fathers justified their own efforts to overcome the barbarous style of the scholastics

[33] *Quincuplex psalterium* (Paris, H. Estienne, 1509), ai^r.

so too the simple biblical piety they attributed to the Fathers justified their aversion to scholastic method, their insistence on a return to the sources in their original languages, the normally exegetical form of their own theological works, and, finally, the end they sought: an eloquent and vibrant personal piety joined to moral probity.

It was natural, in this context, that Lefèvre's circle should have attributed to the Fathers a peculiar authority. Assessing the significance of the *Corpus Dionysiacum* in 1497, Lefèvre laid down the fundamental principle on which he founded their pre-eminence: "The more nearly a light approximates the intensity of the sun, the more brightly it shines . . . and the closer a thing is to its origin, the more purely it retains its own nature. . . . It follows that of all writings the Holy Gospels are recognized as having the greatest dignity, splendor, and authority, as writings which have emanated directly from God and been infused into ready minds." After the gospels in authority, he continues, comes the remainder of the New and Old Testaments. Then the apostolic writers, closer than any others to the source of divine light: Ignatius; Hegesippus, "vir apostolicus et apostolorum temporibus vicinus"; the pseudo-Clementine writings which Lefèvre published in 1504 because he had learned from Pico della Mirandola that they contained apostolic doctrine; and above all, Dionysius the Areopagite. These works, "which have come down to us from apostolic times, seem to differ from others as living things differ from the dead, heavenly from earthly, mortal from immortal; for they are works which preserve in themselves a living force and a marvellous light beyond all others."[34]

---

[34] I, Aiii^r: *Dionysiaca*, pp. cx–cxi. For Hegesippus and the pseudo-Clementine literature see Appendix 1, Nos. ii and vi. Lefèvre's image of Ignatius as an apostolic mystic emerges clearly from the *Argumentum* with which he prefaced the epistles (1, 102^v): "Ignatius . . . scripsit epistolas undecim, sua vincula pro Christo continentes, plenas sancti spiritus fervore sacrum eius pectus suaviter agitantis. Quapropter pie legendae et pronuntiandae sunt, non laxe, non remisse, enervo emollitoque animo, sed cum fervore; sic enim et eas scripsit totus ardens, totus gestiens, totus flammatus, cupiens dissolvi et esse cum Christo sacratissimus martyr, divino iam amore inebriatus. Delicias etenim paradisi in extasi et amatoriae mentis excessu aliquando ipsum expertum posteris reliquit antiquitas."

Neither Lefèvre nor his followers, however, went on to picture the entire subsequent history of ecclesiastical literature as one of continuous decline from apostolic times. They rather grouped all the Fathers after Ignatius and Clement in a third category and assigned them a substantially equal authority and function. Their function was to mediate the light of Scripture and guide future generations in grasping its spiritual and unifying intelligence. Their authority, derived from their proximity to the source of light, was as unquestionable as that formerly assigned to Pythagoras by his disciples.[35] It followed that because their doctrine was a *vetus doctrina*, it was solid and pure and better than the moderns'; and because their ethical teaching reflected *mores antiqui*, it was chaste and holy and also better than the moderns'.[36]

It was left to Lefèvre's enemies to draw the full consequences of this statement of the relative merits of the ancients and moderns. In his *Annotationes* of 1526, Noël Béda, syndic of the Sorbonne, called Erasmus and Lefèvre *humanistae theologizantes*; and he tells us how they arrogantly pretended "to drink from rivers which flow close to the very source of divine wisdom and not from those rivulets which have degenerated because of their great distance from that source; that is to say, they always have in their hands Origen, Tertullian, Cyprian, Basil, Hilary, Chrysostom, Ambrose, Jerome, and others like them; but never scholastics like Peter Lombard, Alexander Hales, Albertus, Thomas, Bonaventura, Ockam, and so on. Thus do the humanists boast in their own words."[37] Lefèvre himself was never so explicit; but Béda, at least in this instance, has not distorted his real meaning and his real belief.

[35] xv, ai^v: Renouard, *Badius Ascensius*, II, 146.

[36] vII, ai^v: Appendix II (1), ll. 4–6. Not all the moderns, however; only the scholastics. Lefèvre prized Cusanus and several medieval mystics so highly that he sometimes ranked them even above the Fathers.

[37] *Annotationes Natalis Bedae Doctoris Theologii Parisiensis in Jacobum Fabrum Stapulensem libri duo: et in Desiderium Erasmum Roterodamum liber unus* (Paris, Badius Ascensius, 1526), preface. My attention was called to this passage by D. P. Walker, "Origène en France," pp. 110–11.

Lefèvre d'Étaples and his circle thus saw the Fathers primarily as the intellectual leaders of the primitive church, at once the heirs of the classical literary tradition and the oldest and most authoritative teachers of the meaning of Scripture. On the other hand, several younger members of Lefèvre's circle (I am thinking of Bovillus, Beatus Rhenanus, and the still very little known Alanus Varenius[38]) found in them a further attractive satisfaction: philosophical doctrines which seemed to them to support their own humanist conception of man. All three had been trained in the humanist Aristotelianism Lefèvre had imported from Italy; and all were profoundly marked too by the influence of Nicholas of Cusa and the Florentine Neoplatonists. These tastes, and a rather more secular point of view, opened their eyes to aspects of patristic thought, especially Greek patristic thought, infrequently dwelt on by their elders.

The long letter to Lefèvre with which Beatus Rhenanus prefaced his 1512 edition of Nemesius of Emesa's *De natura hominis*[39] suggests the kind of philosophical material in the Fathers which impressed the younger generation. It illustrates too, since the *De natura hominis* was well-known to the high scholastics, the different ways in which a Greek patristic work of the late fourth

[38] Alanus Varenius was a pupil of Lefèvre and Clichtove and a friend and correspondent of Bovillus. He is a minor figure of some interest. I have seen the following works: (1) *Alani Varenii Montalbani Tholosatis De Luce Intelligibili Dialogus Vnus* (Bologna, Giovanni Benedetti called Platonides, Feb. 8, 1503). [B.M.] Dedicated to Jean de Pins. The interlocutors are Iacobus [Stapulensis] and Carolus [Bovillus]. (2) *Alani Varenii Montalbani Tholosatis De Amore dialogus vnus* (Bologna, Giovanni Benedetti called Platonides, April 13, 1503). [B.N.] (3) *In hoc opere contenta. De amore dialogus I. De luce dialogi II. De harmonia dialogus I. De harmonie elementis liber I. De rerum precipue diuinarum vnitate dialogus I. De diuina magnitudine dialogus I. De pulchritudine dialogus I. De septem virtutibus liber I. De oppositis monstris liber I. De amicitia precipue diuina liber I. De rerum trinitate liber I. Oratio habita in frequenti ecclesiasticorum virorum consessu. Epistolae complures* (Paris, Henri Estienne, [1512]). [B.N.] (4) *In hoc opere contenta. In Canticum canticorum Homiliae quindecim. In aliquot Psalmos Dauidicos oratiunculae siue breues Homiliae octo et quadraginta. In supersanctam dei genitricem Mariam panegyrici siue laudatiui sermones quinque* (Paris, Henri Estienne, May 21, 1515). [B.M.; Seville, Colombina.]

[39] Text in *Briefwechsel des B. R.*, pp. 41–5.

century could be read in the high Middle Ages and in the Renaissance.

In his preface Beatus Rhenanus listed the philosophical doctrines in Nemesius' book he considered most important. If we compare this summary with the text itself of the *De natura hominis*, it becomes clear that he was most attracted by the first chapter, in which Nemesius had developed at length the themes of the dignity of man, of man as the link between the physical and intellectual worlds, of macrocosm and microcosm; by Nemesius' polemic in Chapters 2 and 3 against the Aristotelian doctrine of the soul as the entelechy of the body and his arguments in favor of the Platonic conception of the soul as a separate spiritual substance ruling the body; and by his emphasis on the freedom of the will, an argument almost as strong as Origen's and developed in directions that could hardly help appealing to someone who knew and admired Bovillus' *De sapiente*: man is a largely autonomous moral agent, containing in his own nature the possibility of the most varied development, who can, by free choice, become akin to any being, become like a rock or plant or beast if he turn toward evil, like the angels if he turn toward good. "We may conclude from reading this book," Beatus ends, "that the man who recognizes his own dignity learns from this to live well. For if he considers seriously his own dignity, he will be easily induced to flee all vices like the worst pest. Indeed, men sin so much precisely because they forget their own dignity. . . . Therefore, who will not greatly praise philosophy, since it leads man to self-knowledge? Even more praiseworthy is that philosophy, flowing forth from Christian thinkers, which also reminds us of those things which pertain to man's salvation."[40]

---

[40] *Briefwechsel des B. R.*, pp. 43-4: "Is itaque divinissimus pater omnium primum de homine philosophatur deque creationis tum ordine tum ratione. Ubi ostendit, quanto ingenio supramundanus opifex hominem praesertim et reliqua produxerit, quae legentem eo perfectionis ducunt, ut miram illam decentissimamque sensilium conditionem suspiciens in conditoris admirationem subvehatur. Nam quemadmodum in excellenti opere industriam suam exprimit artifex, ita et deus sapientiam suam maxime in hominis effictione non obscure declaravit, ut Nicolaus Cusanus, omnium pie philosophantium princeps, multis

Beatus Rhenanus obviously read his text as a philosophy of the dignity of man; and if we look in Nemesius for the passage which most nearly suggests itself as the inspiration of his reading, then it is the remarkable encomium of man which closes the first chapter, a passage whose direct source, significantly, is Origen's *Commentary on Genesis* (of which only fragments survive), where he mingled Christian themes with themes from Posidonius' *Hymn to Man* (partially preserved in Cicero's *De natura deorum*) to forge an important link in that tradition which extends from the celebrated chorus in Sophocles' *Antigone* to Pico's *Oration*:

> Who can fittingly admire the dignity of man, who joins in himself the mortal and immortal, the rational and irrational; who bears in his own nature the image of the whole creation (and for this reason is called a microcosm or little world); who is God's special care and for whose sake God made all things and Himself became man? . . . Who can enumerate the excellence and ornaments of the nature of man? He crosses the seas, he penetrates the heavens with the eye of the mind, he understands

in lucis commonstrat. Hunc etenim utriusque mundi copulam constituens praeclarissimis dotibus insignivit, intellectum enim ei tribuit et liberum arbitrium, excellentissimum munus et summae libertatis, qua deus cuncta creavit, nobile vestigium. Deinde de anima contra Aristotelem et aliʊ̣ ⁿhilosophos acriter disputat, ut pulchriora hiis nusquam me legisse crediderim. Postquam elementorum naturam ac animae vires virtutesque sensuum et organa recenset, subiungens mox de electione voluntarioque et involuntario dissertationem, quam liber de fato excipit, dignissimo sermone de providentia finem operi imponente. Quae omnia mihi ad hoc conferre videntur, ut homo dignitatem suam agnoscens bene vivere discat. Quam si diligenter consideraret, facile induceretur, ut cuncta vitia veluti teterrimam pestem defugeret. Et certe cur homines plerumque peccent, in causa est propriae dignitatis oblivio. Solus enim homo inter res creatas saepiuscule a suo fine aberrat, reliquis omnibus in suis officiis continenter perstantibus, ad quae natura producta sunt. Idcirco quis non philosophiam vel maxime laudarit, cum haec hominem in sui ipsius cognitionem adducat. Laudabiliorem tamen censeo, quae a christianis profluens eorum, quae ad hominis salutem attinent, simul admonet, velut haec subtilissima divini Gregorii Nysseni doctrina, quae cum multorum errores coarguat, solidae veritati innititur." For further details on Nemesius in the Renaissance see E. Garin, "La 'dignitas hominis' e la letteratura patristica," *La Rinascita*, I (1938), 102–46, esp. pp. 112 ff.

the course of the stars and their intervals and sizes . . . no science, art, or doctrine escapes his penetration . . . he foresees the future; he rules over all, he dominates all, enjoys all; speaks with angels and with God; commands at his pleasure all other creatures; subjugates the demons; learnedly investigates the natural world and the essence of God, becomes a house and temple of God and achieves all this by piety and virtue.[41]

Now, Beatus Rhenanus knew that the *De natura hominis* had been often cited by Aquinas: thirty-nine times in the *Summa Theologiae*, to be precise.[42] It is interesting to compare the passages which interested *him* with those singled out for emphasis by Beatus. One is immediately struck by the fact that Aquinas made no use of Chapter 1 and did not quote Nemesius on the dignity of man or on man's place in the *kosmos*. Nor did he mention, even in the objections, the extended Platonic analysis of the soul and its relation to the body. Aquinas' exclusive interest was focused on a very narrow section of the book, that part of the discussion of the freedom of the will which concerns voluntary and involuntary actions and which is, in fact, a reworking of Book III, Chapters 1–8 of Aristotle's *Ethics*. Even Nemesius' discussion of free will, in other words, attracted Aquinas only in

---

[41] Migne, *P.G.*, XL, 532C–533B. Text and German translation in Gilson-Böhner, *Christliche Philosophie* (2nd ed., Paderborn, 1954), pp. 129–30. See also Werner Jaeger, *Nemesios von Emesa* (Berlin, 1914), pp. 133–6; E. Skard, *Nemesiosstudien* (1936, *Symbolae Osloenses* 15–16), pp. 35–40; and David Amand, *Fatalisme et liberté dans l'antiquité grecque* (Louvain, 1945), pp. 549–69.

[42] Cono of Nürnberg to Beatus Rhenanus, *Briefwechsel des B. R.*, pp. 49–50: "Veniam deinde ad nostros Latinos, sanctum illum doctorem inprimis Thomam Aquinatem, clarum ecclesiae catholicae lumen . . . cui tanta Nysseni Gregorii [i.e., Nemesii] visa est authoritas, ut in multis etiam difficillimis hunc in robur suarum probationum adducat. . . . Albertus quoque Magnus tum libro secundo de mirabili scientia dei tum in libro de homine, huius venerandi patris ex hoc opere plurima loca in probationis testimonium allegat." See also Emil Dobler, *Nemesius von Emesa und die Psychologie des menschlichen Aktes bei Thomas von Aquin* (Werthenstein, Luz., 1950). This valuable study lists in detail the passages from Nemesius referred to by Aquinas (pp. 15–17). Further evidence of probable knowledge of the *De natura hominis* in the twelfth and thirteenth centuries has been collected by Father Ignatius Brady, "Remigius-Nemesius," *Franciscan Studies*, N.S. VIII (1948), 275–84.

its Aristotelian source, not for what he had taken from Origen or Gregory of Nyssa.

Why these particular passages (and only these) attracted Aquinas is clear enough: they justified a Christian philosopher's use of Aristotle.[43] Humanists quoted the Fathers to justify an identical preoccupation with pagan philosophy. Indeed, Beatus Rhenanus dedicated two letters of Gregory Nazianzen to Clichtove for the single reason that they were addressed to the peripatetic philosopher Themistius and spoke of him with praise and friendship.[44] But if in these cases Aquinas and Beatus Rhenanus pillaged the past for similar reasons, they pillaged different texts and put them to different uses. For St. Thomas used Nemesius to help him construct a theological *scientia* based on Aristotelian principles; Beatus Rhenanus quoted him to defend, and sharpen, a Renaissance conception of the dignity of man.

In France, in Lefèvre's circle, the rich variety of patristic literature had been only tentatively mined by the end of the second decade of the sixteenth century. Lefèvre's collaborators knew little Greek.[45] Their critical and historical sense was weak. Enthusiastic dating assigned fifth- and sixth-century works to the apostolic period. They attributed Origen's *Commentary on*

[43] Dobler, *op. cit.*, pp. 135–7. [44] *Briefwechsel des B. R.*, pp. 52–3.

[45] No work by a Greek Father was published in France in this period in the original Greek. Direct translations from the Greek were limited to Lefèvre's of the *De fide orthodoxa* of John of Damascus (Paris, 1507) and Budé's of a letter of Basil the Great. The Greek Fathers were normally published sometimes in ancient Latin translations, sometimes in medieval translations, and sometimes in the recent translations of *Quattrocento* Italian scholars. Thus Clichtove published Origen's *Commentary on Leviticus* in the translation of Rufinus; Lefèvre published Ignatius in a translation which dates from the sixth century, Hegesippus in a translation he attributed to St. Ambrose, and the *Historia Lausiaca* of Palladius in the revised text of the Roman deacon Paschasius. The text of Nemesius' *De natura hominis* was a humanist recension of the most common medieval translation, that of Burgundio of Pisa. More important were the patristic translations of the Italian Renaissance. Lefèvre used the translation of Ambrogio Traversari for his edition of the Dionysian writings and Clichtove published Cyril of Alexandria in the translations of George of Trebizond. Badius' large edition of the works of Basil the Great is typical: the *Regula* translated by Rufinus, the *Hexameron* by Argyropulos, the sermons and letters by R. Volaterranus, and the *Adversus Eunomium* by George of Trebizond.

Leviticus to Cyril of Alexandria and followed a medieval tradition
in confusing Nemesius of Emesa with Gregory of Nyssa. Lefèvre,
unlike Valla, accepted the Dionysian myth in the final, extravagant form given it by Hilduin of St. Denis; defended the *comma
Johanneum* against Erasmus from a text of Jerome which was itself
a forgery;[46] and in order to correct the Vulgate of the Pauline
epistles piquantly felt compelled to prove that it was not by
Jerome at all.[47] Finally, they were intimately dependent on
Quattrocento Italian patristic scholarship: for texts, for translations,
for their knowledge of new works. Without exception the real
novelties of Christian antiquity became known in France through
Italian intermediaries; and it is no doubt the most important
single contribution of Lefèvre's circle to have made these novelties
—the *Thesaurus* and *Commentary on John* of Cyril of Alexandria,
Basil's *Contra Eunomium*, the *De curatione Graecarum affectionum*
of Theodoret of Cyrus, Olympiodorus' *Commentary on Ecclesiastes*
—more widely available.

Yet even in this early stage, the significance French humanists
gave to the reappropriation of Christian antiquity was becoming
increasingly apparent. The Fathers offered Lefèvre and his friends
a Christian vision of antiquity, a Christian eloquence, a Christian
philosophy, and an "ancient and true theology," that "union of
piety and wisdom with eloquence" which they sought, a vision
which seemed necessarily to reconcile the tensions between
Christianity and the ideals of classical culture and to prove that
such a reconciliation continued to be possible; which seemed
consequently to solve the central problem of early French humanism (the problem of Gaguin and Budé, as it was of Lefèvre
d'Étaples): the proper relation between an enthusiasm for the
antique and a firm commitment to Christian values.

[46] *Commentarii in epistolas Catholicas* (Basil, 1527), fol. *3r.
[47] *Apologia quod vetus interpretatio epistolarum beatissimi Pauli quae passim legitur
non sit tralatio Hieronymi*, in *Epistole divi Pauli apostoli* (Paris, 1512), aiiv–aiiiv.

10 A Re-Evaluation of Hellenism in the French Renaissance [1]

LINTON C. STEVENS

SINCE the pioneer work of Émile Egger, *L'Hellénisme en France* of 1869, a large number of monographs and books dealing with particular aspects of Greek influence have enriched our understanding of the significant contributions which the students of the Greek language, literature, and philosophy have made to French culture.[2] Two major problems have yet to be clarified. The first problem is the separation of three related influences, which, in spite of their apparent similarities, present significant differences: the Byzantine, the classical, and the hellenistic traditions. It cannot be claimed that these influences can be completely separated in any one period, but certain dominant tendencies may at least be pointed out. The second question involves the comprehension of classical concepts, the shift in emphasis and attitude which marks each generation of Greek students, and the gradual diffusion of hellenism. What had once been the esoteric learning of a few became the necessary appanage of every educated man. Even some women had acquired this "manne céleste de bonne doctrine."

[1] The preparation of this article was made possible by a grant-in-aid of the Research Committee of the University of Alabama.

[2] The best general surveys of this field are those of Gilbert Highet, *The Classical Tradition* (New York: Oxford University Press, 1949) and R. R. Bolgar, *The Classical Heritage and its Beneficiaries* (Cambridge, England: Cambridge University Press, 1954). See also "The Classics in Sixteenth Century France," by James Hutton, in *The Classical Weekly*, XLIII, No. 9 (Jan. 30, 1950), 131–9; Linton C. Stevens, "How the French Humanists of the Renaissance learned Greek," *PMLA*, LXV, No. 2 (1950); "The Motivation for Hellenic Studies in the French Renaissance," *Studies in Philology*, XLVII, 2 (1950); "The Critical Appreciation of Greek Literature in the French Renaissance," *South Atlantic Studies for Sturgis E. Leavitt* (Washington, D.C.: Scarecrow Press, 1953); and Börje Knös, *Un Ambassadeur de l'hellénisme, Janus Lascaris* (Paris, 1945).

Denys Lambin wrote to his feminine friends in Latin and Greek; Jeanne de Lestonac, the sister of Montaigne, spoke and understood Greek better than did many contemporary hellenists.[3] It is evident that the whole field of hellenism in the Renaissance cannot be adequately treated in one article. Hence it is necessary to exclude from the outset certain large areas. No attempt will be made to review the study of the Greek language, the activity of the translators, or the history of Aristotelianism and Platonism.[4] Nevertheless, a few translators whose interpretations have some special significance will be mentioned. Our principal aim is to survey the present state of knowledge on the subjects indicated above and to suggest some of the lacunae.

We may note that the evolution of hellenism in the Renaissance presents certain characteristics which do not permit any rigid chronological categories to be established, yet perhaps four generations of hellenists may be discerned. In the first generation, from 1485 to 1515, which includes Lascaris, Tissard, Aléandre, and Jacques Lefèvre d'Étaples, the Byzantine tradition predominates. Interest is concentrated upon grammar, philology, and the publication of Greek texts. Judgments based upon stylistic, literary, and philosophical values could hardly be expected from those who were suddenly confronted with a bewildering variety of authors whose range of interests greatly surpassed the more limited scope of derivative Latin literature. The only exception is Lefèvre, whose interest in philosophy, almost unique in his generation, leads him to seek a new interpretation of Aristotle and Plato. The second generation, from 1515 to 1545, includes Budé, Rabelais, Lazare de Baïf, Robert Estienne, Étienne Dolet, Pierre Danès, Clenardus, Melchoir Volmar, and Alciati. These men were

[3] See Henri Potez et Francois Préchac, *Lettres Galantes de Denys Lambin* (Paris, 1941), p. xiii; Fortunat Strowski, *Montaigne* (Paris, 1938), p. 20.

[4] See Walter Mönch, *Die italienische Platonrenaissance und ihre Bedeutung für Frankreichs Literatur- und Geistesgeschichte* (Berlin, 1936); R. V. Merrill and R. J. Clements, *Platonism in French Renaissance Poetry* (New York, 1957). The most informative, succinct account of Aristotelian and Platonic influence is to be found in Paul Oskar Kristeller's *The Classics and Renaissance Thought* (Cambridge: Harvard University Press, 1955).

chiefly concerned with classical literature. They read Aeschylus, Sophocles, Euripides, and Aristophanes; among the orators they preferred Isocrates, and among the historians, Herodotus. The third generation, from 1545 to 1575, was probably the most brilliant, since Greek studies had acquired a prestige which attracted men of all professions. Among the most famous were Pierre Ramus, Vicomercato, Jean Dorat, Denys Lambin, Amyot, Muretus, Adrien Turnèbe, and Loys Le Roy. It embraces the men of the *Pléiade*, the professors of the Collège Royal, printers, the humanist jurists, and even a secretary of Marguerite of Navarre, Bonaventure des Péviers. While they read the popular hellenistic writers such as Lucian, Plutarch, and Lycophron, they also read Aristophanes, whose political satire made him a dangerous author. The sons of Jean Wier heard Turnèbe lecture on Aristophanes, and Rabelais did not hesitate to borrow ideas and themes from him. Dorat explained Aristophanes to his students and Alciati referred to him in his letters.[5] The fourth (and last) generation of hellenists, at the end of the century, includes Montaigne, Florent Chrestien, Joseph Scaliger, Henri Estienne, and Casaubon. Montaigne drew most of his Greek illustrations from hellenistic writers, although in his later essays he began to appreciate Plato.[6]

Any discussion of French humanists who devoted themselves to the study and spread of Greek culture in the first quarter of the sixteenth century would be incomplete without mention of the influence of Erasmus. In spite of his prodigious learning, his mastery of Greek and Latin, and his dazzling versatility, Erasmus was more of a philologist and a rhetorician than a thinker. His contributions to humanistic education, to textual criticism, and his interpretation of Greek culture must be treated with some reserve. Menéndez Pelayo compared him to Voltaire in respect

---

[5] See L. Delaruelle, "L'étude du grec à Paris," *RSS*, IX (1922), 51–62 and 132–49. See also Humphredus Hodius, *De Graecis illustribus linguae graecae literarumque humaniorum instauratoribus* (London, 1742); Walter J. Ong, *Ramus, Method and Decay of Dialogue* (Cambridge, 1958).

[6] See Hugo Friedrich, *Montaigne* (Berne, 1949), pp. 417 ff.

to the verve of his satiric style and his skill in polemical argument.[7] Gonzague de Reynold goes even further in his criticism of Erasmus. He asserts that Erasmus was primarily interested in ancient wisdom as a guide to social life, but knew nothing of Greek religion, its mystery, its profundity, and its philosophical import.[8] Since Erasmus translated the *Hecuba* and the *Iphigenia* of Euripides in 1506, it is to be presumed that he was familiar with the other plays of this dramatist. We may wonder, therefore, how he could have failed to appreciate the sincere piety of the *Hippolytus*, which so closely resembles Christian ideas. Erasmus, like the Greeks, loved society, as we can see from his correspondence and his continual peregrinations.[9] The isolation and the contemplative life of the monastery held no charm for him. He preferred the amenities of Oxford and the society of More and Colet.

Guillaume Budé, who was a close friend of Erasmus, had a similar view of Greek literature, but since his Catholic beliefs were much more orthodox than those of Erasmus, he found greater

[7] See *Historia de los Heterodoxos españoles*, III (Santander, 1947), 43–59. Menéndez Pelayo states (p. 43): "En lo poco que trató de filosofía es un escritor insignificante, sobre todo al lado de Luis Vives." See also A. Renaudet, *Préréforme et humanisme à Paris* (Paris, 1953), p. 380: ". . . moins attiré par les doctrines des anciens que par leurs mœurs et leurs usages, il préfère à l'étude de la science et de la métaphysique renaissantes d'Athènes et d'Alexandrie, la lecture des orateurs et des poètes, qui ont fixé en traits éternels quelques-uns des caractéres permanents de l'humanité." Renaudet indicates the limitations of Erasmus in his last book, *Humanisme et Renaissance* (Genève: Droz, 1958), p. 166: "Helléniste, Erasme ne semble lire assidûment ni Homère ni Sophocle, auquel il préfère Euripide; ni Aristote, trop difficilement conciliable, malgré Saint Thomas, avec les dogmes chrétiens de la création et de l'âme immortelle; ni Platon, auquel il ne veut emprunter que des mythes et des symboles."

[8] See *L'Hellénisme et le génie européen* (Fribourg, 1944), p. 239. The author is perhaps too severe when he says (p. 243): "Le cosmopolitisme est un trait grec, nous le savons, mais l'européanisme itinérant est une habitude médiévale. Erasme est un *clericus vagus*."

[9] See André-Jean Festugière, *Personal Religion among the Greeks* (Los Angeles: University of California Press, 1954). Festugière, in concluding his remarks on the *Hippolytus*, adds (p. 17): "Personal piety, when it is fervent and deep, is a peculiarity; it sets a man apart. The intensely religious man is wont to withdraw from the world in order to contemplate at leisure. He appears therefore to be solitary, odd, unsociable. And nothing was more odious in classical Athens than unsociability."

difficulty in reconciling his love of the ancients with Christian doctrine. His ambivalent attitude is shown most clearly in his *De transitu Hellenismi ad christianismum* (Paris, 1535). His narrow conception of Greek philosophy is not much more enlightened than that of Noël Béda. Theology and philosophy go hand in hand.

> Quapropter ab Hellenismo errorum praeceptore, simulachorum cultore, nugarum opifice, ad veritatis cultum atque simplicitatis, philosophia nos revocare clara voce videtur, utpote quae theosophiae, germana sit et socia.[10]

Budé fails to understand what the Greeks meant by *paideia* and would limit it to rhetoric.

> Caeterum paediam, nos literarum peritiam iustam dicimus: quae choro disciplinarum liberalium constat, quam tamen et ipsam tyrocinium aliquandiu facere oportet in limine sapientiae, sermonisque symbolico aureis initiare.[11]

In answer to the question whether the truth of Christianity is comparable to the truth of ancient philosophy, Budé gives an equivocal opinion. He condemns on the one hand the polytheism of the ancients, while on the other hand he asserts that the roots of a purer philosophy are also to be found in pagan culture.[12]

The Byzantine scholars who introduced French humanists to Greek culture at the beginning of the French Renaissance have been rather severely and perhaps unjustly criticized. Renan said that the majority were very mediocre men like Philelphus whose

---

[10] *De transitu*, p. 76.

[11] *De studio literarum recte et commode instituendo,ad invictissimum et potentissimum Principem Franciscum, Regem Franciae. Excudebat Iodocus Badius Ascensius* (Paris, 1533). p. xxvii. Cf. the definitions of *paideia* given by Werner Jaeger, *Paideia* (New York: Oxford University Press, 1939), i, iii and 283.

[12] Josef Bohatec, *Budé und Calvin* (Graz, 1950), p. 29. See also Ernst Walser, *Gesammelte Studien zur Geistesgeschichte der Renaissance* (Basle, 1932), who criticizes Budé as follows (p. 87): "Ein ästhetisches Erfassen der Antike ist bei ihm kaum bemerkbar: politischer Kosmopolitismus, hochmütige Studien-aristokratie gegenüber dem grossen Haufen, republikanische oder gar religiös indifferente Gefühle, die man so gemeinhin als die 'charakterischen Merkmale' der Renaissance haben möchte, sind ihm alle gleich fremd."

only interest was the money they could receive from their lessons.[13] The Byzantine culture was said to be sterile and uninspired. The professors who came from Italy were, for the most part (with the exception of George Hermonymus), competent in the Greek language, but they devoted all their efforts to philology, rhetoric, and poetics. They neither understood nor appreciated philosophy, in spite of their disputations concerning the merits of Aristotle and Plato.[14] On the positive side, one must give credit to those pioneers who provided their disciples with texts, grammars, and dictionaries. The students of Greek welcomed with equal enthusiasm authors of all periods. Hence it is difficult to distinguish Byzantine from hellenistic influences, but it is possible to make a few generalizations. Christian apologetics and Neoplatonism were stimulated and encouraged by the lectures and books of the Byzantine Greeks.[15] A hellenistic author such as Plutarch, who has been called "the tutor of the Renaissance" and who exercised such a decisive influence upon Montaigne, was studied and read in the Byzantine schools. Unknown in the Middle Ages, he was only revealed to the West in the fifteenth century by the exiled Greeks. Thus it was the Byzantine scholars who introduced him to France.[16] The Byzantine author Psellus enjoyed a certain popularity throughout the century since there was much interest in magic and demons. His *de operatione daemonum dialogus* was Ronsard's source for the

[13] E. Renan, *Œuvres complètes* (ed. H. Psichari, Paris, 1949), III, 824.

[14] See Carl Neumann, "Byzantinische Kultur und Renaissancekultur," *Historische Zeitschrift* (Munich, 1903), p. 218; Börje Knös, *op. cit.*, pp. 10–11; Bolgar, *op. cit.*, p. 284; see also August Heisenberg, "Das Problem der Renaissance in Byzanz," *Historische Zeitschrift* (Munich, 1926), p. 399.

[15] For the theological interrelationships between Hellenism and Byzantine tradition, see Dr. Endre Ivánka, *Hellenisches und christliches im frühbyzantinischen Geistesleben* (Vienna, 1948). See also C. Huit, "Note sur l'état des études grecques en Italie et en France du XIVe au XVIe siècle," *Revue des études grecques*, XIV (Paris, 1901), 143: "Mais la remarque en a été faite maintes fois, si le byzantinisme était l'héritier naturel de l'hellénisme, c'était d'un hellénisme hellénistique et non purement grec, héritier d'ailleurs insouciant et incapable, tout particulièrement en ce qui avait porté si haut le nom de l'ancienne Grèce, à savoir la poésie, la science et les arts."

[16] See Börje Knös, *op. cit.*, p. 94.

Hymne des daimons. Ronsard accepted the existence of demons as a scientific fact and he attempted to define their nature.[17] Jean Wier mentions Psellus in his *Histoires, disputes et discours des illusions et impostures des diables* (1579).

Although among the first generation of humanists, Jacques Lefèvre d'Étaples is an illustrious example of an early interpreter of the Greek tradition, despite the fact that he possessed little Greek and was far inferior to other Greek scholars of his time in knowledge of the language. But this enigmatic figure, whose range of interests included classical authors (Aristotle, Plato) as well as the works of the Byzantine Dionysius the Areopagite and a treatise on natural magic, had a better understanding of Greek philosophy than his congeners. Bolgar thinks that he deserves to rank among the forerunners of Bacon and Galileo.[18] Renaudet praises his commentary on the Nicomachean Ethics and his encyclopedic erudition as well as his intelligent interpretation of hellenism.[19] With the exception of Lefèvre, the literary influence of classical authors is scarcely noticeable before the generation of 1515.

The various imitations, motifs, and transmutations of hellenic thought in Ronsard and Du Bellay have been thoroughly explored, but the work of Jean-Antoine de Baïf has not yet received the attention it deserves.[20] Antoine de Baïf was probably the best Greek student of the *Pléiade.* He heard Dorat explain

[17] Pierre de Ronsard, *Hymne des daimons, Edition critique et commentaire* par Albert-Marie Schmidt (Paris, 1938), p. 6.

[18] Bolgar, *op. cit.,* p. 289.

[19] *Préréforme et humanisme à Paris,* p. 282: "Mais, pour illustrer l'Ethique Aristotélicienne, il avait relu les poétes, les orateurs, les historiens de l'antiquité.... Son livre manifestait une connaissance de la pensée, de la civilisation, de la vie grecque et romaine, que nul encore, en France, n'avait atteinte, que seuls dépassèrent, au XVIe siècle, Erasme et Budé." See also Renaudet's "Un problème historique: la pensée religieuse de J. Lefèvre d'Étaples," *Medioevo e rinascimento, studi in onore di Bruno Nardi* (Florence, 1955), II, 628.

[20] See especially Isadore Silver, *The Pindaric Odes of Ronsard* (Paris, 1937); "Du Bellay and Hellenic Poetry," *PMLA,* IX, No. 4 (1945), 949–58; "Ronsard Comparatist Studies, Achievements and Perspectives," *Comparative Literature,* VI (Spring 1954), 2; "A flame among the faggots: Ronsard on his education as a hellenist," *Mélanges Henri Chamard* (Paris, 1951), p. 81. See also James Hutton, *The Greek Anthology in France* (New York, 1946), pp. 350–74.

Sophocles in 1558. He translated the *Women of Trachis* and the *Antigone* of Sophocles, the *Medea* and the *Helena* of Euripides, but published only his *Antigone* and the prologue of the *Helena*.[21] Creizenach gives rather extravagant praise to Baïf's version of *Antigone*. Even though he admits that Baïf has sometimes misinterpreted the original and occasionally left out some essential ideas, he claims that Baïf has surpassed all his predecessors in power of expression, fluency, and metrical skill.[22] Marie Delcourt has a few reservations. She finds that he renders the abstract speeches rather inadequately, but, following the example of his father, Lazare, in translating word for word, is generally faithful to his model. His use of stichomythy is excellent. Occasionally he suppresses historical allusions or weakens an image.[23] The importance of translation as a criterion in estimating the competency of Greek scholars and their intelligent transmission of Greek concepts has not yet been adequately treated. The whole question is intimately related to the interpretation of hellenism.[24] The five requirements that must be fulfilled by the ideal translator as described by Étienne Dolet are just as valid today, but they were not often observed by the humanists of the sixteenth century, who preferred a rather free rendering and frequently indulged in unnecessary amplification by using several synonyms for one word, and who paid little attention to the nuances of the Greek particle.[25]

[21] See Raymond Lebègue, *La Tragédie française de la renaissance* (Brussels, 1944), p. 18.

[22] Wilhelm Creizenach, *Geschichte des neueren Dramas* (Halle, 1919), Bd. II, 424.

[23] See Marie Delcourt, *Étude sur les traductions des tragiques grecs et latins en France depuis la renaissance* (Brussels, 1925), pp. 74–81.

[24] See Frédéric Hennebert, *Histoire des traductions françaises d'auteurs grecs et latins pendant le XVIe et le XVIIe siècles* (Brussels, 1861); Justin Bellanger, *Histoire de la traduction en France (auteurs grecs et latins)* (Paris, 1892); Pierre de Nolhac, "Le premier travail français sur Euripide: la traduction de François Tissard," *Mélanges Henri Weil* (Paris, 1898); Johann Dassenbacher, *Amyot als Übersetzer der Lebensbeschreibung des Pericles von Plutarch* (Prague, 1887); René Sturel, *Jacques Amyot, Traducteur des vies parallèles de Plutarque* (Paris, 1909); see also his "Essai sur les traductions du théâtre grec en français avant 1550," *RHL* (1913), pp. 269–96 and 637–66.

[25] See Dolet's *La Manière de bien traduire d'une langue en autre* (Lyon, 1540).

A comparison of Baïf's translation with a few passages from Sophocles' *Antigone* will show that Baïf has failed to grasp the vigor of the original and has so weakened the force of certain key words that the poetic and dramatic effects of Sophocles' diction completely disappear.[26] For verses 37–8, Jebb translates:

> and thou wilt soon show whether thou art nobly bred,
> or the base daughter of a noble line.

Baïf renders this:

> Et tu pourras bien tost nous montrer s'il te plaist,
> Que des tiens à bon droit la fille lon te die
> ou n'avoir rien de ceux dont tu te dis sortie.

The two strong words εὐγενής (of noble birth) and ἐσθλός (honest, virtuous, courageous) are replaced by a vague circumlocution. For line 4 in Jebb's version:

> Nothing painful is there, nothing fraught with
> ruin, no shame, no dishonor, that I have not seen
> in thy woes and mine,

Baïf translated:

> car nous n'avons rien vu, qui nous soit arrivé
> ou à toy ou à moy, que nous n'ayons trouvé
> Plein de grieve douleur, plein d'ennuy, plein de peine,
> Plein de deshonneur, plein de honte vilaine.

Four words of the Greek, ἀλγεινὸν ἄτης αἰσχρον ἄτιμόν, are represented by five words in French. But the word *ennui*, although a strong word in the sixteenth century (sorrow, grief, anguish), does not adequately convey the meaning of ἄτης. William Chase Greene in *Moira: Fate, Good and Evil in Greek Thought* (Cambridge, Mass., 1944) cites Euripides, *Medea*, 279, 979, 987 for the use of *Até* as ruin. In 530 of the *Troiades*, δόλιον ἔσχον ἄταν represents the trick of the Trojan horse and is translated by Parmentier and

---

[26] The editions used are *Sophoclis fabulae*, ed. by A. C. Pearson (Oxford, 1950); Ian Antoine de Baïf, *Œuvres en rime*, ed. Marty-Laveaux (Paris, 1886); R. C. Jebb, *Sophocles: The Plays and Fragments* (Cambridge, 1885–1902).

Grégoire in the Budé edition as "l'embouche fatale." Werner
Jaeger states that *Até* in the *Iliad* evokes a mighty religious
conception, the madness of doom.[27] In line 20 of Sophocles we
find: "δηλοῖς γάρ τι καλχαίνουϲ' ἔπος." Jebb translates this: " 'Tis
plain that thou art brooding on some dark tidings." Baïf gives us a
banal version: "me voudrois-tu grande chose conter?" The word
καλχαίνω with its double meaning (to be purple, to be in doubt, in
trouble, to meditate deeply) is well expressed by Jebb, but Baïf's
insipid and trivial *grande chose* edulcorates a word that suggests
dark forebodings and tragedy.

The influence of Greek drama upon French tragedy has been
small. Raymond Lebègue claims that only Buchanan and Théo-
dore de Bèze reflect the Greek tradition. Jodelle borrowed from
Greek tragedies the form of the choruses in *Cléopâtre*; Peletier
suggests that Sophocles and Euripides should be taken as models
rather than Seneca, but most of the dramatists appear to be satisfied with the latter. George Buchanan, the Scottish humanist
and poet, was an important figure in sixteenth-century France.
Henri Estienne honored him on the title page of one of Bèze's
works with the description "poetarum sui saeculi facile princeps."
He wrote two Latin tragedies modeled on the Greek—*Jephthes*
and *Baptista* (biblical dramas), and two plays translated from
Euripides—*Medea* and *Alcestis*. Of these, the *Jephthes*, modeled on
the *Iphigenia at Aulis* and the *Hecuba*, is the most original as well
as the most Greek in inspiration and treatment. It was so successful
that it was translated into five languages. Although there is no
division into acts, the monologues and speeches are interrupted by
numerous choruses in which Buchanan displays his lyrical gifts.
The main scene, in which Jephthé resists the supplications of his
wife and daugher, owes much to Euripides.[28]

The importance of Greek studies for the jurists can hard y be
overestimated. Budé in his *Annotationes in pandectarum libros*
had revolutionized the science of jurisprudence by applying the

[27] Werner Jaeger, *op. cit.*, I, 25.
[28] See Lebègue, *op. cit.*, p. 18; Bolgar, *op. cit.*, p. 363; Paul van Tieghem,
La Littérature latine de la renaissance (Paris, 1944), p. 181.

historical method to the interpretation of the laws and by using philological criteria to establish the exact meaning of technical terms. His most brilliant disciple in this humanistic revolt against the medieval commentators was Andrea Alciati, who had left Italy in 1518 to teach at Avignon. His learning was encyclopedic. As a scholar, a man of letters, a moralist, and a jurist, he was convinced that Greek was indispensable to any jurist who aimed at distinction. The program of studies which he advocated was not confined to a narrow professional training, but embraced philosophy and literature as well as a mastery of Latin and Greek:

Superest, ut et graecanicae literaturae cognitionem, iuris civilis candidato oppido necessariam iuxta ac utilem esse ostendam. Primo omnium, bonam partem legum civilium, quas in Pandectarum libris consutas habemus, e Graecorum, Platonis, Aristotelis, Demosthenis, Homeri denique libris collectas, tam Manifestam est, quam quod manifestissimum. Iam quanvis πρὸς τὰ ἄλφιτα non conducit, tamen mire leges intelligibiles reddit, e quibus fontibus emanarunt, compertum habere.[29]

Alciati's literary reputation is limited for us to his *Emblemata*, but many of his unpublished poems and dramatic works were known and appreciated by his friends. He wrote some Greek epigrams which were included in an anthology published by Bebel at Basle in 1529. He translated the *Clouds* of Aristophanes into Latin and wrote a comedy entitled *Philargyrus*.

Vides, opinor, me efutire tragica, nam, si nescis, factus sum ὁ μέγιστος κωμικός et nec Aristophani quidem ipsi dignor cedere: perveni fere ad catastrophen fabulae quam Philargyrum inscripsi, superestque una aut altera tantum scenula, ut deinde supremam illi manum imponam.[30]

[29] *Andreae Alciati mediolanensis viri undecunque doctissimi Iudiciarii Processus Compendium, atque adeo iuris utriusque praxis expeditissima* (Parisiis, 1537), p. 268. See also Gian Luigi Barni, *Le Lettere di Andrea Alciato giureconsulto* (Florence, 1953), p. xxxiii; Ernst V. Moeller, *Ein Beitrag zur Entstehungsgeschichte der modernen Jurisprudenz* (Breslau, 1907), p. 96; Slavomir Condanari, "Humanismus und Rechtswissenschaft," *Ewiger Humanismus*, VIII (1947), 11; Paul Émile Viard, *André Alciat* (Paris, 1926), p. 253.

[30] Barni, *op. cit.*, p. 60, lettera 33 (1523).

He claims that the humanistic and literary culture of jurists is in no way inferior to that of theologians and doctors.[31]

Loys Le Roy, far from possessing the erudition of Turnèbe, nevertheless had read all of Plato and Aristotle. He was more interested in ideas than in lexicography. Becker believed that his translation of the *Phaedo* was superior to most of the translations of the century. Le Roy devoted himself to the ideas without neglecting the appropriate graces of expression. The philosophic part of the dialogue particularly aroused his admiration and stimulated him to acquire a new insight into the Greek mind. That he was unable to understand the historical development of ancient thought was no fault of his own. The prevailing climate of opinion was opposed to freedom of thought and unbiased scientific inquiry. The constant struggle to protect oneself against the suspicion of heresy inhibited the free expression of personal opinion and discouraged unorthodoxy. He has been reproached for following too closely Ficino's Latin translation of Plato, but he attempted to render the special style of each dialogue and to convey the flavor of Socrates' familiar irony and the eloquence of Diotima.[32] His errors in translation, like those of Amyot, can be attributed less to his ignorance of Greek than to an excess of zeal. He thought that he might make his versions more palatable to the general reader by gallicizing unfamiliar concepts.

Florent Chrestian (1541–96) was one of the most distinguished hellenists of his generation. A disciple of Henri Estienne, he

[31] *Ibid.*, p. 254, lettera 168: "Quod si videmus aetate nostra coeteras artes iam non paulo politiores esse, graece latineque disputare praestantes theologos, Aristotelem, Platonem, Aphrodisieum, Plotinum, Porphirium, Hammonium eleganter loqui, medicos, et in primis Dioscoridem, Galenum et Aeginae tam magna cura puriori sermone redditos, quae tandem invidia est, ut non et nobis iurisconsultis id concedatur? qui aliorum duces, si autores nostros imitaremur, esse debueramus."

[32] See A. Henri Becker, *Un humaniste au XVIe siècle. Loys Le Roy* (Paris, 1896), pp. 107, 120. See also Franco Simone, *Guillaume Fichet retore ed umanista* (Turin, 1938), p. 37: "Platone era seguito non tanto per il suo pensiero quanto per la sua arte di esporre codesto pensiero: insomma esso diventava come Cicerone un maestro dell'arte di unire l'eloquenza e la filosofia."

became the tutor of the young prince of Béarn who was later to come to the French throne as Henri IV. His activities as a translator aroused the admiration of his contemporaries, who compared him to Budé, Turnèbe, and Casaubon. He translated selected epigrams from the Greek anthology into Latin verse, three plays of Aristophanes—the *Wasps*, *Peace*, and *Lysistrata*; the *Andromache* and *Cyclops* of Euripides; the *Seven against Thebes* of Aeschylus; and the *Philoctetes* of Sophocles. Scaliger, De Thou, and Sainte-Marthe thought that his Greek and Latin verses were superior to those of the moderns and equal to those of the ancients.[33]

The fact that hellenistic authors were more popular than any others during the sixteenth century can be explained by the *zeitgeist*. Since all the Greek students had received a thorough training in Latin and since the medieval interest in oratory was still sustained by its practical utility in diplomatic affairs, the rhetoric of declamation so highly cultivated in Alexandrian schools was particularly attractive to hellenists. Writers on moral philosophy appealed to the students of Cicero and Seneca. Metaphysics, unless it was mingled with the mystic and quasi-religious interpretations of Neoplatonism, found few readers. The French hellenists were particularly fond of Lucian, for his mockery of Greek gods and mythology suited Christian prejudices, and his imitation of Attic Greek was instructive to those who felt ill at ease with the great classic authors. The Alexandrian historians and the scholarly commentators with their conscious archaizing were natural models for those who were trying to familiarize themselves with an alien world.

If we glance at the catalogues of some of the sixteenth-century libraries, such as those of Guillaume Pelicier or Jacques Cujas, we note that hellenistic authors are most numerous. The reading of a theologian who was neither a distinguished hellenist nor a member of any learned *cénacle* may reveal which authors were

[33] See C. Brainne, J. Debarbouiller, Ch. F. Lapierre, *Les Hommes illustres de l'Orléanais*, I (Orléans, 1852), 190–1. See also James Hutton, *The Greek Anthology in France*, pp. 167–71.

most popular. Guillaume de la Mare (1451–1525), rector of the University of Caen, was trained in civil and canon law. His knowledge of Greek was small, but he translated the *Amours de Léandre et de Héro* from Greek into Latin. He quotes Homer, Euripides, Aristotle, Demosthenes, Isocrates, Xenophon, Plutarch, Diogenes Laertius, Epictetus, Hippocrates, Porphyry, Lucian, Josephus, and Dionysius of Halicarnassus.[34] Among the 1,312 books of Cujas's library (of which only 192 were legal works), the classics are represented by Hesiod, Sophocles, Euripides, Plato, Aristotle, and Isocrates; the hellenistic authors by Heliodorus, Epictetus, Apollonias Rhodius, Callimachus, Longinus, Aratus, Dioscorides, and Ptolemy (his *geographia*); among the Byzantine authors were Basil, Chrysostom, and Moschopoulus.[35] Since the list is rather long, the authors mentioned are only a few typical selections. This balance of classic, hellenistic, and Byzantine authors is fairly characteristic for all Renaissance students of Greek, save the major hellenists.

The attitude toward Greek studies was modified by a notable shift of opinion between 1500 and 1550. Whereas in 1523 Greek was under suspicion as heretical, and Rabelais's Greek books were confiscated, the increased interest in the church Fathers, the efforts at conciliating the moral ideas of the Greeks with the Christian religion, and the importance of Greek for theological and for juristic purposes brought about a complete revision of pedagogical practice. The emphasis upon Greek in the Reformed schools caused critics of scholasticism to make some invidious comparisons. This was reflected in the recommendations of the Jesuits, whose schools were soon to become the best in France.[36] Bolgar

[34] See Ch. Fierville, *Étude sur la Vie et les Œuvres de Guillaume de la Mare* (Paris, 1893), p. 55.

[35] See *Greci enumeratio liborum domini Cujacii* (fonds latin MS 4552, B.N.). See also Pierre Mesnard, "La place de Cujas dans la querelle de l'humanisme juridique," *Revue historique de droit français et étranger* (Paris, 1950), pp. 521–37.

[36] See *Ratio Studiorum et institutiones scholasticae Societatis Jesu*, pub. by G. M. Pachtler (Berlin, 1887–94), 4 vols. *Monumenta Germaniae paedagogica*. T. II, p. 161: "Magnas ac multiplices esse Graecae linguae utilitatis ambigit nullus. Nam praeterquam, quod praecipui fere autores omnium disciplinarum Graece scripserunt, ut patet in medicina, in Philosophia, in mathematicis, in Graecis

is perhaps too skeptical of the claims of the Jesuit teachers. Even though the Collège de Guyenne, under the leadership of André de Gouvéa and known to be somewhat favorable to Protestant ideas, may have been rather exceptional, the program of studies pursued there indicates educational trends which were not unique for the time. At this school between 1550 and 1575, Nicolas de Grouchy, followed by Mathieu Béroalde and Salignac, lectured in Greek on Aristotle. This would imply rather more than an elementary knowledge of Greek in his auditors. Paul Porteau pointed out that Latin texts were translated into several dialects of Greek even during the youth of Montaigne.[37]

We may conclude that the influence of hellenism in France during the Renaissance is manifested in three types of "innutrition." The literary influence is most clearly revealed in the members of the *Pléiade* and in the *cénacle* of Lyons under the leadership of Maurice Scève. This consists of borrowing metrical techniques, mythological allusions, images, and words. The second type is constituted by the philosophical and scientific heritage, derived partly from Greek sources and partly from the intermediation of Italian and Byzantine scholars: Neoplatonism, astrology, and medical works.[38] The third type, which only appears toward the close of the century, is the political tradition,

Bibliis, in Conciliis et Patribus, quorum veram ac germanam sententiam vix assequi possumus ipse adhuc sermo Latinus Graecis literis non parum indiget. Non enim possunt peti nisi Graeco fonte multarum rerum nomina et nominum proprietates etymologiae, accentus, quantitas syllabarum. Ipsa etiam Graecorum Poetarum, oratorum, Historicorum lectio atque imitatio uberiorem reddit et locupletiorem Latinam eloquantiam poesim et historiam. Magnae igitur et multae sunt Graecarum litterarum utilitates: at, nisi discuntur a puero et cum primis Grammaticae elementis, apte distributis pro numero classium Graecae Grammaticae partibus, vix unquam discuntur. . . . Quarto turpe est in ea re vinci ab haereticis, qui a teneris annis Graece instituti contemnunt Catholicos Graeci sermonis imperitos, et ad Graecos fontes provocare solent non sine Catholicorum ignominia."

[37] See Ernest Gaullieu, *Histoire du Collège de Guyenne* (Paris, 1874), p. 231; Porteau, *Montaigne et la vie pédagogique de son temps* (Paris, 1935), p. 287.

[38] See especially for the details of scientific influence, George Sarton, *The Appreciation of Ancient and Mediaeval Science During the Renaissance* (Philadelphia, 1955), and *Six Wings: Men of Science in the Renaissance* (London, 1958).

exemplified by La Boétie and Bodin. La Boétie found the inspiration for the title of his *Servitude volontaire* in Plato's ἐθελοδουλεία, which may be defined as a friendship founded on the cult of virtue and the desire to become better.[39] The *Oeconomicus* of Xenophon, which La Boétie had translated in 1563, provided him with some of his arguments against tyrants. In addition to his frequent borrowings from Plutarch, he makes effective use of Pausanias and Dio Chrysostom.[40] His conception of natural law is close to that of the Greeks.

> Premièrement, cela est, comme je crois, hors de doute que, si nous vivions avec les droits que la nature nous a donnés et avec les enseignements qu'elle nous apprend, nous serions naturellement obéissants aux parents, sujets à la raison, et serfs de personne.[41]

This may be compared to the statement of Periphanakis: "Le droit naturel dans la pensée grecque s'identifie presque avec la loi morale universelle (appelée aussi loi divine)."[42] On the first page of his *République*, Bodin says: "République est un droit gouvernement de plusieurs mesnages, et de ce qui leur est commun, avec puissance souveraine." As Mesnard interprets this passage, "droit gouvernement" refers to Bodin's idea of justice, which dominates his conception of government.[43] From Hesiod to Aristotle, the faith in justice was the foundation of political thought. The frequent occurrence of δίκη and δικαιοσύνη in the works of the Greek dramatists bears witness to the importance of this idea[1] in Greek culture.

---

[39] See Joseph Barrière, *L'Humanisme et la Politique dans le Discours de la Servitude volontaire* (Paris, 1923), p. 16.

[40] *Ibid.*, pp. 34, 40.

[41] *La Servitude volontaire* (ed. Paul Bonnefon, Paris, 1922), p. 60.

[42] See Constantin Periphanakis, *La théorie grecque du droit et le classicisme actuel* (Athens, 1946), p. 17.

[43] See Pierre Mesnard, *L'essor de la philosophie politique au XVIᵉ siècle* (Paris, 1952), p. 481.

11 Christian Interpretations of Pagan Authors

RAYMOND LEBÈGUE

THE fact that I have so often concerned myself with Christian thought under Francis I is probably a subconscious reaction against the opinions which held sway about forty years ago among historians of the Renaissance. Despite the work of Imbart de la Tour and Renaudet, it had been asserted that the Renaissance was essentially a laicization of the human intellect and a liberation from religious beliefs; and that paganism had reawakened and triumphed over Christianity. This is no exaggeration. One has only to think of the interpretations given to the ideas of Rabelais, Ronsard, and Montaigne; and also, more recently, of the violent reactions stirred up by a book with the provocative title of *La religion de Rabelais*. Pierre Champion gave the title *Paganisme et réforme* to one of his books, just as though the only people who existed before the Counter-Reformation were Protestants and "pagans." It has taken much determined effort to correct this highly oversimplified view of the Renaissance.[1]

In this discourse I should like to take a comparatively restricted field and use it to consider the great problem of pagan humanism. What was the attitude toward pagan works at the beginning of the Renaissance in France, among editors, translators, and commentators? For our present purpose these works can be classified as follows: those which were anti-Semitic and anti-Christian, those which were hostile to all religion (Lucian and Lucretius), those which could be reconciled with Christian doctrine, and those which could not. As this is only a short discourse I shall rest content with a few examples which seem to me to be significant.

---

[1] All the same, I am quite sure that a certain number of French thinkers in the sixteenth century were rightly described as *achristes*.

LUCIAN

There is no existing sixteenth-century work on Lucian, which is a pity, as it would have thrown much light on a curious intellectual evolution. From the very beginning, genuinely Christian humanists used to read, edit, and translate Lucian without any anxiety or scruple; in their view there was nothing atheistic about savoring his language and his talent for comedy and satire. Among Lucian's first translators were Erasmus and his friend Thomas More. In their prefaces they claimed to find Lucian's writings helpful in their work of purifying and refining Christianity. In the preface to his translation of the *Toxaris*, Erasmus asserted that the truest and most perfect form of friendship was Christianity.

At the beginning of the translation of Alexander or the pseudo-Divine, Erasmus wrote to the bishop of Chartres:

> ... quo nemo sit utilior ad depraehendendas coarguendasque quorundam istorum imposturas: qui nunc quoque vel magicis miraculis, vel ficta religione, vel adsimulatis condonationibus, aliisque id genus praestigiis vulgo fucum facere solent.[2]

The same tendency is to be found in Thomas More. Against the irreligiousness of Lucian he set the Christian faith, but he thought it unnecessary to labor the point unduly: "Why should I concern myself with the opinion of a pagan in these matters which are to be reckoned among the principal Christian mysteries?"

Like the Bollandists after him, he appealed to Lucian when recommending that hagiographies be written in a more critical spirit:

> Nullam fere martyris, nullam virginis vitam, praetermiserunt, in quam non aliquid hujusmodi mendaciorum inseruerint, pie

[2] "... than whom none is more useful for detecting and refuting the impostures of certain of these people: who, with the aid either of magical miracles or of made-up religion or of pretended forgiveness, and other tricks of this sort, are wont to make a dissimulation in public." The reference is to the "scoundrel" of the pseudo-Divine.

scilicet. . . . Nec veriti sunt eam religionem contaminare figmentis.[3]

Here is an example of a fundamentally irreligious pagan being used by two renowned humanists in their attempt to discern the true from the false in religious practices and Christian literature.

THE APHORISTS

Few pagan books have performed such long educational service in Christendom as the *Distichs* of Dionysius Cato, and the introduction of printing spread them far and wide. Of the numerous editions which appeared in the sixteenth century here are a few examples.

a) Erasmus did not fail to slip a few Christian precepts into his commentary, as well as some satirical references to contemporary abuses. When Cato censured the offering of bloody sacrifices to the gods, the Dutch humanist took occasion to criticize extravagance in Christian ceremonial, for God wished to be worshiped in spirit. When Cato showed his disapproval of gambling, Erasmus added the comment that this was the pastime of Christian princes and even a number of priests.

b) *Les motz Dorez de Cathon* contained the original verses together with a French translation by Pierre Grosnet. The translator deliberately christianized the precepts. Not only did he render *peccata* by "sins," and *sanctus* by "saint," but also *carmina* by "Holy Scripture." He recalled the Ten Commandments in his paraphrase of *Aliena concupiscere noli*:

> Et ne couvoite aulcunement
> Les biens, ne la femme d'altruy.

He introduced the word "Christian":

> Infantem nudum cum te natura creavit.
> Chrestiens viennent nuds sur terre.

---

[3] "Scarcely any life of martyr or virgin goes by in which they have not inserted one or more falsehoods of this description, for pious reasons, of course.... And they did not scruple to contaminate that religion with mere figments."

And another significant gloss:

> Ut sapiens vivas, audi que discere possis.
> Aprens de vivre saigement
> En lisant la saincte escripture.

c) Mathurin Cordier was a great Protestant teacher who, in 1533, as a professor at Nevers, gave out a scholarly edition of the *Distichs*. It was an educational classic in French-speaking lands, and there were no less than thirty editions before 1600. His Christian scruples appeared in the dedicatory letter to Robert Estienne: his pupils, he wrote, had obliged him to explain this work to them, even though it often went against his piety as a Christian. In 1556 he wrote a new preface in which he expressed his regret that the *Distichs* had been prescribed for study. For this reason the Latin text in his book is followed not only by a word-for-word translation but also by an *admonitio*, or warning, intended often as an antidote. When Cato referred to blind Fortune, Cordier hastened to correct him:

> His est error Ethnicorum, qui fortunam esse deam putaverunt: eamque deam caecam appellarunt.
> (This was the error of the heathens, who thought of Fortune as a goddess: and they called her the blind goddess.)

Cato's conjugal morality was only partially acceptable:

> Uxorem fuge, ne ducas sub nomine dotis, Nec retinere velis si ceperit esse molesta. Admonitio: Imo ad mortem usque retinenda est ea quam semel duxeris, etiam si fuerit molestissima. Nam Christiana lege non licet uxorem relinquere, nisi propter ejus adulterium.
> (Avoid a wife, and do not marry one because of her dowry; and do not think to keep her if she starts to become irksome. Admonition: Once you have taken a woman to wife you must keep her until death, however irksome she may become. For according to the Christian law it is not permitted to leave one's wife, unless she commits adultery.)

Cato was not aware of Christian charity, so Cordier underlined the difference:

Dilige sic alios, ut sis tibi charus amicus. Admonitio: Ethnicorum doctrina haec est: Christianis autem sic est praeceptum: Diliges proximum tuum sicut teipsum. Proximus tuus, omnis homo est, ait Augustinus.
(Love others in such a way that you may become your own best friend. Admonition: This is the teaching of the heathens: but for Christians the precept is: Love your neighbor as yourself. And your neighbor, as Augustine says, is every man.)

Semper tibi proximus esto. Admonitio: Sed contra hoc praeceptum, est illud D. Pauli: Charitas non quaerit quae sua sunt.
(Always be your own nearest neighbor. Admonition: But opposed to this precept is that of St. Paul: Charity does not seek its own.)

d) A mediocre and highly prolific poet named François Habert was among those Renaissance moralists who reconciled the morality of one pagan or another with Christian doctrine. In his edition too every distich was followed by a French translation in four-line stanzas and an epigram corresponding to Cordier's *admonitio*. His commentaries were written with those of Cordier in mind. Presented with the precept: *Litem inferre cave cum quo tibi gratia juncta est*, he composed this epigram:

> Ce propos là de ne prendre querelle
> A son amy, c'est un propos chrestien:
> Car il contient l'amytié mutuelle
> De qui les bons observent l'entretien . . . .

Like Cordier, he took offense at *sis tibi charus amicus*:

> L'enseignement de Caton en ce lieu
> N'est pas comprins en doctrine fidele:
> Car il repugne aux sainctz edictz de Dieu
> Lequel au lien mutuel nous apelle,
> Et (qui est plus) ce poinct il nous revele
> Non seulement de bien faire aux amys:
> Mais d'estre pleins de charité la belle
> Et de bien faire à tous noz ennemys.

His commentary on *Uxorem fuge* was also inspired by Cordier's:

> Le premier poinct envers les bons a lieu,
> De n'espouser femme pour son douaire.
> Le second poinct est du tout contre Dieu,
> Et à la loy de Jésus-Christ contraire:
> Car du lien conjugal se distraire
> Est deffendu voire jusque à la mort,
> Et n'a pouvoir le mary de ce faire,
> Si son espouse adultere ne mord.

Cato was not the only aphoristic writer whom attempts had been made to christianize. In 1596 the translator of the *Vers dorés* of Pythagoras was to claim that his rendering was faithful, "except where he has tried to tone down somewhat the parts which spring from the paganism of Pythagoras."

THE PHILOSOPHERS

All the pagan philosophers were treated according to the nature of their particular teachings. Seneca commended himself to Christian readers because of the correspondence he entered into with St. Paul. The first printed translation of one of his works—that by Laurent de Premierfaict—bore the title *Des epistres de Senecque et S. Paul lesquels furent moult amys et familliers entre eulx*.

No pagan philosopher has ever been brought into line with Christianity with more patient perseverance than has Plato. It is as though all his commentators had adopted the words of Pascal: "Platon pour disposer au christianisme". Marsilio Ficino had set the example for the French humanists of the sixteenth century. Du Val, bishop of Séez and translator of the *Crito*, expressed the generally accepted opinion when he wrote: "Ses propos approchent fort de la doctrine de Jésus-Christ." His commentators would see grace in the divine fury, identify the World Spirit with Christ, and happily mix together quotations from Plato's dialogues, the Apostles, and the Fathers.[4]

All this is well known, and it would be better, therefore, to linger a little on the translations of Cicero. Among the men of letters then living in Dieppe was a certain David Miffant, the governor of the city, who in 1502 published in Paris a translation of De Officiis, the moral purpose of which was set out in full on the title page:

> ... auquel livre chascun homme pourra prendre vrays enseigne-mens de bien et honnestement vivre en société humaine selon vertu moralle, moyennant laquelle avecques foy pourra parvenir en la gloire eternelle de paradis, qui est la fin et souverain bien où consiste felicité humaine.

His preface invited all Christians to draw "profitable doctrines" from this book. To read the De Officiis and put its precepts into practice was a means—together with the aid of faith—whereby one might merit paradise.

In 1537 there appeared a translation of the De Amicitia. In his preface the translator, one Jean Collin, appealed to passages from St. Matthew and St. Paul, and justified his choice "because the nature of this book is closely united to the law of the gospels."

THE POETS

Since the poets had enclosed a moral lesson beneath the veil of fiction, it was recommended that an allegorical interpretation be given to their works. This is what Josse Bade did in 1501 in a commentary on Vergil, which was frequently reprinted: the Georgics use the example of the bees to teach us the principles of a well-organized state; the first six books of the Aeneid offer an allegorical representation of the six ages of man's life (the fourth, which tells the story of an ill-fated love, is juventus, youth; and the sixth, in which Aeneas holds converse with the dead, is

---

[4] Cf. my account of Platonism in France during the sixteenth century, in Actes du Ve Congrès de l'Association G. Budé, 1954, pp. 341–2.

senectus, old age).[5] He connected the Fourth Eclogue with the predictions of Isaiah and the Sibyl and detected in it an obscure presentiment of the coming of Christ.

This allegorical method was applied with untiring ingenuity by a translator from Touraine called Guillaume Michel.[6] His renderings of the Latin authors do not seem to have met with much success, but it is important to spend a little time over them because they bear witness to a state of mind which had lingered on from the Middle Ages. In 1516 he published his translation of the *Bucolics*, and three years later published the *Georgics*— "translatées et moralisées."

In his *Bucolics* he made reference to the historical interpretation of the Fourth Eclogue, though he himself preferred the Christian one: "But this applies better to Jesus Christ . . . but some more rightly understand this to refer to Jesus Christ . . . but these things can be understood better of Christ." He extracted an allegorical meaning from a number of lines: for line 13 he referred to the *Expurgate vetus fermentum* of St. Paul. In line 41 he recognized Christ; and he thought to see, in the *Varios lana colores* of the next line, "the apostles of all colors." "Thorns shall bear grapes" in line 30 was taken to mean that "the heretics shall be converted to the full measure of the faith." And the famous *risu cognoscere matrem* called forth the following association: "Jesus Christ is born in great joyousness." The First Eclogue gave Michel a chance to bring in the *Crescite et multiplicamini* from the Book of Genesis.

Just as Ovid's *Metamorphoses* had been "moralized," so Michel too "moralized" the *Georgics*. Each of the four cantos formed an allegory of one of the cardinal virtues. Vergil's exhortation to cultivate, manure, and irrigate the soil meant that one had to cultivate prudence, fertilize, and enrich it through the reading of the Holy Scriptures, and keep it watered with the thought of those

[5] Cf. Mme. Hulubei, "Virgile en France au XVIe siècle," in *Revue du XVIe siècle*, XVIII, 7–13.

[6] Cf. Hulubei, *op. cit.*, pp. 29–33; Bernard Weinberg, "Guillaume Michel dit de Tours," in *Bibliothèque d'Humanisme et Renaissance*, XI, 72–85.

things which are to come. In the second canto the transformation of the wild trees into domestic ones is an allegory of the sinner's conversion through grace. Fatten the cattle in order to sacrifice them to the gods means: Let us humble our thoughts before the Lord. As for the horse-drawn chariot, this is the Church of God, upon which the four Evangelists perform the office of wheels.

The episode of the bees in the fourth canto provided Guillaume Michel with many an allegory. The king bee was the king of justices, and thus Christ. The pejorative meaning attached in the everyday language of the time to the word *veau* (calf) did not prevent the imaginative exegete from seeing the calf as Christ, "compared to a calf all because of his humility." This led to the subtle explanation of the birth of legless bees from out of the calf as "the new men regenerated in the blood of Jesus Christ, with no power of their own to walk and make progress along the path of virtue."

That the tradition of moralizing Ovid persisted right up to the height of the Renaissance needs no other proof than the fact that our friend François Habert dedicated a translation of the *Metamorphoses* to Henry II in 1557. His letter to the king was filled with moral and religious allegories, which form a very droll contrast with the amoralism of the Latin poet: Daphne becomes the symbol of modesty and Phaeton a model for the education of children; Arachne proves that ingratitude toward God is punished, and Deucalion is an image of the omnipotent Savior of the world.

Several conclusions can be drawn from these texts.

In the commentaries and dedicatory letters of editors or translators, references to the Bible and the Fathers are interspersed with quotations from pagan works.

The Aphorists who had been prescribed for study in colleges were brought into line with Christian morality.

The works of the philosophers were compared with the principles of Christianity; where there was an irreducible contradiction the error in question was condemned.[7] The most frequently christianized philosopher was Plato.

A number of humanists continued with the "moralization" of Vergil and Ovid and discovered allegories with a Christian meaning in their works.

And finally, Erasmus and Thomas More drew Dionysius Cato, and Lucian into the religious polemics of the early sixteenth century.

This study has been intentionally restricted to a single country and to a limited period of time, but it could well be extended. It would be useful to take a single author and find out how long his works continued to be allegorized or given a Christian interpretation; it would also be valuable to study the part played in this by the Jesuits, the Protestant humanists, and others. In this way much light could be shed on a little-known aspect of ancient culture in the modern world.

---

[7] For instance, one of the most eminent representatives of Christian humanism, Lefèvre d'Étaples, appended a list of "absurd Socratic laws" to his anthology of Plato's *Laws* and *Republic*. (Cf. my article, "La République de Platon et la Renaissance française," in *Les Lettres d'humanité*, II, 159.)

PART FIVE

French Humanism and the Arts

1. Il Rosso Fiorentino: THE DEATH OF ADONIS
   Fontainebleau, Galerie François I

2. Il Rosso Fiorentino: VERTUMNUS AND POMONA
   Pen drawing. Paris, Louvre

3. French Master of the Second Quarter of the Sixteenth Century:
A GARDEN FESTIVAL
Drawing. Paris, Louvre

4. Bernard Salomon: THE SHOWER
Woodcut

5. Francesco Primaticcio: DIANA AND ACTAEON
   Drawing. Paris, Louvre

6. Francesco Primaticcio: THE MASQUERADE OF PERSEPOLIS
   Drawing. Paris, Louvre

DEO MAGNO AETERNO,
ET BLANDE SCATVRIENTIB·RVBIACIS
NIMPHIS
SVIQ·NOMINIS MEMORIAE PERENNI
GABRIEL SYMEONVS FLOR·ΕΥΔΟΚΙΑΣ
D·S·P·C·

ROIAG

7. Bernard Salomon: THE FOUNTAIN OF ROAIG
   Woodcut

8. Jean Duvet: THE VISION OF THE CANDLESTICKS
Engraving from the 'Apocalypse'

9. Germain Pilon: MATER DOLOROSA
Paris, Louvre

Pienue belange.

10. Jacques Bellange: THE MARYS AT THE TOMB
Red chalk drawing. Vienna, Albertina

11. School of Fontainebleau: THE HARVEST
   Fontainebleau Castle
12. Jacques Bellange: STAG HUNT
   Pen and brush drawing. Nancy, Musée Historique Lorrain

12 The Ancient and the Gothic Revival in French Art and Literature

OTTO BENESCH

THE country which had taken the lead in the art and culture of the Middle Ages, France, did not play so prominent a role about 1500 as did Italy, Germany, and the Netherlands. It almost looks as if France, which had spent her force throughout the centuries in an uninterrupted stream, slackened at the end of the fifteenth century, when in the neighboring countries a concentration of the creative forces occurred. France was filled with that refined languishing echo of the Middle Ages which the French themselves call *détente*, and which found its best expression in some works of sculpture. A poetic tenderness is perhaps the foremost quality of the works of the *deténte*. This was to become of great importance for the future. After a brief fallow period, the sixteenth century brought forth a new crop in which poetry had no inconsiderable share. The fine arts were not impaired as they were in Germany by Reformation problems, but they had to share their prominence with literature. And it was mainly in literature that the French made their great national contribution to the sixteenth century. Therefore, a joint consideration will prove helpful for the understanding of both.

The movement was more closely linked with the cultural program of the rulers than in any other country. It was not the individual struggle of artists and scholars alone, as in Germany and the Netherlands, which brought about the discussion of the new achievements of the Italian Renaissance. It was more the planned activity of the sovereigns which opened new possibilities to artists and writers. French culture in the sixteenth century was not a culture of burghers as in Germany and the Netherlands, but a court culture—and thus far, a continuation of the medieval order. King Francis I's patronage of the fine arts gave a decisive turn to the whole development. His sister Marguerite of Navarre fostered humanism and literature. Henry II reaped the fruits of what his predecessors had planted.

If we consider the revival of classical antiquity as a significant feature of the new Renaissance culture, France was retarded in comparison with the other countries. The climax of this revival was reached in France about the middle of the sixteenth century, when it had passed the summit elsewhere. *It is embodied in the arts by the school of Fontainebleau: in literature by the poets of the Pléiade.* Although the greater importance rests with the poets, the painters have the priority in time and were of the greatest influence on the development of the poetical imagery. In order to understand the situation at the time of Henry II, we have to study the foundations laid by Francis and Marguerite in the first half of the century.

Francis I considered himself a connoisseur of painting, and he had the enthusiasm of a great collector. He saw his artistic ideal in the Italian Renaissance. When he was a young man, his expeditions and travels brought him in close contact with its sources. His agents in Italy tried to procure as many works of art as they could and transfer them to France. Francis even tried to transplant the masters themselves. Leonardo da Vinci spent the last years of his life in Cloux. Andrea del Sarto was in the service of the monarch for one year. A systematic colonization of France by Italian artists began after 1528, when the king rebuilt the old castle in the idyllic surroundings of the forests and ponds of Fontainebleau. It was his favorite place; going to Fontainebleau he called "going home." The king succeeded in making Fontainebleau a concrete symbol of the new fashion. It was praised as a "new Rome" by Vasari, the authoritative Italian critic of the sixteenth century. This success was due to the large-scale activity of Italian masters in Fontainebleau.[1] They settled in the country,

[1] We owe the most extensive and important research on the school of Fontainebleau to L. Dimier. See *Le Primatice, peintre, sculpteur et architecte des rois de France* (Paris, 1900); *French Painting in the Sixteenth Century* (London, 1904);

permeated it with a new artistic gospel, and at the same time assimilated themselves to its tradition. Thus an artistic culture of quite unique flavor arose, based on Italian Renaissance in form, on Latinism and Grecism in literary content, and on the French heritage in spirit.

Marguerite of Navarre, a noble and liberal-minded character, was open to all progressive thought in the humanities and literature. She was one of the most educated women of her time. She studied not only the modern but also the ancient languages. Despériers translated Plato's dialogue *Lysis* for her. She favored Clément Marot as a poet. But she was also, with all the mystic and loving fervor of her soul, a protector of religious reformers like Calvin. She left a considerable literary work, best known among it the *Heptameron*, which follows the novels of Boccaccio. With her began the enthusiasm for the simple, unspoiled charm of nature, for the bucolic, which was to play such an important part in the poetry of the *Pléiade*.

Florentine painting had a considerable influence on the royal taste. Contact with Leonardo and Andrea educated Francis in the appreciation of Florentine art. The first phase of the school of Fontainebleau was in the Florentine tradition. In 1531 Giovanni Battista Rosso, called Il Rosso Fiorentino,[2] arrived at Fontainebleau and became the undisputed leader of the artistic enterprises there. Rosso's art was under the dual influence of Michelangelo and Andrea del Sarto. He developed from the mode of his models a highly expressive, almost exaggerated style with elongated figures, harsh contrasts, acute angles, opposing all harmonious roundness and balance. His compositions like the "Deposition from the Cross" in Volterra, 1521, reveal a tendency toward

---

"Les Origines de l'Art Français," *Les Arts* (Paris, 1905); *Fontainebleau* (Paris, 1925); *Histoire de la Peinture Française des Origines au Retour de Vouet, 1300 à 1627* (Paris, 1925). In recent years Mme. Sylvie Béguin has treated this field with particular success. See *L'École de Fontainebleau* (Paris, 1960); *Niccolò dell'Abbate en France*, Art de France, II (1962), pp. 113 ff.; *Toussaint Dubreuil*, Art de France IV (Paris, 1964).

[2] K. Kusenberg, *Le Rosso* (Paris, 1931).

the transcendental and superhuman. They rise in Gothic steepness and clearly work out the medieval tendencies in the art of Michelangelo. We notice the same tendency in the art of another artist of the same age, Pontormo, whose compositions rise flamingly and longingly toward heaven. With Pontormo and Rosso begins what we call Mannerism in Italian art.[3] Mannerism was more than a particular group or fraction of the general development.[4] The art of the Mannerists in the north and south clearly developed features which were valid in various transformations for almost a century. In the history of art it is thus customary to call the long era of late Renaissance which follows the very short, almost episodelike era of high Renaissance also the era of Mannerism. Mannerism lasted from the 1520's until the beginning of the seventeenth century.

As French art of the sixteenth century kept Gothic tendencies alive underground, it was a matter of course that Rosso's art would appeal to the French taste. The Italian influence on French art in the sixteenth century was a predominantly Manneristic one. The first work which was begun in the castle was the Gallery of Francis I, a long corridor adorned with frescoes which are framed by a profuse decoration in wood and stucco, carvings and moldings. The impression is that of splendor and magnificence, and at the same time of a fantastic crowding which lends to the southern forms something of the unsurveyable, entangled aspect of northern sculpture of the late Middle Ages. Rosso was responsible for the whole design, of which the figure composition forms only a part. Dispersed among the architectonic elements are nudes in contorted counterpoises, struggling in the narrow space allotted to them. They are seemingly inspired by Michelangelo's Sistine ceiling and the allegorical figures of the Medici tombs. The subjects of the murals are taken from classical

[3] W. Friedländer, "Die Entstehung des antiklassischen Stils," *Repertorium für Kunstwissenschaft*, XLVI (1925), 49 ff.

[4] The basic definition of Mannerism as a great chapter of the history of ideas was given by Max Dvořák, "Über Greco und den Manierismus," *Kunstgeschichte als Geistesgeschichte*, Munich, 1924, pp. 261 ff.

mythology, history, and poetry. Homer's *Iliad* and *Odyssey*, Herodotus' and Valerius Maximus' writings, Apuleius' *Amor and Psyche*, and Ovid's *Metamorphoses* are the literary sources. The compositions, like the "Death of Adonis," are developed in sharp, splintery forms which also lend to the nudes a decorative and unreal appearance. It is the same quality which we see in Rosso's cool and clear-colored easel paintings. As the frescoes have suffered rather much through later overpainting, we may use the original drawings as a help in reconstructing the genuine rhythm of these works. Many of them have survived. The "Instruction of Achilles by the Centaur Chiron" (Paris, École des Beaux-Arts) in fighting, riding, and swimming proves the master's great ability to concentrate on agitated composition in a limited field to a graceful pattern. Pictorial qualities are far from this art; most of its effect rests with the eloquence of line. Therefore, these delicate preparatory drawings give a perfect idea of the artistic aim striven for. The Mannerists were outstanding draughtsmen. We may also gain an idea of the original splendor of this work from another source. I have already mentioned the importance of the art of tapestry to the northern countries. A set of tapestries in the Museum of Vienna[5] reproduces the various sections of the gallery of Francis I. It is marvelous how the harmonious richness of these creations, full of a subdued luster and sparkle of gold, transfers the heavy contrasts of architecture, sculpture, and paint into the dreamlike, imaginary realm of the Gobelin—an enhanced poetry such as was the final aim of this art (Plate 1).

The poetical quality of the inventions increases. A garden house, the Pavilion of Pomona, was adorned with fresco cycles by the Italian masters. The story of Vertumnus and Pomona taken from Ovid was illustrated by Rosso. The building no longer exists, but Rosso's delicate designs give an excellent idea of the fanciful and whimsical work.[6] Vertumnus, the God of Autumn, in the disguise of an old woman, ardently tries to

[5] See O. Benesch, *The Art of the Renaissance in Northern Europe*, Ch. VI, note 1.
[6] P. Lavallée, *Le Dessin Français du XIIIe au XVIe Siècle* (Paris, 1930), p. 92.

persuade Pomona, the Goddess of the fruit-bearing trees, who ponders over his proposals with a naïve and girlish gesture (Plate 2). A female genius with butterfly wings and several *amoretti* who take the beauty under a crossfire of their arrows are grouped near. A fence, a garden door, a pond, and maskerons with fruit garlands complete the setting of a bucolic and courtly stage on which the scene takes place. The poetical imagination creates an atmosphere in which a fancied past and contemporary fashion blend.

One of the most beautiful illustrations of the legend of Vertumnus and Pomona is a series of tapestries woven after designs of the Flemish artist J. C. Vermeyen in the style of Fontainebleau, where the enchanting story is played on the stage of a magnificent garden which interlaces architectural design and natural growth in a fascinating totality.[7] This is the cult of garden and nature which became reality in the social life of the French aristocracy during the time of Francis I and Henry II. We see it delineated in a beautiful, large, still unidentified drawing which the author discovered among the treasures of the Cabinet des Dessins in the Louvre (Plate 3). Horseback riders and hawkers arrive at a garden festivity. Noblemen greet with grand gestures ladies accompanied by pet dogs like the little Peloton whose eulogy was sung by Joachim du Bellay in a charming poem. Clipped hedges, tunnels, and domes of living foliage lead into the depth of the garden. Singers, lute players, musicians, and banqueters populate them. Despite the general gaiety of the scene, the figures have the same Gothic slenderness and almost spectral haughtiness which we notice in the works done by the Italian Mannerists for this society—a secret Gothic. And this society is the same which is sung of in the works of the French lyrical poets, in which the imagery of the painters became word and musical sound. Clément Marot portrayed it in the following lines:

> Mais soulz belle umbre en chambre et galeries
> Nous pourmenons, livres et railleries,

[7] M. Crick-Kuntziger, "L'auteur des cartons de 'Vertumne et Pomone,'" *Oud Holland*, XLIV (1927), pp. 159 ff.

Dames et bains, seroient les passetemps,
Lieux et labeurs de nos espritz contens.[8]

Clément Marot forms a beginning. He not only admired
Petrarch and Boccaccio but also attempted to trans'ate Vergil,
Ovid, and Catullus. We are in the time of Erasmus, whose *Adagia*
was printed in Paris. Medieval naïveté still slips into Marot's classi-
cality. In the poem on his own childhood, "L'enfance de Marot,"
he describes the charms of the French countryside in a way which
suggests the calendar illustrations in the illuminated books. We
mentioned before that in the works of his patroness, Marguerite
of Navarre, a similar naïve feeling of nature prevails. A long
narrative poem entitled "The Coach" describes how she rides
into the open country, enjoying valley and forest, talking to
simple people. Three noble ladies emerge from the forest and
utter their amorous complaints. They do this in such a rhetorical
length and shed so many tears that they charge the sky with the
moisture of clouds, and a heavy shower finally pours down,
breaking up the elegiac party (Plate 4). In spite of the cloudburst,
they leave the rustic stage to join the coach in a very dignified
manner. The great illustrator Bernard Salomon has represented
this scene in a delicate little woodcut which adorns Jean de
Tournes' edition of Marguerite's poems.[9]

In this early phase of French Renaissance, nature and antiquity
go side by side, intermingled in a casual, piecemeal way as in the
Netherlandish painting of the early sixteenth century. A real
fusion of both to a new imaginative totality did not come about
before the *Pléiade*. The *Pléiade* was a group of seven like-minded
poets and scholars of the era of Henry II who, following the
example of a group of ancient poets who lived in Alexandria
in the third century B.C., took this name from the sign of the

[8] Épigrammes à l'imitation de Martial, livre V, no. 18.
[9] *Marguerites de la Marguerite des Princesses, Tres illustre Royne de Navarre.
A Lyon, par Jean de Tournes 1547.* Our reproductions, Plates 4 and 7, are
taken from the volumes of the Frances Hofer Collection, deposited with the
Houghton Library, Harvard University. We are indebted to Mr. and Mrs.
Philip Hofer for the permission of reproduction.

zodiac. They were led by Pierre de Ronsard and Joachim du Bellay as stars of first order, with Remi Belleau, Jean-Antoine de Baïf, Estienne Jodelle, Jean Daurat, and Pontus de Thyard the *stellae minores*.

The poetry of the *Pléiade* is distinguished by two main features. In the first place, it is learned, scholarly poetry which develops its proper artistic and linguistic program and establishes a poetical theory with definite principles. It follows up a literary ideal. In all these respects it may be compared with the works of the painters of the school of Fontainebleau, who were scholarly artists following rules and principles, and who appealed to the taste of educated connoisseurs. In the second place, owing to the superior mastery of its representatives, the poetry of the *Pléiade* was able to vivify the scholarly achievements. They remained no dead archeological requisites, but became the vehicle of a new attitude toward life imbued with poetical spirit. This poetical enhancement and elevation made human nature, scenery, mythology, past, and present appear in a different light—not as facts of a firmly established hierarchic order, but as reflections of the creative poetical mind.

The poets of the *Pléiade* acquired a thorough knowledge of ancient languages and literature. Ronsard studied Greek with the Hellenist Daurat. Homer, Pindar, Vergil, Ovid, Horace, Tibullus, Propertius, and the great Italians were the models. The poets of the *Pléiade* held in contempt the old poets of ballads who worked "only by nature, without art and doctrine." They introduced the Alexandrine. The ode and the sonnet were among their favorite forms of poetry. Yet they actively opposed the humanists, who believed they could write like Greeks and Romans. Their aim was to regenerate the French language, that it might acquire a flexibility and expressiveness matching the ancients. Du Bellay published in 1549 his *Défense et Illustration de la Langue Française*, the theoretical creed of the group in which we read the following sentence: "I cannot blame too strongly the rashness of some of our countrymen who, being anything rather than Greeks or Latins, depreciate and reject everything written in French." The native language should acquire a musical perfection, and Ronsard's poems were indeed favored as texts by sixteenth-century composers.

In his poem "L'enfer" Marot had already described a world of ancient deities which is reminiscent of the gallery of Francis I. Pleading before Minos, the judge of the dead, the poet enumerates all the pagan deities to whom he is known:

> En la mer suis connu des plus hauts dieux,
> Jusqu'aux Tritons et jusqu'aux Néréides
> En terre aussi des Faunes et Hymnides
> Connu je suis. Connu je suis d'Orphée,
> De mainte nymphe et mainte noble fée.

The subjects of the frescoes of the gallery pass by in this poem. But it was not until Ronsard that poetry depicted the ancient deities of that lofty, elevated style which we know from the paintings of Fontainebleau. In the verses of a festival entitled "Les Sereines," performed at the canal of Fontainebleau, Ronsard made the pagan deities mix with earthly men, as many a painting of the Fontainebleau school shows:

> Quand nos ayeuls n'estoyent tels que nous sommes,
> Apparoissoyent les Nymphes et les Dieux,
> Et sans avoir une voile sur les yeux,
> Ne desdaignoyent la presence des hommes.
> Par les forests les Sylvains habitoyent,
> Et sur les monts dansoyent les Oreades;
> La mer avoit son Glauque et son Neptun,
> Desur les bords venoit jouer Portun,
> Et les ruisseaux abondoyent des Naiades.

The most cherished object of this poetical cult was Diana, the virgin goddess, tall, slender, youthful, who roamed through the forests. She and her maidens and nymphs embody a new canon of beauty, blending feminine with masculine features, a canon celebrated by Primaticcio in endless variations. Francesco Primaticcio of Bologna had arrived in 1532, and became the artistic dictator in Fontainebleau after Rosso's death. With him, the current of Italian Mannerism which derives from Raphael and the Roman school entered French art. Primaticcio, who had worked for six years under Giulio Romano at the Palazzo del Té in Mantua, was a universally gifted artist, an inventive genius of great style. His canon of forms dominated Fontainebleau in the second phase, and through it, Europe. From the middle of the sixteenth century onward, Fontainebleau became the center and source of power of many Italianizing trends in northern European art.

Primaticcio replaced the expressive harshness of Rosso with an elongated, languishing grace. This is the beauty which Ronsard praised in his verses on Eurymedon and Callirrhoë,[10] who was changed into a well in the forest:

> Je voudrois ce jourd'huy, par bonne destinée,
> Me changer d'homme en femme, ainsi que fit Coenée,
> Coenée qui tournant par miracle sa peau,
> Estoit tantost pucelle, et tantost jouvenceau.
> Je verrois dans le baing la belle Callirée:
> Je faux, mais je verrois la belle Cythérée.

Diana, the maidenly goddess, surprised by Actaeon while bathing with her nymphs, was a standard topic of the artists and poets.

> O beau crystal murmurant,
> Que le ciel est azurant
> D'une belle coleur blue,
> Où ma Dame toute nue
> Lave son beau teint vermeil
> Qui retenoit le Soleil . . .

sings Ronsard in Ode XIII of Le Cinquiesme Livre des Odes. Primaticcio decorated the bathing apartments in Fontainebleau with murals representing this subject; we know the composition from original drawings (Plate 5). Artificial grottos like the Grotte des Pins were erected in the garden under the poetical device of "Diana's bathing place."[11] The tall, slender, long-legged female type occurs as well in the works of Jean Goujon, which

---

[10] "Les Vers d'Eurymedon et de Calliree: Le Baing de Calliree."
[11] M. L. Gothein, History of Garden Art, I (London, 1928), 400.

represents the style of Fontainebleau in French sculpture. Famous is his group of "Diana with the Hart," which he executed between 1547 and 1549 for the Fountain of the Nymphs in the Castle Anet, the residence of Diane de Poitiers, mistress of Henry II.

As Mannerism liked the elegant, floating, balancing grace of figure, it also liked the ambiguous, changing character of shape. Permutations and transformations were quite to its taste, and therefore subjects from Ovid's *Metamorphoses* were much in favor. Bernard Salomon's 1557 illustrations for Ovid charmingly show how human and animal shapes change into trees and bushes. The poetical story of Prince Ciparisse of Cyprus[12] recounts how the boy adorned his favorite animal, a tame hart, with gold and flowers. He killed it by mistake while hunting. As he could not live without the animal, Apollo transformed both into trees.

The two largest works which Primaticcio did in Fontainebleau were the Gallery of Ulysses (destroyed in the eighteenth century) and the large ballroom, both completed in the era of Henry II, who in 1547 followed Francis I on the throne. Primaticcio adorned the spandrels with mythological frescoes, for the execution of which he had already used the help of the third outstanding Italian painter working in Fontainebleau, Niccolò dell'Abbate, who had arrived in 1552 and introduced the precious Mannerism of Parmigianino. There the decorative splendor of Primaticcio's style comes to full development. The "Wedding Feast of Peleus and Thetis," where Discord throws the apple amid the guests, presents the banqueters most effectfully grouped in the triangular space. Primaticcio's drawings surpass even the executed frescoes in beauty.

A speciality of French court life of the sixteenth century were the festivals, the so-called masquerades, performed in the halls of the palace or in the open air of the park. Rosso and Primaticcio were the producers, who delivered the design not only for the whole setting but for every archaeological and costume detail. Ronsard wrote the verses which the mythological characters had

[12] Ovid, *Metamorphoses* (Lyon, Jean de Tournes, French edition, 1557), p. 136 "Ciparisse en Cipre."

to recite. Occasional poems of this kind form a considerable portion of his work. What these performances were like we may guess not only from costume designs, but also from Primaticcio's drawing for a fresco in the Chambre of the Duchesse d'Étampes, representing Alexander's Masquerade in Persepolis (Plate 6). The actors pass by with stilted, tiptoeing steps, a solemn choir of tall, flaming figures rising to heaven in fantastic disguise which is supposed to be ancient, but is imaginary and fanciful like antiquity in Ronsard's poetry.

We mentioned before that the poets of the *Pléiade* tried to evoke from scholarly achievements a genuine poetical spirit, and gain new poetical aspects of life. This comes to the fore most vividly in the lyrical poems, in which the poet strips off the ancient cothurnus and just pours the mood of his soul, tuned by surroundings and scenery, into verses. The feeling of nature expressed thus is of pagan serenity, at the same time related to the late medieval enjoyment of nature. There, the spirit of Fontainebleau turns completely French and national. I should like to quote some of Ronsard's odes—this, for example, on the selection of his tomb (Livre IV, Ode IV):

> Antres, et vous, fontaines
> De ces roches hautaines
> Qui tombez contre-bas
> D'un glissant pas,
>
> Et vous, forests et ondes
> Par ces prez vagabondes
> Et vous, rives et bois,
> Oyez ma vois.

In art also the style of the school of Fontainebleau gradually became a national French manner, as we see in the picturesque woodcut of a fountain in Auvergne by Bernard Salomon (Plate 7), almost an illustration of Ronsard's ode.[13] Another artist in

[13] This woodcut is added to an Italian treatise by Gabriel Symeon on the nature of the moon and the names given to the Goddess Diana by classical authors. *La Natura et Effetti della Luna nelle cose humane, passando per i XII Segni del Cielo, Insieme co i nomi che gl' Autori Greci & Latini hanno attribuiti a Diana. La Fontana di Roiag in Overnia* (1558).

whose art the international style of Fontainebleau turned specifically French was Jean Cousin the Younger, whose *œuvre* of drawings
the author was able to reconstruct from many scattered sketches
wrongly attributed to various Italian and Netherlandish masters.[14]
A rich pen drawing in the Albertina, delicately washed with
purple, places the story of Diana and Endymion in an enchanting
bosquet with curly trees, much in the style of the Dutch painter
Jan van Scorel, whom Francis I tried in vain to draw to his court.
This *bosquet* is like Ronsard's "Forest de Gastine":

> Tes bocages soient tousjours pleins
> D'amoureuses brigades,
> De Satyres et de Sylvains,
> La crainte des Naiades.

> En toy habite desormais
> Des Muses le college,
> Et ton bois ne sente jamais
> La flame sacrilege.

Diana as goddess of the moon, "torch bearer, only heir and
daughter of the shadows of the night," was sung of in sonnets by
Remi Belleau and Louise Labbé, a poetess who wrote love songs
of wonderful depth.

The profoundest poet of the *Pléiade* was Joachim du Bellay,
who, admiring the antiquities of Rome, consumed himself in
nostalgia for his native Anjou. Walter Pater devoted one of his
finest studies to him.[15] Du Bellay's visions of scenery are perhaps
the most poetical and soulful ones. When we look at the painting
of the "Harvest"[16] in Fontainebleau (Plate 11) where a courtly
couple enjoy the rustic life in the open, windswept country, it

[14] O. Benesch, "Jean Cousin fils dessinateur," *Promethée*, I (Paris, 1939), 271 ff.
The drawn *œuvre* of Jean Cousin fils has in the meanwhile been considerably
increased by new finds.

[15] *The Renaissance* (1873).

[16] The painting was mostly attributed to Niccolò dell'Abbate. S. Béguin
ventures an attribution to Niccolò dell'Abbate's son Giulio Camillo (*L'École
de Fontainebleau*, pp. 65–7). She published another painting of the same artist
with rural scenes in the Riechers Collection, Paris.

brings to our mind Du Bellay's "Song of a Winnower of Wheat to the Winds":

> A vous, troupe légère,
> Qui d'aile passagère
> Par le monde volez,
> Et d'un sifflant murmure
> L'ombrageuse verdure
> Doucement ébranlez,
>
> J'offre ces violettes,
> Ces lis et ces fleurettes,
> Et ces roses ici,
> Ces vermeillettes roses,
> Tout fraîchement écloses,
> Et ces œillets aussi.
>
> De votre douce haleine
> Éventez cette plaine,
> Éventez ce séjour,
> Cependant que j'ahanne
> A mon blé que je vanne
> A la chaleur du jour.

The splendid and festive trend of the ancient revival which stands out so conspicuously in France's artistic and literary culture of the sixteenth century was not the only, nor even always the dominating, one. It paralleled another equally strong and equally important trend, the revival of the medieval spirit. We took occasion to point out the secret Gothic tendency in the Mannerism of the school of Fontainebleau, the rebirth of the fifteenth-century enjoyment of nature in the lyrical poetry. Without doubt, both trends influenced each other strongly. The medieval tradition was never completely interrupted. Yet the Gothic trend in French art and literature was more than a shadowy afterlife of a bygone era. The mysticism of Marguerite of Navarre, the powerful versification of the Psalms by Marot, prove a newly awakened interest in the religious spirit of the Middle Ages. We saw similar trends in the other European countries. In a gloomy poem, "La Mort aux

Hommes," Marot makes Death speak to man as in the Gothic *danses macabres*, murals in the French cemeteries. The poem begins with the lines:

> Incontinent que la mort entendit
> Que l'on voulait inutile la dire,
> Son bras tout sec en arrière étendit,
> Et fièrement son dard mortel brandit,
> Pour République en frapper par grande ire.

With these lines who would not think of Ligier Richier's "Epitaph for René de Chalon" in the Church of Saint-Pierre at Bar-le-Duc? Death appears there in the terrifying realism of at skeleton alive. And Death speaks to man in Marot's poem:

> L'âme est le feu, le corps est le tison;
> L'âme est d'en haut, et le corps inutile
> N'est autre cas qu'une basse prison
> En qui languit l'âme noble et gentille.

A longing for the beyond, for that which the Middle Ages considered the only good, speaks in these verses. They clearly prove the dual influence of thought under which the French poets and artists worked. The serious note of the transitoriness of earthly pleasures was often sounded by the poets of the *Pléiade* too, especially by Du Bellay.

The revived medieval spirit found its most grandiose expression in the works of Jean Duvet, a goldsmith and engraver who was born in 1485 and died after 1561. Duvet had studied the masters of the Renaissance in Italy. He was acquainted with the works of Leonardo, Mantegna, and Raphael. His grammar of forms fits well into that of the Renaissance of Francis I's era. But how different is the spirit to which these forms are subservient! Duvet's compositions completely disregard all natural or rational space relations. They are patternlike, crowded in a medieval *horror vacui* like tapestries or sixteenth-century enamels, a kind of work Duvet executed as well. Even poetical subjects like the "Story of the Unicorn,"[17] offer a strange, dreamlike aspect, unreal and heavy

[17] A. P. F. Robert-Dumesnil, *Le Peintre-graveur français*, 11 Vols. (Paris, 1835), Vol. 5, Nos. 54–9.

like a nightmare. His greatest and most expressive work is the "Apocalypse,"[18] which he engraved on order of Francis I and Henry II in the years 1546 to 1555. The medieval grandeur of Dürer's "Apocalypse" inspired these engravings, yet they have a visionary power quite their own. The angel who stands with columns of fire on sea and earth makes the Evangelist swallow the book. His body concretes from billowy clouds; his head sends a cross of rays into space which is constricted by rising rocks, trees, palaces, floating ships, and angels, one above the other in a dream-like profusion. Even Dürer tried to make real the unreal, in order to make it convincing. Duvet seems to deprive classical Renaissance forms of all real effects, as, for instance, extension in space, logical connection, tectonic accents. The seven-headed dragon which carries the Babylonian harlot on his back rises like lingering columns of smoke. The flaming cities and the wondering men are pressed into the intervals wherever uncovered space gaped. Oppressive peril, threatening cataclysm, and conflagration of the world impend. William Blake's visions are anticipated. The "Vision of the Seven Candlesticks" (Plate 8) roars with the swings of ellipses and circles. The mystical intersections of the circuits of celestial bodies rather than southern tectonics are the ruling laws of this composition. The figures are swerving orna-ments instead of tactile solids, but ornaments which speak, which express something—fear, terror, majesty, but also glowing fervor and soothing grace.

Nothing can be compared to the arousing visionariness of Duvet's works except a few things in Old German art. Yet they must have found a deep response in the contemporary mind. The Gothic craving for expression is indelible in northern art. It breaks through even in the work of a foreigner like the somber, pathetic "Lamentation for Christ" which Il Rosso painted for the Castle of Écouen shortly before his death.

The Gothic trend in French Renaissance art increased in the second half of the sixteenth century and finally reached its climax

[18] Robert-Dumesnil, Nos. 27–49.

about 1600. The more the serenity of spirit which dominated the era of Francis I was replaced by a serious, contemplative, mournful mood (the general mood of the Western world in the era of the Counter-Reformation), the more the shadows of the Middle Ages raised their gigantic heads. The body is a prison from which the soul longs to be freed. The enjoyment of physical beauty and nature recedes. If the forms transcend nature, it is not in order to obey a canon of beauty, but to convey expression of soul, depth of sentiment. The light which illuminates the way of men is not sun and moon shining on *bosquets* with nymphs and fauns, but the light of religion, of faith, of the beyond, the light which shines with a supernatural glare at the end of the long, dark tunnel of earthly life. This feeling found its strongest expression in France in the sculptures of Germain Pilon, in the etchings and drawings of Jacques Bellange, and in the writings of St. François de Sales.

Germain Pilon, born in 1535, had passed through Fontainebleau in his youth.[19] He carved several decorative sculptures for the garden. Yet in contrast to Goujon, whose main works were of profane character and served decorative purposes, Pilon struck the serious and solemn note in the style of Fontainebleau. So he turned to ecclesiastic and funereal sculpture. From 1560 to 1563 he carved the three genii who carry the urn with the embalmed heart of Henry II (Louvre). Pilon's works keep a royal pomp, especially the large tombs, but they grow in devout somberness, expressiveness, and realism. Medieval qualities increasingly penetrate the Renaissance nobility. These sculptures are mementos of the vanity of earthly splendor. The "Tomb of Valentine Balbiani" (Louvre), begun in 1572, shows the deceased in her most beautiful array, accompanied by her little pet dog, resting on the slab;[20] a bas-relief

[19] J. Babelon, *Germain Pilon* (Paris, 1927).

[20] Flavinio de Birague wrote this eulogy on the little animal (Babelon, *op. cit.*, p. 67):

Épitaphe d'un petit chien de Madame la chancelière de Birague

Ce petit chien aima tellement sa maistresse,
Qu'après qu'elle eut quitté la terre pour les cieux,
Le regret causa tant en son cœur de tristesse,
Qu'après trois jours laissa le vivre soucieux.

on the sarcophagus represents her in repelling realism, lying in the coffin, naked, a decaying corpse, almost a skeleton. The large tomb of Henry II and Catherine de Medici in the Abbey Church of St. Denis, on which Pilon worked from 1563 to 1570, shows the deceased in their royal state kneeling on the platform of the chapel. Inside, they lie naked on the pall, stripped of all their splendor, human wrecks like any poor beggar. The realism has the sole purpose of directing the minds of the onlookers toward the beyond. Akin to El Greco in spirit is the "Mater Dolorosa" in the Church of St. Paul in Paris, perhaps the most sublime and spiritualized work of this greatest French sculptor of the century (Plate 9).[21] Out of a mass of drapery, the noble, straight silhouette of her body frees itself, rising like a Gothic tower. Her head is bent in silent mourning. There the most beautiful works of French Gothic come to life again. As ecstatic in expression is the kneeling St. Francis in the Church St. Jean-St. François. He receives the stigmata, enraptured in sacred inspiration, giving up himself to the vision of the Crucified. The marble seems to be pervaded by an inner light, the light of religious fervor and devotion. Both works were done in the 1580's and are worthy contemporaries of El Greco's altar paintings.

The highest degree of spiritualization, of expressive transformation of reality, and of estrangement from nature was reached in the art of Jacques Bellange. It is the very quintessence of Mannerism, refined to the utmost subtlety and losing all earthly weight. Bellange's figures seem to glide like flames over the ground without touching it. We know little about his life. Bellange was court painter to the Duke of Lorraine. His traceable activity covers the years from 1602 to 1619. He was a belated artist, working far into the seventeenth century, which followed up ideals different from his. His work was a late fruit of Mannerism—this may explain its unmatched expressive refinement. He executed decorative paintings for the Palace of Nancy and altarpieces for the

[21] The terra-cotta model for the marble sculpture in St. Paul, in original size, is preserved in the Louvre. Pilon received the marble block for the sculpture, an order of Catherine de Medici, on April 4, 1586. Babelon, op. cit., p. 68.

churches of the city. Nothing has survived of them; only the delightful proofs of his draughtsmanship and graphic art are preserved. The decorative paintings of festivals and masquerades followed the program of Fontainebleau. Yet we may assume from the drawings that all features of classical beauty in them were distorted as in a magic mirror to a fantastic, ghostlike world (Plate 12).[22] Figures seem to be no longer those of human beings but of exotic flowers and plants. They palpitate and flare.

The same strangeness of form was applied by Bellange to his religious works. The final aim of this Mannerism was not a superficial play of formal devices, but expression of soul, as tender and delicate as may be imagined. An admirable red chalk drawing in the Albertina (Plate 10)[23] shows the "Three Marys at the Sepulchre," mystical souls whose subtle emotions are revealed in the touch of their long fingers. They are the very embodiment of that beauty of the soul of which St. François de Sales wrote in his *Philothée* or *Introduction a la Vie dévote*, published in 1609.[24] Philothée is a noble lady whom the saint instructs in keeping the

[22] In 1924 a highly important one of these drawings passed unrecognized through a sale in Paris. "Dessins anciens," Collection de M. X***, Hotel Drouot, vendredi 11 avril, 1924, No. 37, "Hendrik Goltzius, La chasse au cerf." It was of considerable size (405 × 500 mm.) and represented a stag hunt in the style of the courtly tapestries. Rich washes, which anticipated much of the technique of Callot, lent a magic chiaroscuro effect to it. After publication of the first edition of the present book the drawing turned up again and was acquired by the Musée Historique Lorrain, Nancy.

The present author was also able to form a little group of easel paintings by J. Bellange with the "Annunciation of the Virgin" in Karlsruhe as a nucleus. To this group belong: the "Carrying of the Cross," Graz, Museum Joanneum (attributed by the present author to Bellange in *Blätter für Heimatkunde* 7. g., Heft 5, Graz, 1929, p. 72); the "Banquet of Herod" in the Alte Pinakothek, Munich; the huge "Banquet of Herod" in the Prado, Madrid (oral attribution by Ludwig Burchard).

[23] O. Benesch, *Meisterzeichnungen der Albertina*, Salzburg, 1964, No. 208 and plate.

[24] The inner affinity of Bellange's art to the mystical trend in the thought of St. François de Sales was pointed out by Dvořák, "Über Greco," p. 272. St. François' religious thought had also a rational aspect which found its parallels in the works of Bellange's follower Jacques Callot. See O. Benesch, *Artistic and Intellectual Trends from Rubens to Daumier* (Harvard College Library, 1943), p. 20.

soul untouched amid the conventions of social life and directed toward the higher spiritual realm. She is taught how to meditate, to place herself in the presence of the Lord, to purify herself from affectations. The tendency of this book is toward a mystical yielding to God, as glowing and boundless as that of the great mystics of the fourteenth century, yet more intimate, more personal, keeping within the framework of style and fashion of the time. We may imagine Philothée to be like one of the three damosels who converse with the angel at the tomb after the Resurrection.[25] They rise like strange tulips in the Lord's flower garden. Their coiffures, their flowing silk robes, accord with the taste of the time. The small heads are burdened with fluffy wigs, the hands twist in precious gestures.

Do these mundane traits mean a profanation of a sacred subject? Far from that. In their courtly exquisiteness, they are intended to impart the miraculous, mysterious supernatural of the holy event. The perfume of their beautiful souls extinguishes the difference of coarse matters. Nude skin and garment merge into one unity which is neither flesh nor cloth but a new purified substance, an emanation of the mystical feeling. Religious art of the international style about 1400 produced similar forms.

In the large etching the "Carrying of the Cross,"[26] a mighty choir of such extravagant figures rises, weightless and uncorporeal, like pouring columns of smoke, out of which faces emerge as if seen in a dream. Bellange had been in Italy and learned from the works of the Sienese Mannerists, who presented similar mystical tendencies, but his boundless subjectivism dismissed the last vestiges of formal logic indispensable with Italian art.

The art of Bellange in its expressive climax seems to bring about the very last fulfillment of Mannerism as the penetration of the ancient revival with the spirituality of the Middle Ages.

[25] Etching, Robert-Dumesnil, Vol. 5, No. 9.
[26] Robert-Dumesnil, No. 7.

13 At Amiens: From the Renaissance to the Counter-Reformation[1]

LUCIEN FEBVRE

EVERY age has its own style—or, perhaps, its own climate, to use a more modest and yet at the same time more embracing term. And this is not only true of art and literature. If historians were to concern themselves with something better than mere parrotry they would certainly find that this notion of style or climate would enable them to characterize more clearly the successive periods in the life of a human community or group—and, what is very much to the point, to characterize them in terms of something genuinely intrinsic. This intrinsic element may seem to be too intimate and secret to be accurately defined; nonetheless, it is clearly to be seen in everything about a particular country in a particular age—its material or intellectual achievements, its political systems or philosophical theories, its religious beliefs or social activities.

But what is the best way to give an account of the changes of style (or climate) which take place when one "age" moves into the next? This is rather like trying to find a keyboard on which to move one's fingers at a constant speed from one end of the register to the other while listening carefully for all the possible different tones. The obvious place is an archive, which offers whole series of documents in order, and where comparisons can be made over a long period of time. For example, much light can be thrown on politics by the debates held in assemblies, law courts, or town councils. And again, other useful information can be found in a set of inventories of furniture or from inventories of a dead man's estate.

Historians up to now have not profited as much from such

[1] Article published in *Annales d'histoire sociale*, III (1941), 41–55.

documents as they both could and should have.[2] There is a
tendency to consider them as so much bric-à-brac, especially
among historians who frequent the big, imposing archives—the
archives which make the self-important historian conversant with
governments, sovereigns, and state secrets. Bric-à-brac they may
be, and there is certainly a bit of everything to be found in them.
And yet, as will be seen, there are also some remarkable documents
which make it possible to trace the course of religious, intellectual,
and moral history.

To take one example among any number of others, consider the
municipal archives of Amiens, the principal city of the Somme.
Amiens is in Picardy, a frontier province which has borne the
brunt of many battles. It is a city which has kept up its connections,
in an easy, comfortable sort of way, with Paris, which is not too
near and not too far; yet at the same time it never made, nor was
it ever in a position to make, those endless wishful comparisons
with the capital in that spirit of rivalry which occupied such a
large part of Rouen's history under the *ancien régime*.[3] It is a rich,
active, agricultural city, the city of gardens, and a busy center of
trade and production, as well as the capital of the French fine-cloth
industry. It was also one of the principal centers for river traffic.
Above all, it was always open to attack. Anyone who wants to
find out more about the history of the word "frontier" should go
through the documents of Amiens. He would find them most
revealing. Situated very near to the Low Countries, and to
England also, it was always threatened and often occupied. Until
a rather late date, it was the place to which all those who nourished
political schemes in France turned. Even at the beginning of the
seventeenth century, for instance, in June, 1611, Concini had

---

[2] But some of these collections have proved their worth; every historian of
Burgundy, for example, knows how much there is to be drawn from the
inventories published by Prost.

[3] It was encouraged in this by its claim to be the second city of the realm.
Cf. Louis Huygens (1655) in his "Journal de voyage" (*Gazette des Beaux-Arts*,
II [1937], 93): "From what we were able to judge, it is much greater than any
city in Holland, except for Amsterdam, to which, as is generally believed, it
concedes very little. After Paris it is thought to be the first in size in all France."

himself appointed governor of the city. In 1619 Luynes succeeded the Duc de Longueville there as governor of Picardy. The king, the queen, and all the princes made a point of stopping there to make their presence felt. Amiens is an excellent witness of French history.

The city has in its archives an admirable series of estate inventories, covering a fairly large period—from the end of the fifteenth century to the French Revolution. Running parallel to these is a fine collection of municipal debates and a complete set of accounts. The three series are excellently spaced out in such a way as to complete and confirm one another. And, what is more, they have all been catalogued, perhaps with some prolixity, by one of those painstaking archivists who have rendered such sterling services to the study of history;[4] services which owing to the failings of historians, have sometimes remained in vain. "Copiousness" might be a better word than "prolixity" in this instance; this abundance has proven very useful, because we are not going back to the originals themselves. The present aim is not to compose an archival study as such, but to address an exhortation to future researchers. Reference will be made here only to inventories, and a single example will suffice to show what can be learned from them.

The impressive series of inventories starts from the middle of the fifteenth century. There are the usual mentions of movable furniture, implements, provisions of all sorts, linen, clothes, and all the many other things which accumulate in long-established households. But there are also books to be found, together with what might be called works of art, though this is sometimes too ambitious a term,[5] and *objets d'art*.

[4] Amiens, Communal Archives before 1790. Vols. II and III, series BB, by G. Durand, Amiens (1894–7), quarto; *ibid.*, Vols. IV and V, series CC (1901–5); *ibid.*, Vols. VI and VII, series FF (1911–25).

[5] In this sketch I propose to leave aside everything concerned specifically with the history of art. The names of the painters and sculptors then at work in Amiens, the artistic value of works appearing in the inventories and their origins—there is no time to go into all this. But anyone who made the effort would find himself well repaid.

As for works of art and antiques, it is instructive to follow the inventory abstracts, starting from the first two or three decades of the sixteenth century. About 1560–70 there seems to be a change of tone.[6]

Before this turning point, between about 1545 and 1550, there are few if any secular representations. There are no landscapes, no family portraits—at least in the households of burghers—nor even any portraits of French monarchs. But the Virgin Mary is to be found everywhere, painted, carved, or engraved; occasionally only one, but mostly two or three, and of various sorts: Our Lady of Pity, Our Lady of the Seven Dolors, but much more rarely any depiction of the Annunciation or of Mary with other saints, such as St. Bernard or St. Joseph. Among representations of the Divinity, the Crucifixion was to be found very nearly everywhere (though every now and again there was a Holy Shroud of cloth brought back from a pilgrimage, a miniature Calvary, a Holy Sepulcher and a Veronica); also, now and then, an *Ecce Homo* or a *Pietà*. And then, naturally, there were the familiar figures of men and women saints: heads of St. John, mainly against the setting of Amiens, the city which since 1206 had prided itself on its possession

[6] This might well be the place for a fine debate about methodology, but I have no intention of entering into one. I am taking it absolutely for granted that all readers of the *Annales* are possessed of common sense, and I do not intend to lay down the law about the attitude they should adopt. There is obviously only one precise date furnished by an inventory of a dead man's estate—the date of his death. After all, an old man who died in 1620 would not have bought all his effects, pictures (if any), or books in 1619; moreover, he would not have purchased all that he possessed, since many things would have been inherited. All this goes without saying. But it is always possible to give a date to books: a book published in 1560 would not have been bought in 1530. Fashions in art can also be dated, not quite so rigorously, but in terms of general trends. A wooden table with convoluted legs, decorated with stylized dragonfly heads, with a top inlaid with a tracery of wild bryony—this can be dated without any hesitation as 1900 (school of Nancy). It might be 1898, or 1904, or even 1910. But there is no need to be too finicky—this is, broadly speaking, 1900. It is not bad to be able to date styles to within ten years, and one would be very lucky to be able to do the same when it came to ideas or moral attitudes. As for *objets d'art*, there is nothing whatever to stop the historian from turning, when need arises, to the best local antiquarian for advice. After all, a good antiquarian will have seen a great deal and may even have remembered a great deal.

of the front of St. John the Baptist's skull; likewise Michael, James, Nicholas, Jerome, Christopher, and Sebastian, all of whom were subjects of devotion for easily understandable reasons, whether of profession or of circumstance. St. Jerome was the great patron of clerics; St. Sebastian of archers (hardly surprising in Picardy), and at the same time one of the great protectors against the plague; St. Christopher afforded protection against sudden death, and so on. Everything was very straightforward.

As for women saints, St. Barbara with her tower came first, then St. Catherine and her wheel, St. Margaret, the patron of mothers in labor, and, already, two or three Mary Magdalens. All this, of course, is only a very quick survey and makes no claim to statistical accuracy; the sole purpose is to provide a basis for comparison.

But after the turning point between 1560–70, a sudden expansion and change of direction are to be seen; these constitute a minor iconographic revolution.

Pictures of the divinity were there as always: the *Ecce Homo* (though not as common as before), and everywhere, of course, the Crucifixion. But everywhere, also, there was a hitherto unusual number of pictures of Christ, both as a man and, more frequently, as a child, together with *Agnus Deis* and depictions of scenes from the Passion, such as Christ carrying his cross, Veronica, and occasionally a Calvary and a Garden of Olives.

There were more pictures of the Virgin Mary than ever. Our Lady of the Seven Dolors had recently become popular and was very frequently to be found from about 1560 to 1565, as well as depictions of Our Lady stemming from the various centers of pilgrimage, such as Notre-Dame de Liesse, Notre-Dame du Puy, or Notre-Dame de Boulogne. Yet clearly the most popular of all was the cult of the Virgin of Pity, which had probably been revived about this time by Annibale Carracci, who had followed Correggio and broken with the old traditions of the fifteenth century.

As for the saints, the head of St. John was as common as ever, but St. Michael was not far behind. St. James seems to have been less in favor after 1565, but Jerome, Nicholas, and Sebastian still figured. And at about this time appeared a very popular newcomer —St. Claude, the miracle-worker of the Jura. To find out whether this popularity was temporary, accidental, or fairly widespread it would be necessary to make a comparison with other similar studies;[7] but the Amiens records seem to suggest that it was at its height from 1580 onward. Among women saints, Mary Magdalen came into very real favor and was soon to become the patron saint *par excellence* of the beautiful penitents of the Fronde who, having sinned boldly, knew how to repent in the grand style.[8] But even around this time she was starting to take a real hold on people's affections. St. Barbara remained as popular as ever, though St. Margaret appears to have lost ground.

At this point it might be a good idea to set all these pictures of men and women saints alongside the Christian names of those who were inventoried about this time. This is easy enough to do, though it requires patience.

I myself took from these inventories between 1520 and 1540 a total of 861 individuals—597 men and 264 women; among the 597 men there were 91 different Christian names (of which 19 appeared only once). Moreover, from the period 1600 to 1622 I took down the Christian names of 1,983 individuals: 1,256 men (104 Christian names) and 727 women (60 Christian names). In the first group (1520–40) there was an overwhelming predominance of Jean, in all 174. Then Pierre (72), Jacques (38), Nicolas, or occasionally Nicole (35), Guillaume (31), Antoine (20), Robert

---

[7] My own knowledge of the subject is not of very great assistance: St. Claude belonged essentially to the people of the Franche-Comté, and the texts here give little information about his popularity. There is, however, no question about his popularity in Amiens. Cf. series FF, II, 722–3 (1579), 792 (1588), 803–4 (1591–2), and so on.

[8] Bremond has written interestingly on the cult of Mary Magdalen in seventeenth-century France, as well as on its development and significance. Epic poems were already being composed in her honor (1606, 1608, 1617, 1628); cf. the statistics given by R. Toinet (*Quelques Recherches autour des poèmes héroïques-épiques*, Tulle, 1897–1907).

(16), Adrien (13), François and Simon (both 10), Firmin (9), and Mathieu (9). It is important not to be sidetracked by certain others, though these could hardly help being of the greatest interest to a student of Picardy and its traditions. This list of Christian names is a veritable storehouse of keepsakes, lit up by some very singular *hapax legomena*, such as a Vespasien; this, however, is nothing compared with the Saturne which, in all its magnificence, could be seen attached in 1494 to one Saturne Karuel, an Amiens tavern-keeper.[9] And then, the women. Jeanne was first (73), followed by Marie (only 39) and Marguerite (19), which means that about one girl in three was called Jeanne, one in six Marie, and one in twelve Marguerite. Then there were Colaye (13), Catherine and Isabeau (both 12), Antoinette (9), Barbe (only 5), and Madeleine (4). It can be seen that the presence of images of male and female saints in a household was very far from being explained by the popular choices of Christian names. Jeanne and Colaye are never represented among the pictures of saints to be found in the effects of households in Amiens; at the same time, despite the rarity of the name Barbe, there were many pictures of St. Barbara to be found. It was certainly the men who in the main instituted the domestic cult of women saints, though it is open to question whether this was intended as a mark of honor to their wives. In the same way, although there were any number of statues, pictures, and engravings of St. Jerome, St. Christopher, and St. Sebastian in the houses, one would probably not have encountered very many men called Jerome, Christophe, or Sebastien walking about in the streets.

[9] Most probably a form of Saturnin—St. Saturinus, protector of the ovine race. Among the *hapax legomena* are to be found Betremieu, Ernoul, Enguerran, Eletre, Flourens, Guérard, Gentian, Hutin, Ildevert, Jacotin, Raoulant, Saturnin, Tassin, and Valent. In Amiens, as can be seen, there were not only old inhabitants faithful to the glories of their diocese: St. Firminius, set up on the door of the cathedral, who seems, by his very air of deep certitude, to be imparting a blessing; the martyrs Gentian, Fuscian, and Victorix; the ancient bishops, with St. Honorius at their head; also Domice and Geoffroy, and, for the women, Ulphe. Information about all this can be found in Corblet, *Hagiographie du diocèse d'Amiens*. (From 1610 to 1622 there were 18 Firmins, 3 Fuscians, 1 Honoré, and 1 Gentian.)

This study cannot be taken just as it stands—it needs to be carried further with the help of cross-checks and comparisons, and always with the lightest possible touch.

Now let us turn to the second group, the Christian names taken from the inventories between 1600 and 1622. Jean (246) and Pierre (115) were still in first place, but Pierre was followed very closely by Antoine (105). In the first group Antoine and Pierre were respectively 20 and 72, but in the second 105 and 115; an age of hermits. After this come Nicolas (85), Jacques (71), and a sudden resurgence of François (42), which might be a sign of loyalty to the royal house. But Henri was scarcely to be found (only 7 out of 1,256); this would seem to suggest that the monarch who was defeated at Saint-Quentin and who allowed himself to be despoiled at Cateau was not especially popular in Amiens. Whatever the reason, it is quite probable that a fair proportion of those named François in these documents had received the name out of devotion to the Poverello of Assisi, patron of the Observantines (or "Cordeliers") and Capuchins, rather than to King Francis. Claude had become more numerous than in earlier years (33), which links up with the observation made earlier about the multiplication of devotional objects in honor of St. Claude: there were only two Claudes in the 1520–40 group. As against this, Michel was hardly represented (11 out of 1,256).

Among the women's names the first thing to note is a complete overthrow: the Virgin Mary had effectively ousted St. Joan, with 180 against 98, respectively. Considering the date, this could lead to some very interesting reflections. In fourth place comes Françoise, to go with the 51 François just mentioned: this is a considerable jump from the 5 (out of 264) of the preceding period. Then there are Catherine (39), Antoinette (33, to go with the 105 Antoines) and Anne (29)—but the 28 Madeleines confirm the new popularity of Mary Magdalen, since there were only 4 (out of 264) in the earlier period.

All this, of course, raises problems which cannot be considered here, since this is a sketch and not a detailed study. But one thing is worth noting. We are all too easily inclined to forget the particular hold which the religious orders had on the men and women of other ages. How is their influence to be measured? Time and again, after a given date, there can be found evidence of particular devotions associated with particular saints' names, and it is here that the influence of the religious orders can be seen: the Minims for St. Francis de Paul [their fifteenth-century founder], and the Augustinians for the evocation of St. Nicholas of Tolentino, patron of the souls in purgatory and protector against the plague— just like St. Louis. In the same way, there was that form of the Passion cult which consisted in calling to mind certain topographical details of the Holy Land—this points to the Franciscans, the guardians of the Holy Sepulcher, who organized the *Via crucis*, along which the pilgrims would go, starting from the house of Pilate, passing by the place where St. Veronica performed her pious office, and finishing up at Calvary. Over the years this gradually became codified into the fourteen classic Stations of the Cross. It is possible to piece together a whole series of such groupings and, so to speak, hagiographical families, sometimes very unexpected, like the devotion to St. Louis which the Franciscans were so fond of propagating—the pious king, according to tradition, had become a Franciscan tertiary. The Archangel Michael was very close to their hearts and figured greatly in their devotions, which is a reminder of how faithfully he had been honored by St. Francis himself.

All this is worthy of examination and close study, and I am convinced that such work would be repaid by very substantial results. But—and this must be repeated—only on one condition; several similar parallel studies should be undertaken at the same time. They need not be restricted to the sixteenth century, since the period 1540–80 was not the only one, either in France or elsewhere, to see changes of style. At the present time I am in a position to make only one other comparison: the Franche-Comté under Charles V and Philip II.[10] This particular comparison—

[10] Cf. Lucien Febvre, *Philippe II et la Franche-Comté* (Paris: Champion, 1911), Chapters x and xi ("La vie bourgeoise," "La vie noble").

insufficient as it is (for various reasons)—has led me to believe that the results of five or six studies carried out simultaneously in very different places (e.g., Bordeaux, Toulouse, Grenoble, and Lyons, then Tours, Rouen, Amiens, and Beauvais—and I am suggesting these places without any previous examination of the documents they have to offer) would be of the utmost interest and would lead to some very important conclusions about the history both of religious devotions and of the people's loyalty to king or region.

It is now time to close this excursion into the realm of Christian names and return to our domestic iconography of the years following 1560. At first there were numerous allegories, evidence of that renewal of taste for symbols which had spread all over Christendom from Italy. There were the four elements, the seven liberal arts, the three theological virtues, and an abundance (not to say a luxuriance) of Roman charities.[11] But there was a new addition: in all the inventories there were now "stories." Stories from pagan antiquity, such as the Judgment of Paris, Hero and Leander, chaste Lucretia, Lycaon, Bacchus, Venus, and so forth. Sacred stories, above all scenes from the Old Testament, and illustrations of "sacred history": the Creation of Man, Adam and Eve, the Flood, Abraham offering sacrifice, Isaac and Jacob, Jonah and the Whale, Tobias and the Angel, Lot and his daughters, Susannah and the elders, that holy man Job, Solomon and the Queen of Sheba, Judith (and Holofernes), Esther, and finally the Prodigal Son, the prodigious growth in whose popularity at this

[11] The following, for instance, can be found in 1585 in the inventory of Pierre Poitevin: four pictures on wood, representing the Last Supper, the story of Lot, the three virtues, and Apollo and the seven liberal arts. Provided all necessary allowances are made for the lapse of time, it can be seen that this burgher reproduced the interesting medley of taste to be found in the rich collection of the widow of the high and powerful Adrien de Pisseleu, Mme. Charlotte d'Ailly, who had been inventoried in 1575: four pictures painted on wood, consisting of a girl offering her breast to her father; King Francis; Lucretia; the Comte de Rhingrave; "the old man who used his two daughters"; and Adam and Eve. Also two pictures, one of Mary Magdalen, the other of Venus, etc.

time needs no reminder. And this is only a random selection of the subjects depicted as shown by the inventories.[12]

This is a change of climate indeed, though it should not be forgotten that these subjects, which the local painters, inhabitants and visitors alike so loved to treat, and which were sometimes drawn into the margins of Amiens documents, had a meaning for the people of Amiens—and a very clear meaning, at that. Amiens Cathedral, after all, was the "messianic cathedral" par excellence, the prophetic cathedral in which every arch, portal, and window seemed to foretell the coming of the Lord. Adam, Solomon, Abraham, Tobias, Judith, Esther—all were the most familiar and popular prefigurations of John and Mary. This lively taste for scenes from sacred history might almost be better described as a revival than as something new, were it not for so many other considerations from the history of literature and religion; for instance, the fascination for the Old Testament among the teachers of the Reformation, who drew the Catholic controversialists along in their train and at the same time set in motion an army of playwrights (about whom details have been made available in recent studies on the theater, notably those of Lebègue).[13] In any case, one both can and must talk of a new climate—the atmosphere and, if the expression is not too strong, the décor of prayer had changed.

The inventories of 1520, 1530, and 1540 still enable one to evoke the silent, modest dialogue which the faithful of that age, receptive above all to the appeal of the New Testament, held in their homes

[12] Here are some samples: 1578, the wife of an elected official: "Two pictures painted on canvas (Solomon and the Queen of Sheba, a dying man and a Mary Magdalen)." 1578, the wife of a burgher: "A picture of painted canvas upon which is depicted Charity; a canvas upon which is painted . . . the story of Queen Esther; a picture painted on wood, upon which is . . . the story of Susannah." 1578, a notary's wife: "A canvas upon which is painted the miracle of the seven barley loaves; six leaves of paper upon which is painted the story of St. Paul." There are frequent mentions of these "leaves of painted paper": e.g., 1585, six pieces of paper, painted, comprising the stories of Tobias and Job.

[13] Theater, art, and devotion—these offer a whole new series of studies to be undertaken, both at this date and throughout the period. The tools are to hand, at least for the theater; only the workers are needed.

before a deeply moving picture of the *Pietà*, Our Lady, or some
favorite member of the Heavenly Court of Paradise. But from the
inventories of 1600, 1610, and 1620 it can clearly be seen in
Amiens, in the houses of the poor as well as those of the com-
fortably rich, that piety had taken on a new coloring. One very
typical example is the depiction of the Divinity. From 1540
onward there appeared, at first only very occasionally, then
gradually in increasing numbers, and finally as a matter of course,
the mention of "petits Jésus," gilded, clothed, and embellished.
The following, from 1561, belonged to a painter of modest means
named Pierre Cado: "An image of Jesus in wood, painted and
gilded, clad in a robe of damask and a shift of linen trimmed with
false gold." Among the rich the imitation gold became genuine
gold; and very often the piety of people in Amiens did not rest
content with one "petit Jésus" in gilded wood. There is frequently
mention of two, or even three, as in the case of Marie de Sachy
(d. 1594): "An image of Jesus clad in a robe of yellow velvet;
another image of Jesus, clad in cloth of gold; another, clad in a
robe of red velvet, and adorned with a head ornament." But the
normal thing was to have two statuettes, dressed either exactly
alike or in deliberate, careful contrast.[14] And then a new fashion
became established: the "little jars for nosegays," intended for
nosegays of artificial flowers, or nosegays of silk and gold thread,
and sometimes even carved nosegays in gilded wood—in other
words, the sort of thing one would expect to find in little wayside
altars, of a rather doll-like type, completely new in style and

[14] The following will serve as examples: 1540 (probably for the very first
time): "A little Jesus, gilded, with two little robes of silk satin and satin from
Bruges" (belonging to a merchant). Also 1540 (a goldsmith): "A little Jesus and
an image of Our Lady, the whole in gilded wood." 1541: "A Jesus clad in a
robe of red damask and with a bonnet of crimson velvet." For the two images,
cf. 1587: "Two images of Jesus in wood painted and gilded, each adorned with
a vestment, the one in a robe of violet velvet, figured, and stitched with gold
thread; the other in a robe of grey damask, likewise stitched with gold thread."
1595: "Two images of Jesus, adorned with two caps of velvet, accoutred in red
silk satin." 1598 (Marie Cantereine, a merchant's wife): "In a cabinet of wood
lined with Ascot serge, two little Jesuses clad in their robes, with a crown." And
so on.

somewhat finical in taste.[15] It was a taste for embellishment, gilt, and prettiness, and also, as the Old Testament scenes suggest, for stage trappings and theatrical presentation. It came from Flanders (and the Amiens documents say so expressly, since they mention little statuettes of Jesus "after the fashion of Flanders," and silk nosegays "after the fashion of Flanders"), from that citadel of baroque art, pompous and somewhat carnal, all lit up with gilt, which seemed to want to turn churches into triumphal arches. . *Ad majorem Dei gloriam.* It is worth remarking that this cult of the "little Jesus" in many ways preceded, without in any way recalling, the cult of the Child Jesus in the seventeenth century, the most engaging account of which was given by Henri Bremond in his great work, *Histoire littéraire du sentiment religieux en France.* The statuettes of the "little Jesus" in Amiens at the end of the sixteenth century and those of the little King of Glory of Sister Margaret of the Blessed Sacrament had nothing in common; here, too, there was a complete break and a change of climate.

There must be no mistake about the effigies from the end of the sixteenth century—they definitely reveal a change of taste, a clear sign of which, surely, is that sudden influx of "landscapes" (generally forming pairs or pendants)[16] among the effects inventoried from 1560-5 onward. "Six painted canvases, framed in wood, called landscapes": so runs a document of 1566 (FF 339). Landscapes, Old Testament scenes—which, in accordance with the fashion of the time, were almost half landscape—and colored devotional pictures, the sort of thing loved by old maids and by those who liked their piety aroused by an appeal to the flesh and

[15] 1578: "Two little jars of blue glass for the placing of nosegays." 1587: "Two images of Jesus . . . two large nosegays of silk, after the fashion of Flanders." Also 1587: "Two little jars for nosegays adorned with gold and silk, and several little dolls and nosegays of gold and silk." 1589: "An image of the Virgin Mary with several nosegays of silk; another in gold, and several nosegays in silk and gold thread." 1610: "A cabinet of oak wood, covered with glass, in which is an image of Jesus, with other little images and silken nosegays." And so on.

[16] Cf. 1566: "Two landscapes"; 1568: "Two landscapes"; 1580: "A large picture of painted canvas upon which is depicted a landscape"; 1595: "A picture upon which is represented a landscape."

the senses, pretty-pretty and somewhat infantile: all these go to form a climate. And again, the appearance in the inventories of objects such as "a little picture in silver, being the effigy of Cardinal Borromeo," or "the spoon of St. Francis de Paul," and an oil portrait of St. Francis de Paul, all direct our attention, as if that were needed toward historical and local origins.

The Amiens inventories do not contain only effigies or pictures. There are always books to be found, either very few or a great number. It is very rare for an inventory not to mention at least one or two, and such "solitaries" are often very curious indeed: generally they were not modern books but cast-outs, old books (sometimes odd), the remains of unwanted incunabula, or manuscripts, which had all ended up among people of rather humble station.[17]

The following are to be found for the years from 1530 to 1550. Throughout the inventories were French Bibles and New Testaments. In a priest's house, the Passion in French. *L'Exposition des Épîtres et Évangiles de l'année* in French was very common, and *L'Exposition de Oraison dominicale*, also in French. Beside these were devotional books: the *Légende Dorée*, often reprinted; the *Internelle Consolation*, which was the French version of the Latin *Imitation of Christ*; the long-established *Art de bien mourir*, which still had a long run ahead of it; the Psalter with Lira's commentary—and the Books of Hours.

It would be as well to leave aside the professional books, the books of law and civil procedure, the *Somme rurale*, the *Propriétaire des choses*, and the *Calendrier des bergers*. There was no shortage of classical authors, either in Latin or in French: Cicero, Vergil, Ovid, Catullus, and Aristotle's *Ethics*; from 1540 onward there were some copies of Erasmus and the *De elegantia linguae latinae* of Laurenzo

---

[17] E.g., in 1603, belonging to a lead-worker, the *Chroniques de France* "in scrolls, with a wooden cover." The *Annales de France* often finished their days among people of humble station: in 1583 a carpenter; in 1598 a master carpenter, together with a Bible, and so on. Nearly everywhere the *Vie des saints* was to be found in homes with only one book.

Valla, but no Plutarch. Classical literature had not ousted the old French literature, and the romances were always represented: the *Roman de la Rose*, the Round Table, Lancelot of the Lake, the Destruction of Troy, Ogier the Dane, Valentine and Orson, and so forth. Occasionally there was a copy of the *Cent Nouvelles*. There were very few histories: now and again a *Mer des chroniques*, a *Fleur des histoires*, and a *Rosier des histoires* (of France).

But in 1608 comes the inventory of a wealthy burgher, Jean Bultel (FF 588). A Greek-Latin New Testament bears witness to the intellectual quality of the deceased.[18] Erasmus had disappeared, and Scaliger was there instead; and Plutarch took his place beside Pliny. An interest in geography is revealed, most notably by the *Cosmographie* of Belleforest and the short *Description du monde* by this same plagiarizer of [Sebastian] Munster. An interest in history, too, for here are to be found the two folios of the *Grandes Annales et histoires générales de France* by the same Belleforest (1579). There is also the *Histoire des troubles*, together with a Froissard and a Commynes. Poetical relaxation was afforded by copies of Baïf, du Bartas and Pontus de Tyard.

An interesting comparison is provided in 1611 by the inventory of a squire, François de Louvencourt (FF 651). There was no Bible or New Testament; the great standby was that voluminous work of the famous Père Coton, S.J., the *Institution catholique* (1610), intended as an antidote to Calvin's *Institution chrétienne*. Side by side with these was the *Justes grandeurs de l'Église romaine*. An oil portrait of St. Francis de Paul, the founder of the Minims, gave some final touches to the general picture of this great Catholic figure of the Counter-Reformation. There was no Erasmus here either, but instead Scaliger, Justus Lipsius, and Tacitus. Amyot's Plutarch was represented here as everywhere else at the time. To satisfy the interest of the deceased in geography, there was the

---

[18] The New Testament in Greek and Latin was often to be met with in the homes of booksellers or lettered men: in 1538, Marie Cousin, a bookseller's wife; and in 1587, the lawyer Fournier, together with Erasmus, Vivès, Ramus, Alciati's *Emblèmes*, the *Decameron*, and Rabelais.

Théâtre des provinces et cités du monde of Ortelius, without detriment, of course, to J. Hugue's *Navigation*.

It would be well to go on marking out the main trends. The reader must not go away feeling that the idea of a "change of style" is an empty phrase; nor must the historian think that he is being confronted merely by the fancies of one or two individuals rather than by a new and widespread set of thoughts and sentiments. For instance, in 1617 we find a lawyer, Jean Danès (FF 662). There was no Bible in his home, nor any New Testament;[19] instead, the *Histoire d'une mission de Capucins* and Jean Bodin's *Démonomanie*, which immediately show us exactly where we are. Danès too had an interest in geography: Jean Thevet's *Cosmographie universelle*, Belleforest's *Cosmographie universelle* and Leo the African's *Description de l'Afrique*. For his historical requirements, Danès read Belleforest's *Neuf Rois Charles*, Du Haillant's *Histoire générale des rois de France*, Guicciardini's *Histoire des Albigeois* and *Histoire des guerres d'Italie*, Martin du Bellay's *Mémoires*, and the *Histoire des princes de Pologne* and the *Antiquités et syngularités des villes de France*. He even dipped into contemporary sociology, since he possessed Jean Bodin's *République* and Simler's *République des Suisses*. As a little light relief from this heavyweight reading there were Boccaccio's *Decameron* (presumably in Antoine Le Maçon's translation), Ronsard's *Carmes*, and Garnier's *Tragédies*.

It would be rather tedious to continue this catalogue, since the same entries are to be found everywhere. There was a widening of outlook and more books catering for individual interests and pursuits. Worth mentioning also is a desire for scientific accuracy, starting now to make itself felt in the choice of words: after 1540, for instance, the older *"mesureur"* (measurer) was replaced by *"géomètre"*: "To Master Noël Gremer, Geometer . . . To Master Robert Dufour, likewise Geometer. . . ."[20] Later, in 1551, came

[19] The Bible seemed to become more and more the appanage and distinguishing mark of Protestants. It was to be found frequently in the homes of artisans (e.g., 1612, a master weaver, together with a Du Bartas).

[20] CC 136, f° 112, 1540.

the first reference to an "architect,"[21] hitherto always "master mason"; Rabelais' neologism had made great strides. Moreover, there was the curious personage who in 1551 bestowed upon himself the grandiose title of "master architect," and who, in one and the same year (1558), was able to draw up a map of Picardy, Boullenois, and Artois, and "with the aid of a compass to make a map" of the city of Amiens and its surroundings. With equal accuracy he helped the cause of justice by doing "portraits" of murder victims, thereby fulfilling such functions of a "police laboratory" as the judges of Picardy thought necessary at the time. Finally, in 1566, comes the first reference to an "engineer": "the engineer being then at Doullens. . . ." This means, of course, a military engineer.[22]

The geometer, the architect, and the engineer; the making of maps with compasses and the development of sophisticated cartography—all these form a point of departure for, and even represent the first fruits of, a culture influenced by scientific accuracy, an accuracy which had already left its mark on the men of those times. The way was being quietly paved for the "rational" seventeenth century.

It is now time to join up these scattered items—if the indications provided by the artistic and devotional objects are placed beside the contents of the books, it will be found that the general impression remains the same in both groups. And this impression is a very strong one.

Among the effects inventoried before 1560 there can be found

[21] Zacarie de Celers, "master architect," CC 156, f° 22. The activities of this character are frequently mentioned in the documents, and very varied they were. One day he was gilding and upholstering with gold and azure the fireplace of the council chamber (1545), on another he was assisting the cause of justice by drawing the place where a man and his wife had been found dead; he also made plans and did surveys for fortifications, which did not prevent him from devoting his attentions to archery targets, parish banners, and suchlike.

[22] CC 164, f° 27. Cf., later, 1574 (CC 201, f° 14 v°): "The portrait which the Sieur Belamat the younger, engineer, had commenced of the surroundings and fortress of the said city of Amiens."

things which aided people to pray to God in spirit, to put themselves in his presence, as represented by some serene or sorrowful effigy, and to pray directly and silently, without any ostentation. In the same way, the libraries before 1560 are witnesses to a worshiping in spirit, and their contents were conducive to this. Everywhere one finds the simplicity of the gospel, the sobriety of Lefèvre d'Étaples, and the slightly cold clarity of Erasmus, the Dutchman whose heart was rarely moved and who did not lend himself very easily to an aura. But after 1560 everything evidences a need for décor, pomp, and gilding, and a clear invitation to sensibility—a sensibility which was not without a certain eloquence. But was it not also around this time that the Amiens registers stopped referring to the king as "sire" or as "the King our master,"[23] and introduced the more stately and solemn "the King's Majesty?" Yet the libraries collected the mystics, the eloquent humanists, and the flowery literature of an age which could not think of the spirit alone without the flesh; an age which no longer cared to look upon the object of its devotion in all its nakedness, but wished to see it dressed up, embellished, framed, and cosily placed in a setting of intimacy. There was also the same feeling about nature, the taste for which remained firmly rooted among these townsmen, stubbornly determined as they were to have their fields and animals with them in the midst of their cities, and among those traveling merchants with so many contacts with faraway places, whose dreams extended beyond the already wide circle of their professional activities, to the fabulous Indies, to savage America, and to high adventure across the sea.

[23] This could well be followed up. My own findings suggest the following formula: "Le Roi notre Sire" until the middle of the sixteenth century (January 5, 1562, in an alderman's discourse, BB 35, f° 37 v°: "Soubs l'auctorité du Roy nostre sire." *Idem*, February, 1562, DD 35, f° 35). But already, in 1558 (CC 169): A Golden Fleece from the emperor went "devers la Majesté du Roy." Such texts could be multiplied. 1574, CC 201, f° 14: "Draw up a report for His Majesty." 1575, CC 203, fo 23 v°: "In a city assessed by His Majesty," and so on.

But this is not all. As we have already seen, there was a taste for history, but mainly French history;[24] and for maps, but mainly maps of the French kingdom. Likenesses of monarchs were starting to make an appearance in people's homes, doubtless the result of reflections on things French during the course of a long crisis. And at the same time, right opposite their kings, the burghers of Amiens would hang up pictures of themselves.[25] And why not? After all, their ancestors had already had the temerity to set up on the buttresses of the North Tower of their cathedral, side by side with the Virgin Mary and St. John (and not a bit smaller), statues of Charles V, the Dauphin (Charles VI), and the Duke of Orleans, and even of such *minores* as Councilor Bureau and Cardinal Lagrange. This introduction of royal portraits into Amiens households may not have been particularly widespread— but it must be remembered that there had been years of disputes and skirmishings, during which the city had been pulled about by the English, the Burgundians, the Spaniards, and the French, with the result that Amiens had never known which side it was supposed to be on (or, more exactly, had never been given much say in the matter)—nonetheless it would be surprising if the royal portraits did not tie up in some way with the taste for history. The link had

[24] And sometimes very contemporary history. The following is from the well-stocked library of Pierre Crocquoison, inventoried in 1580: Guicciardini, the *Discorsi* of Machiavelli, the *Récit de voyage* of King Charles, the *Généalogie des rois*, the *Sommaire des empereurs*, the *Chronique* of Jean Carion, the *République des Turcs*, the *Chronique de Pologne*, the *Discours politiques* of La Noue, and so on. Together with some Erasmus there were an Alciati, the "Marguerite des Marguerites," a Marot, a Rabelais, and the *Decameron*. This was 1580, and therefore before the great polemics of the Wars of Religion; traces of this are to be found everywhere in the inventories of 1600, 1610, and 1620.

[25] 1561, FF 717, 154: An Amiens burgher sued one Jean Prien, a painter, for late delivery of portraits. But it was not until later that portraits of burghers and comparatively humble people appear to any notable extent in the inventories: In 1587 a merchant tanner, a burgher and merchant, and a royal notary ("the portrait of the deceased and Demoiselle Marguerite de Miraulmont his wife"); in 1588 a sergeant of the court; in 1590 a whole tribe ("four pictures painted in oil, upon which are depicted the grandfather, grandmother, father, and mother of the deceased, and the father and mother of the minors of the family"— this was a burgher).

been forged in the Wars of Religion and in the crisis which saw the rebirth of France.[26]

But what is meant by France? The debate is endless. There could be no better way of getting our ideas right on this point than by reading through the lists of books in the inventories of two men of this time.

First, the books of Pierre de Famechon, a squire whose estate was inventoried in 1617 (FF 660). Famechon was a reader of Erasmus; he possessed the *Enchiridion*, the *De copia verborum*, the *Apophthegms*, the *Colloquies* and the *De lingua*. There was even the *Grammatica Melanchthonis*. Famechon was a reader of Rabelais, the pride and joy of his library, and of the Sieur Regnier's *Satires*. All these form a distinct group and indicate a definite Gallican loyalty. For Famechon possessed the *Ménipée* and the Edict of Nantes. He

[26] It should be noted that all these novel tastes—history (ancient, recent or contemporary); geography (the interest in cosmographies, accounts of voyages, and atlases); more definite support for the monarchy, helped along by portraits of kings or princes—these are also to be found attested in the same way among the inventoried effects of the more important burghers and newly ennobled rich in the Franche-Comté of Burgundy (whose count was Philip II of Spain). Portraits of the four Valois dukes of Burgundy "with their wives," Charles V, Philip II, Maria of Hungary, and so forth; family portraits, maps (of Germany, Gallic territory, and the comté), and, in the libraries, the ancient historians (though no trace of the pedant or the school); Plutarch, of course; the *Republic* of Plato, side by side with that of Bodin; no Cicero, but all the burning curiosity of the Renaissance about man, nature, and the inhabited world (the fine *Cosmographie* of Munster); the *Theatrum Orbis* of Ortelius; Thevet's *Cosmographie*, and so forth; as for history, mainly chronicles, the *Nef des histoires*, the *Mer des chroniques*, Froissard, the *Chroniques* of Saint-Loys, Olivier de la Marche, the Loyal Serviteur; then the provincial histories and the memoirs (*La Bretagne* of Argenteau, the *Annales d'Anjou*, Belleforest's *Histoire des neuf Charles*, Martin du Bellay's *Mémoires*, La Noue's *Discours*, the *Histoire de Berry*, Paradin, Saint-Julien-de-Balleure, and others); and above all, histories of more distant peoples (Olaüs Magnus, *De Gentibus Septentrionalibus*, Cromerus, *De Gestis Polonorum*, the *République des Suisses*, the *Histoire des Médicis*, the *République des Turcs*, together with Colombus, Thevet, and Georges Castriot, not forgetting Andrea Vesalius and Paracelsus. This was the library of the Gauthiot d'Ancier family—and it can be seen that, although they were not French subjects, they had the same interests as the men of Amiens. (Cf. L. Febvre, *Philippe II et la Franche-Comté*, pp. 355 ff.)

approved of the *Parlement*'s remonstrances against Father Suárez's book and the court verdict which had condemned it. He was against the Jesuits and supported the pacification edict. Apart from these he also possessed the *Figures des rois de France*, and, to do honor to his map of the kingdom, the valuable *Guide des chemins de France* of Charles Estienne. Like everyone else at the time, he was also interested in history and geography. He possessed the *Histoire générale des Indes*, the *Histoire de l'Amérique*, and the *Histoire de la Floride*; there was also Simler's *République des Suisses*, in Gentillet's translation. He read the *État de l'Église sous Charles-Quint* (i.e., Sleidan), Martin du Bellay's *Mémoires*, and the *État de l'histoire de France sous Charles IX*.

But the very same year, 1617, saw the inventory (FF 654) of the library of Martin de Miraulmont, a royal notary. At the head of this stood the *Œuvres spirituelles* of the Reverend Father Louis of Granada: mystical Spain. The famous *Summa Benedicti* sets us firmly in the world of the casuists. Then comes the *Vie des saints*, together with the *Bréviaire d'Amiens* and the *Histoire ecclésiastique* of Nicephorus. Then two books by Pellevé, the cardinal of the League, who was one of the targets of the [*Satire*] *Ménipée*. Miraulmont was clearly on the other side.

Two types of men, indeed—the divided France of Louis XIII's reign. The big question, of course, was which of these two types would prevail and make it possible for Louis XIV to establish himself, at least provisionally, on the ruins of the past? This is an example of the sort of problem which the inventories can make more concrete for those who know how to peruse them.

All this has been nothing more than a quick sketch, and it must be said once more that there was no question of my furnishing a complete, thorough and detailed study. My aim was simply to set an example and to suggest an uncomplicated and relatively easy line of research; though obviously a certain breadth of learning and outlook is indispensable. What can be done so conveniently with the help of the informative documents of Amiens can be done just as conveniently in other places. And be done it must, for only on this condition will it be possible to write a living history of French civilization. Such a history would be sensitive and differentiated and would make it possible to date the really important underlying changes; and it too would have a style of its own.

Suggestions for Further Reading

*Contains useful bibliography.

Blunt, A., *Art and Architecture in France, 1500 to 1700*. Baltimore, 1953.

Bouwsma, W. J., *Concordia Mundi: The Career and Thought of Guillaume Postel (1510–1581)*. Cambridge, Mass., 1957.

*Busson, H., *Les sources et le développement du rationalisme dans la littérature française de la Renaissance*, rev. ed. Paris, 1957.

Church, W. F., *Constitutional Thought in Sixteenth-Century France*. Cambridge, Mass., 1941.

Cioranescu, A., *Vie de Jacques Amyot d'après des documents inédits*. Paris, 1941.

Delaruelle, E., *Guillaume Budé, les origines, les débuts, les idées maîtresses*. Paris, 1907.

Doucet, R., *Les Institutions de la France au XVIe Siècle*. Paris, 1948.

Febvre, L., *Le problème de l'incroyance au XVI siècle*, rev. ed. Paris, 1962.

*Ferguson, W. K., *The Renaissance in Historical Thought*. Boston, 1948.

*Gilmore, M. P., *The World of Humanism, 1453–1517*. New York, 1953.

Gundersheimer, W. L., *The Life and Works of Louis Le Roy*. Geneva, 1966.

Hauser, H., and Renaudet, A., *Les débuts de l'âge moderne*, Vol. VIII in *Peuple et Civilisations*, 4th ed., rev. Paris, 1956.

Haydn, H., *The Counter-Renaissance*. New York, 1950.

Hirsch, R., *Printing, Selling, and Reading, 1450–1550*. Wiesbaden, 1967.

Imbart de la Tour, *Les Origines de la Réforme*. 4 Vols. Paris, 1905–35.

Lavisse, E., *Histoire de la France depuis les origines jusqu'à la révolution*, Vol. V (*1494-1559*), by H. Lemonnier. Paris, 1903–4.

Lefranc, A., *Histoire du Collège de France depuis les origines jusqu'à la fin du Premier Empire*. Paris, 1893.

——, "Le platonisme et la littérature en France à l'époque de la Renaissance (1500–1550)," *Revue d'histoire littéraire de la France*, III (1896).

——, *La vie quotidienne au temps de la Renaissance*. Paris, 1938.

Major, J. R., *Representative Institutions in Renaissance France*. Madison, Wisc., 1960.

Mönch, W., *Die italienische Platonrenaissance und ihre Bedeutung für Frankreichs Literatur- und Geistesgeschichte (1450–1550)*. Berlin, 1956.

Morçay, R. and Müller, A., *La Renaissance*. Paris, 1960.

Ong, W. J., *Ramus, Method, and the Decay of Dialogue*. Cambridge, Mass., 1958.

Plattard, J., *La renaissance des lettres en France de Louis XII à Henri IV*, 3rd ed. Paris, 1925.

Reese, G., *Music in the Renaissance*, rev. ed. New York, 1959.

Renaudet, A., *Humanisme et Renaissance*. Geneva, 1958.

*——, *Préreforme et humanisme à Paris pendant les premières guerres d'Italie*, 2nd rev. ed. Paris, 1953.

Rice, E. F., Jr., *The Renaissance Idea of Wisdom*. Cambridge, Mass., 1958.

Sandys, J. E., *A History of Classical Scholarship*, 3 Vols. (esp. Vol. 2). Cambridge, 1908–21 [reprinted, New York, 1964].

Saulnier, V.-L., *La littérature française de la renaissance, 1500–1610*, 2nd rev. ed. Paris, 1948.

*Simone, F., *Il rinascimento francese*. Turin, 1961 [reprinted 1967].

Taylor, H. O., *Thought and Expression in the Sixteenth Century*, 2 Vols. New York, 1920 [republished after the 2nd rev. ed., 1930].

Tilley, A., *The Literature of the French Renaissance*, 2 Vols. Cambridge, 1904.

Weinberg, B., *Critical Prefaces of the French Renaissance*. Evanston, 1950.

Yates, F. A., *The French Academies of the Sixteenth Century*. London, 1947 [reprinted 1968].

Zanta, L., *La renaissance du stoïcisme au XVIe siècle*. Paris, 1914.

Index

I